D1174208

Autonomy and Rights

Autonomy and Rights

The Moral Foundations of Liberalism

HORACIO SPECTOR

CLARENDON PRESS · OXFORD

1992

Oxford University Press, Walton Street, Oxford OX2 6DP

Oxford New York Toronto
Delhi Bombay Calcutta Madras Karachi
Petaling Jaya Singapore Hong Kong Tokyo
Nairobi Dar es Salaam Cape Town
Melbourne Auckland
and associated companies in
Berlin Ibadan

Oxford is a trade mark of Oxford University Press

Published in the United States
by Oxford University Press. New York

British Library Cataloguing in Publication Data
Data available

Library of Congress Cataloging in Publication Data
Spector, Horacio.
Autonomy and rights : the moral foundations of liberalism /
Horacio Spector.
p.   cm.
Revision of the author's thesis (doctoral)—University of Buenos
Aires, 1989.
Includes bibliographical references and index.
1. Liberalism—Moral and ethical aspects.   2. Liberalism—
Philosophy.   I. Title.
JC571.S743   1992   320.5'12'01—dc20   91-25736
ISBN 0-19-823921-1

Typeset by Graphicraft Typesetters Ltd, Hong Kong
Printed in Great Britain by
Bookcraft (Bath) Ltd,
Midsomer Norton, Avon

To Flora

Acknowledgements

This book has grown out of the thesis I presented for my doctor's degree at the University of Buenos Aires in September 1989. I completed the final version in the winter of 1989–90 while holding a research fellowship from the Alexander von Humboldt Foundation in the Philosophy Seminar at the University of Heidelberg. My thanks are due for the financial support I received from the Alexander von Humboldt Foundation and for the research facilities afforded me at the time by the Philosophy Seminar of Heidelberg University. I must also acknowledge a grant for travelling expenses from the Institute for Humane Studies at George Mason University.

Martín Farrell was my adviser when I was preparing my doctoral dissertation. I am grateful to him for his generous encouragement and illuminating criticism. Oscar Cornblit, Guido Pincione, and Hugo Zuleta worked thoroughly through an earlier draft, making penetrating comments and suggestions. Ignacio Zuberbühler sent me a valuable commentary on a rough copy of Chapter 1 and on the first section of Chapter 4. I likewise owe a debt to Bertram Kienzle for his keen and painstaking revision of the penultimate draft and for his kindly concern that I should enjoy a favourable atmosphere to work in at Heidelberg. There are other colleagues and friends who have helped or encouraged me in diverse ways since 1986 when I first began to take an interest in the moral foundations of liberalism, and in this connection I should like to take the opportunity of mentioning H. Albert, C. Alchourrón, E. Bulygin, E. Garzón Valdés, H. Kliemt, A. Peczenik, J. Raz, and J. Rodríguez Larreta.

Contents

Introduction

The Classical Conception of Liberalism

This book is about the moral foundation of the classical conception of liberalism. The basic idea of this conception is that people have fundamental moral rights the respect for which and protection of which are the necessary condition of the moral legitimacy of government and the decisions it adopts. This is the conception of liberalism embraced by its very founders, notably John Locke, David Hume, Benjamin Constant, and Wilhelm von Humboldt. According to a familiar view, classical liberalism is characterized essentially by maintaining that all or the greater part of the rights which individuals possess are negative ones. Such rights require that the government or private persons should refrain from committing certain actions, as, for example, limiting the use of the Press or confiscating property.[1] By contrast, the so-called economic and social rights are positive ones, i.e. rights that the government shall perform certain actions, as, for example, administering a system of old-age and service pensions or providing transport and communications services.

According to my own view, classical liberalism is not committed to the thesis that all human rights are of a negative kind. I claim that the heart of liberalism is the thesis that each human being has negative rights that always or at least normally prevail over any other moral considerations that are relevant in deciding on the treatment to be given him[2] by government and his fellow beings. So conceived, classical liberalism is logically compatible with the moral standpoint that individuals have positive rights on a hierarchically lower level than that of the negative ones. The assertion that positive rights or other moral considerations lie on

[1] Loren E. Lomasky, *Persons, Rights, and the Moral Community* (New York: Oxford University Press, 1987), 84.

[2] In this book I follow the rule of classical English which prescribes the use of masculine personal pronouns where the sex of the person referred to remains contextually unspecified.

a level hierarchically lower than that of negative rights simply means that negative duties whose fulfilment is necessary to the respect of negative rights override in cases of conflict the duties deriving from positive rights or from other moral considerations. In other words, as I understand it, the central ethical thesis of classical liberalism does not imply that people *do not possess* positive rights, still less that there are not in addition to negative rights other moral reasons that one should ponder over and weigh up in order to determine the ethical legitimacy of a governmental action. Therefore classical liberalism is compatible with a diversity of positions with regard to other moral considerations which may play, in a place subordinate to that of negative liberal rights, a part in establishing the moral rightness or the justice of the political and economic institutions of a society or of the public policies pursued in that society.[3]

Understood in this way, classical liberalism does not imply either that people *possess* positive rights or that there are other moral reasons in addition to negative individual rights. This is to say that liberalism is quite compatible with an ethical standpoint claiming that negative liberal rights exhaust the whole of morality. (A weak variant of this position sees in individual rights all of the moral reasons that may operate in the practical reasonings guiding government action.) Not only is liberal doctrine asserting that there are pre-eminent individual rights not incompatible with this view but the doctrine itself is also a logical consequence of it. For if, as the standpoint claims, there are no moral reasons apart from individual rights, *a fortiori* there are no other moral reasons that rank with them.

Now it is not my intention to hold that the position claiming

---

[3] Nevertheless, given the priority assigned to negative rights, the cash value of its being logically possible for classical liberalism to shelter positive rights or any other moral reasons will depend on the extent and content of negative liberal rights and, in particular, of the right of private property. Indeed, these rights might require so wide a domain of abstentions—i.e. they might guarantee so large a sphere of non-interference—that they would make it morally impermissible to enforce positive duties deriving from positive rights or from other moral considerations. Although this extreme view on the content of negative rights is often accepted implicitly in liberal writings, in my opinion it should not be taken for granted without specific argumentation. Be that as it may, I do not intend in this book to go into an examination of the possible moral considerations about what people should positively do nor about the part such considerations might play in ethical–political deliberation.

that negative rights are the only possible moral reasons is actually alien to classical liberal thought, especially in the weak form that is confined to government action. Obviously this standpoint could not plausibly form part of classical liberal thought if it were assumed that the existence of an individual right can only generate a moral reason to respect it. On this assumption, the way of fulfilling all the moral requirements would be to condemn government to a completely passive role, or else to do away with it altogether. But classical liberalism cannot subscribe to the thesis of the total passivity of government, or to its elimination, because it affirms that government has the duty to *enforce* and *protect* negative individual rights. Clearly, the enforcement and protection of rights, albeit negative ones, involves positive behaviour on the part of government. Admitting, however, that the existence of an individual right gives rise to a reason both to respect it and to create and sustain political institutions for ensuring that it is not transgressed, it must be granted that the view that maintains that only negative individual rights can serve as justification for government action finds support in a number of classical liberal writings which emphasize that the state's action should be restricted to protecting individual rights. For instance, the theory of the minimal state put forward by Robert Nozick in his *Anarchy, State, and Utopia* is said to rest upon the ethical supposition that 'there is only one form of moral wrong, namely violation of individual rights'.[4]

Nevertheless it strikes me that to reconstruct classical liberalism so that it is engaged with the thesis that negative individual rights exhaust the moral universe is to make classical liberalism unnecessarily a theory which is ethically radical and barely credible. The idea that there are not apart from negative individual rights any moral reasons capable of regulating the conduct of moral agents, or the action of the government, presents us with an unjustifiably mean image of moral life. As a matter of fact, our moral experience recognizes in addition to negative duties correlated with individual rights other negative duties which are hardly connected with individual rights, like the duty not to lie. Furthermore, we commonly accept the existence of positive

[4] H. L. A. Hart, 'Between Utility and Rights', in Alan Ryan (ed.), *The Idea of Freedom: Essays in Honour of Isaiah Berlin* (Oxford: Oxford University Press, 1979), 83.

moral duties, some of which, like that of mutual aid, occupy a central position in common-sense morality. That it may be conceptually misleading to maintain that these positive duties are correlative to moral rights is quite another matter. Rather than associate classical liberalism with a moral view as far-fetched as the one I am considering, it is better to interpret the liberal idea that state action does not have to go beyond the protection of individual rights as a political proposal prompted by one of two beliefs: either that individual rights ban such a wide field of human conduct that any government action that does not consist in protecting an individual right will as likely as not constitute in itself a violation of an individual right; or that state action beyond the limits indicated, above all if taken as a rule, will in all likelihood lead to violations of individual rights or to encroachments upon some important value, like freedom or welfare.

When the idea that the state should be restricted to the enforcement of individual rights is interpreted as a political proposal rather than as a thesis about the limits of the moral world, it is equivalent to the famous principle of *laissez-faire* in classical political economy. I will not deny that this proposal may be found in classical liberal writings. Thus, for instance, the fundamental principle of political action for Humboldt is 'that the state refrain altogether from seeing to the positive well-being of citizens and confine itself strictly to watching over their safety from themselves and from foreign enemies, not restricting their freedom with a view to any other ultimate end'.[5] There are, however, legitimate doubts about whether this political principle constitutes an essential ingredient of the liberal tradition. It should be noted that the degree of adherence this principle enjoyed among classical economists is a moot point.[6] Furthermore, undeniably liberal writers, like Adam Smith and John Stuart Mill, explicitly rejected the view that state activity should be

---

[5] Wilhelm von Humboldt, 'Ideen zu einem Versuch, die Gränzen der Wirksamkeit des Staates zu bestimmen', in *Werke*, 5 vols., i (Stuttgart: Cotta, 1960), 90. (The translation is mine; the German original reads: 'Der Staat enthalte sich aller Sorgfalt für den positiven Wohlstand der Bürger, und gehe keinen Schritt weiter, als zu ihrer Sicherstellung gegen sich selbst, und gegen auswärtige Feinde notwendig ist; zu keinem andren Endzwecke beschränke er ihre Freiheit.')

[6] On this point the reader may consult Ellen Franken Paul, '*Laissez-Faire* in Nineteenth Century Britain: Myth or Reality?', *Literature of Liberty*, 3(4) (1980), together with the valuable bibliography there cited.

confined to the prevention and punishment of encroachments upon individual rights. Adam Smith thought that the state has 'the duty of erecting and maintaining certain public works and certain public institutions, which it can never be for the interest of any individual, or small number of individuals, to erect and maintain'.[7] Mill, for his part, distinguished between two sorts of government interference: the 'authoritative' and the 'unauthoritative'. The state acts 'authoritatively', according to Mill, when it prohibits or enjoins a certain kind of conduct, and does so 'unauthoritatively' when it gives advice and promulgates information or 'when, leaving individuals free to use their own means for pursuing any object of general interest ... establishes, side by side with their arrangements, an agency of its own for a like purpose'.[8] I shall not examine here the soundness of this distinction. What I am concerned to point out is that, though Mill seems to agree that authoritative interventions should be restricted to the protection of individual rights, he clearly implies that unauthoritative interventions may exceed the limited sphere of action allotted to the state by *laissez-faire*. In modern economic jargon, both Smith and Mill advocated the intervention of government in the provision of so-called *public goods*.[9]

In my opinion, a further clarification is called for. It is not my intention to assert that classical liberalism, as understood here, is the only possible interpretation of the liberal political tradition. A tradition is not a body of propositions susceptible of being described in a value-free fashion. This is not only because the configuration of a tradition is usually made through the work of several thinkers, who rarely agree about every respect of the tradition. Even the exact determination of the contribution

[7] Adam Smith, *An Inquiry into the Nature and Causes of the Wealth of Nations*, ed. R. H. Campbell and A. S. Skinner, ii (Oxford: Clarendon Press, 1976), 687–8.

[8] John Stuart Mill, 'Principles of Political Economy with Some of their Applications to Social Philosophy', in *Collected Works of John Stuart Mill*, iii, ed. J. M. Robson (Toronto: University of Toronto Press; London: Routledge & Kegan Paul, 1965), 937.

[9] With regard to the notion of public good, see Mancur Olson, *The Logic of Collective Action* (Cambridge, Mass.: Harvard University Press, 1971), 14. Currently, John Gray, a writer sympathetic to liberalism, holds that one of the functions of the state is the provision of public goods; see his 'Public Goods and the Limits of Liberty', communication to the 1986 General Meeting of the Mont Pélerin Society, St Vincent, Italy.

of a single writer to a tradition means embarking on a work of exegesis whose nature is clearly different from the description of empirical phenomena. Like the interpretation of a musical composition or the performance of a play, the content of a tradition cannot be neatly determined in a value-free way. On the contrary, to interpret a tradition is, partly but centrally, to manifest one's own preferences or ideals about the area of human behaviour with which the tradition is concerned. To interpret a tradition is then to take part in its development and enrichment.

Another way of alluding to the same phenomenon is to say that the concept of 'liberalism', in common with a number of other political concepts like 'democracy' or 'justice', is essentially contested.[10] The salient characteristic of essentially contested concepts is that their application gives rise to controversy among different groups claiming that their conception or interpretation of the concept is the right one. The existence of controversies about the application of the essentially contested concepts should not be looked upon as an accidental feature of such concepts; rather, it looks as if the function of these concepts is precisely to channel conflicting appraisements of a certain social practice or tradition in such a way as to enable the confrontation between the antagonistic conceptions to enrich by itself the development of the practice or tradition in question.

The liberal tradition at present recognizes two main interpretative or reconstructive theories. One is precisely the political doctrine that I have already referred to as classical liberalism, and that in recent political philosophy is generally known as *liberta-*

---

[10] John Gray, 'On Liberty, Liberalism and Essential Contestability', *British Journal of Political Science*, 8 (1978), 385–6. The literature dealing with essentially contested concepts (they are sometimes called essentially contestable concepts or interpretive concepts) is wide. The original statement was made by W. B. Gallie, 'Essentially Contested Concepts', *Proceedings of the Aristotelian Society*, 56 (1955–6). Further analyses may be found in the following works: John Rawls, *A Theory of Justice* (Oxford: Clarendon Press, 1972); Steven Lukes, *Power: A Radical View* (London: Macmillan, 1974); Clarke Barry, 'Essentially Contested Concepts', *British Journal of Political Science*, 9 (1979); Christine Swanton, 'On the "Essential Contestedness" of Political Concepts', *Ethics*, 95 (1984–5); Ronald Dworkin, *Law's Empire* (London: Fontana, 1986). For an exposition of the idea of essential contestability and a comparison with the related idea of concepts susceptible of persuasive definition, see my 'Acerca del presunto carácter esencialmente controvertido del concepto de derecho', *Proceedings of the Second International Congress of the Philosophy of Law*, i, La Plata, 1987, 349–59.

rianism. The other theory is so-called *egalitarian liberalism* or *egalitarianism.* Egalitarian liberalism is identified with a political doctrine that denies the government authority either to promote any particular conception of the good life or to assist one conception more than others,[11] or alternatively with the doctrine that holds that individuals possess positive rights comparable to negative ones as regards both their moral 'importance' and the foundations upon which they rest.[12] Despite its great theoretical importance, the examination of egalitarian liberalism is beyond the scope of this study.

The Project

In this book I intend to put forward a theory about the moral foundations of the classical conception of liberalism. However, I do not wish to investigate the moral foundations of any libertarian political theory in particular but rather the moral underpinnings of the most basic thesis common to all possible libertarian political doctrines. This thesis, which I shall call the *basic libertarian thesis,* affirms that individuals have moral rights involving, in some way to be determined, the moral impermissibility of interfering with their choices and actions. The basic libertarian thesis likewise maintains that the negative rights whose existence it asserts (to which I refer indiscriminately in this book by the terms 'negative rights', 'classical individual rights', and 'libertarian rights') prevail as a rule over other possible moral reasons that may compete with them. Thus, the conclusion of this book will coincide with Robert Nozick's point of departure in *Anarchy, State, and Utopia*: 'Individuals have rights, and there are things no person or group may do to them (without violating their rights).'[13]

The best-known theoretical lines that could be followed to justify the basic libertarian thesis are the theory of natural rights, utilitarianism, and contractarianism. In this book I am going to move away from these theoretical strategies and concentrate instead on a liberal justification of the basic libertarian thesis, that

---

[11] Joseph Raz, *The Morality of Freedom* (Oxford: Clarendon Press, 1986), 19.
[12] Lomasky, *Persons, Rights, and the Moral Community*, 84.
[13] Robert Nozick, *Anarchy, State, and Utopia* (Oxford: Blackwell, 1974), p. ix.

is to say, a justification of the existence of libertarian rights starting from the recognition of a distinctively liberal value, like liberty or personal autonomy. In Chapters 1 and 2 I am going to expound and criticize a sort of liberal justification of the basic libertarian thesis that takes as its starting-point the ideal of negative liberty, which I term *negative liberalism*. Although I believe that negative liberalism is in the last instance faulty as a theory justifying the basic libertarian thesis, a critical analysis of it is worth while not only because in my opinion it has actually had a bigger influence on the classical liberal trend than is suggested by its meagre articulation in the literature reflecting this tendency, but also because, as I shall attempt to show, the lessons we may draw from its failure will enable us to work out an alternative liberal justification that may claim to supersede it. In Chapter 3 I shall lay the fundamentals of this new justificatory approach, and in Chapters 4 and 5 will state in detail the main features of the theory of practical rationality forming part of the approach. Lastly, in the Conclusion, the new argument justifying the basic libertarian thesis that results from the alternative approach developed in the three preceding chapters will be presented in complete and articulate shape.

1
Negative Liberalism

I am going to apply the term 'negative liberalism' to a variety of liberal political theories having as a common denominator the recognition that negative freedom is a fundamental social value. The negative liberal holds that the social and political order must be built on the ideal of maximum negative liberty and rejects particularly any attempt to have this role occupied by any form of positive freedom. Even though the meaning of positive freedom is more contested than that of negative freedom, there seems to be widespread agreement that positive freedom is something distinct from and independent of negative freedom, and the notions of negative freedom and positive freedom will be the object of detailed analysis in this chapter.

Negative liberalism harks back to the classical age of liberal thought. As a matter of fact, there are apparently traces of this standpoint in Locke. In section 57 of *The Second Treatise of Government* the principle of the maximization of negative freedom would seem to be propounded as a general criterion to establish the content legal order should have from the liberal viewpoint; Locke says there:

the end of Law is not to abolish or restrain, but *to preserve and enlarge Freedom*: For in all the states of created beings capable of Laws, where *there is no Law, there is no Freedom.* For *Liberty* is to be free from restraint and violence from others which cannot be, where there is no Law.[1]

Kant, for his part, advanced negative liberalism in writing that the biggest problem of mankind is to create a society which should have 'the greatest freedom—therefore a general antagonism among its members—and yet the most precise determination

---

[1] John Locke, *The Second Treatise of Government*, in *Two Treatises of Government*, ed. Peter Laslett (Cambridge: Cambridge University Press, 1970), 324.

and protection of the limits of this freedom, in such a way that it can coexist with the freedom of others'.[2] Negative liberalism likewise crops up in current liberal thought. In his famous lecture *Two Concepts of Liberty* Isaiah Berlin defends the negative conception of freedom and makes an influential criticism of the positivist conceptions of freedom. For Berlin negative freedom is an intrinsic good, albeit not the only one.[3] Friedrich Hayek embraces negative liberalism from the start of his *The Constitution of Liberty* when he observes that in that work he is concerned with 'that condition of men in which coercion of some by others is reduced as much as is possible in society'.[4] Hayek considers the lack of negative freedom as an evil in itself aside from the fact that he also attributes serious adverse consequences to it in terms of the promotion of human welfare.[5] In Germany Hans Albert holds that the protection of (negative) freedom is one of the fundamental regulative ideas of a rational praxis in the political and social sphere. According to Albert, a theory of justice orientated towards the protection of freedom should aim at carrying out the Kantian ideal of a society offering its members the maximum equal freedom.[6]

---

[2] Immanuel Kant, 'Idee zu einer allgemeinen Geschichte in weltbürgerlicher Absicht', in *Kant's Gesammelte Schriften*, ed. Königlich Preussischen Akademie der Wissenschaften, viii (Berlin: Georg Reimer, 1912), 22. (The translation is mine; the German text reads: 'die grösste Freiheit, mithin einen durchgängigen Antagonism ihrer Glieder und doch die genauste Bestimmung und Sicherung der Grenzen dieser Freiheit ... damit sie mit der Freiheit anderer bestehen könne'.) Though this passage suggests that Kant embraced a negative account of social freedom, it should be recalled here that his view of personal freedom as subjection to the moral law is a variant of the positive conception of freedom.

[3] Isaiah Berlin, *Four Essays on Liberty* (Oxford: Oxford University Press, 1969), 125–8 and p. lvi.

[4] F. A. Hayek, *The Constitution of Liberty* (London and Henley: Routledge & Kegan Paul, 1960), 11.

[5] Hayek's theory of the instrumental value of (negative) freedom, put crudely, is that, in guaranteeing that every individual may make full use of his knowledge, particularly of his concrete and often unique knowledge of the special circumstances in which he acts (ibid. 156), freedom provides the proper opportunities for individuals to communicate the knowledge they possess already and for them to bring about useful changes and innovations for the solution of practical problems facing the members of a society, and, in this way, increases human well-being (pp. 22–31).

[6] Hans Albert, *Traktat über rationale Praxis* (Tübingen: J. C. B. Mohr (Paul Siebeck), 1978), 140.

Still more recently, in the 1980s, negative liberalism is a thoroughly vital position. For example, Jan Narveson subscribes unreservedly to the ideal of negative freedom and rejects that of positive freedom, holding that the only proper concern of political institutions is to make people interfere with each other's behaviour as little as possible.[7] And Michael Levin defends negative freedom against positive freedom by arguing that any conception of justice going beyond non-interference would 'play favorites' and must therefore be at variance with an egalitarian distribution.[8]

As I explained in the Introduction, the aim of this book is to provide a sound liberal justification of the libertarian thesis concerning classical individual rights. The purpose of a liberal justification of this thesis is to draw up a correct argument which, starting from the existence of a distinctively liberal social value, will arrive at a conclusion asserting the existence of pre-eminent negative rights. Negative liberalism is of great importance in this connection because it may be regarded as an attempt to offer a liberal justification of the basic libertarian thesis. This attempt is characterized by the fact that the social value from which it departs is negative freedom. Negative liberalism is, as has just been seen, an extended view in liberal philosophy, but it has never been proposed in a perfectly developed form. In this chapter I shall endeavour to present this view in an articulate and convincing manner so that the criticism of it makes sense and is worth while. In Chapter 2 I shall try to show that negative liberalism is not in a position to justify the basic libertarian thesis. In subsequent chapters I shall argue that the core idea of negative liberalism is best captured from an outlook recognizing the value of positive freedom and propounding a deontological conception of the way of giving proper response to this value in the practical reasonings of moral agents.

An articulate presentation of negative liberalism requires the analysis of three central issues: in the first place, the concept of negative freedom. There are serious disagreements about how to analyse this concept properly and, needless to say, the content of

---

[7] Jan Narveson, 'Equality vs. Liberty: Advantage, Liberty', in Ellen Franken Paul *et al.* (eds.), *Liberty and Equality*. (Oxford: Blackwell, 1985), 49–52; and *The Libertarian Idea* (Philadelphia, Pa.: Temple University Press, 1988), 32.

[8] Michael Levin, 'Negative Liberty', in Paul *et al.* (eds.), *Liberty and Equality*.

negative liberalism may vary considerably according to the meaning attached to 'negative freedom'. But we shall not have to analyse the concept of negative freedom only but that of positive freedom as well. The negative liberal supposes that negative freedom and positive freedom exhaust the options a defender of freedom has before him and claims for the former all the value that Western political tradition recognizes in freedom. An important supposition of the view is, then, that positive freedom is something different from, and independent of, negative freedom. This being so, we cannot dispense with an analysis of the concept of positive freedom if we wish to understand fully the position of the negative liberal. Lastly, it should not be forgotten that the aim of the negative liberal is not just that in a society there shall be negative freedom but that there shall be the maximum amount of it. Strictly speaking, the negative liberal's ideal is not negative liberty but maximum negative liberty. Consequently, the third of the questions that I shall have to deal with is the way in which negative freedom is to be measured. The fundamental assumption here is that negative freedom is measurable. But even allowing that negative freedom is susceptible of some form of measurement, it is clear that the position of the negative liberal will change according to the criterion of measurement adopted. And, unsurprisingly, there is no agreement either about how negative freedom is to be measured.

Negative Freedom

The pair of terms 'negative freedom' and 'positive freedom' was coined by Kant.[9] However, the current use of these terms in political theory, which avoids Kantian overtones and which I am following here, goes back to Berlin. For Berlin negative freedom has to do with the question 'What is the area within which the subject . . . is or should be left to do or be what he is able to do or be, without interference by other persons?' Berlin understands by negative freedom basically the Hobbesian idea of freedom as the absence of impediment or external interference. Interference with what? Berlin's position has varied in this respect. In *Two*

---

[9] H. J. Paton, *The Moral Law* (London: Hutchinson's University Library, 1947), 114.

Concepts of Liberty he maintains that the freedom of a person is lost when his wishes are thwarted by means of the deliberate activity of another person; but in the Introduction to *Four Essays on Liberty* he corrects himself and states that he understands by freedom not merely the absence of frustration, but the absence of obstacles (placed by agents or deriving from alterable human practices) with possible choices and activities.[10] Berlin's change of position brings out two important decisions which a negative liberal must adopt in order to present negative freedom as a unique and clearly discernible value. In the first place, whereas in his first definition Berlin was maintaining that unfreedom involves interference with what one wishes to do, he now identifies unfreedom with interference with possible actions, irrespective of whether they are in fact desired or not. The first decision to which I referred is concerned, then, with the object of interference restricting freedom. In the second place, for freedom to be lacking Berlin no longer requires the obstacles to be the fruit of a deliberate human activity; nor does he even demand one action in particular for the curtailment of freedom to take place, provided that the obstacle in question is the result of an alterable human practice. The second decision thus concerns the general sort of human behaviour capable of generating such interference that it may properly be said that freedom is wanting.

Hayek understands by freedom 'the state in which a man is not subject to coercion by the arbitrary will of another or others'.[11] It is worth quoting the passage in which Hayek presents his definition of the concept of coercion, without which his conception of freedom would lack precision:

By 'coercion' we mean such control of the environment or circumstances of a person by another that, in order to avoid greater evil, he is forced to act not according to a coherent plan of his own but to serve the ends of another. Except in the sense of choosing the lesser evil in a situation forced on him by another, he is unable either to use his own intelligence or knowledge or to follow his own aims and beliefs.[12]

In the Hayekian conception the coerced party chooses the act which is forced upon him, but the coercer manipulates the

[10] Berlin, *Four Essays on Liberty*, 123 and pp. xxxix–xl.
[11] Hayek, *The Constitution of Liberty*, 11.
[12] Ibid. 20–1.

alternatives of action of the coerced party in such a way that it may be said that he chooses what the coercer wants. Now, the manipulation of the alternatives of action open to the coerced party is for Hayek a necessary condition of coercion, but not a sufficient one. Coercion implies in addition (1) the threat to do harm and (2) the intention of bringing about in this way a certain conduct by the coerced party.[13]

The contrast between Berlin and Hayek's views of unfreedom places on the *tapis* a third fundamental decision which a negative liberal must take with regard to the concept of negative freedom. Notice that while Berlin appears to make physical compulsion the centre of his attention, especially in his lecture, Hayek concentrates on threats. Both things might be seen as defects of emphasis, for it seems reasonable to think that from the liberal viewpoint as much freedom is lost by threats as by physical compulsion. However, this view is controversial. Specifically, it has been controverted that the non-existence of threats is a necessary condition of freedom as the absence of physical compulsion or impediment surely is. The third decision refers, then, to the shape coercion may take, or, in other words, to the particular sort of intervention that may be characterized as detrimental to freedom. In the following three subsections I shall examine each of the three fundamental decisions that, as I said, a negative liberal should take in order to obtain an adequate and precise concept of negative freedom, suggesting in each case which alternative is the more defensible. I shall begin with the analysis of coercion, continue with the object of interference restricting freedom, and end with the general kind of human behaviour that may give rise to a loss of freedom.

Coercion

The intuitive view that both physical compulsion and threats exclude freedom finds worthy supporters, to be sure. Feinberg, for instance, holds that coercion can take two main forms: physical compulsion or impediment, like prodding with bayonets or imprisoning, and the threat of injury clearly backed up by a

---

[13] Ibid. 133–4.

power of enforcement.[14] Oppenheim adopts a similar position: P is unfree to do X not only to the extent that another person, Q, makes it impossible for P to do X, but also to the extent that Q would carry out an explicit or implied threat of punishment if he found P guilty of having done X.[15] As against this view, sometimes the principle is held that a person cannot be unfree to do something he actually does.[16] This principle implies excluding threats as attacks upon freedom, for Q's threat to P that, if he does X, Q will injure P does not make it impossible for P to do X. It may, however, be said, by way of reply, that this principle cannot be based upon an appeal to standard liberal intuitions, since the most flagrant attacks on individual freedom condemned by liberals consist precisely of tyrannical legal rules threatening subjects with sanctions if they commit certain acts permissible in a free society, such as the expression of ideas contrary to those of the government or the refusal to collaborate in the persecution of dissidents. The *onus probandi* seems to fall here on the one who denies that threats affect freedom.

Hillel Steiner has put forward an elaborate argument to prove that threats do not diminish freedom and that preventing a person from doing something, i.e. making it impossible for him to do so, is the only thing that can be regarded as an encroachment upon freedom.[17] The argument runs as follows. The starting-point is that both threats and offers are interventions affecting the practical deliberations of individuals. What Steiner attempts first to show is that there is no difference in the way in which offers and threats produce this effect. The intuitive idea about the manner in which threats and offers intervene in practical deliberations, which insists that to accept an offer results in an increase of well-being whereas to ignore a threat leads to a decrease of well-being, fails to take account of the fact—says

---

[14] Joel Feinberg, *Social Philosophy* (Englewood Cliffs, NJ: Prentice-Hall, 1973), 7.

[15] Felix E. Oppenheim, *Political Concepts: A Reconstruction* (Oxford: Blackwell, 1981), 57.

[16] C.W. Cassinelli, *Free Activities and Interpersonal Relations* (The Hague: Martinus Nijhoff, 1966), 34; William A. Parent, 'Some Recent Work on the Concept of Liberty', *American Philosophical Quarterly*, 11 (1974), 160.

[17] Hillel Steiner, 'Individual Liberty', in *Proceedings of the Aristotelian Society*, NS, 75 (1974–5), 36–44.

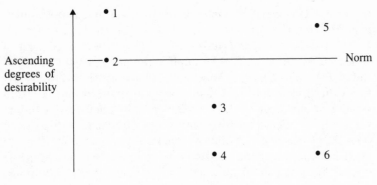

FIG. 1.1

Steiner—that the rejection of an offer produces a relative decrease of well-being whereas succumbing to a threat leads to a relative increase of well-being. To establish a clear difference between the consequences of accepting an offer and the consequences of ignoring a threat, it is necessary to judge the absolute desirability of such consequences, which presupposes a norm or standard. Echoing a proposition of Nozick's,[18] Steiner claims that such a norm is the normal and predictable course of events, that is to say, the course of events the receiver of the intervention would have met with if the intervention had not taken place. Fig. 1.1, which is due to Steiner,[19] shows the configuration of alternative consequences according to the degree of desirability of an offer—for example: 'You may use my car whenever you like' (first column of pairs of dots); a threat, for example: 'Your money or your life' (second column); and what Steiner calls a 'throffer', for example: 'Kill this man and you'll receive £100— fail to kill him and I'll kill you' (third column). The odd-numbered points represent the consequences of succumbing or accepting, while the even-numbered ones represent the consequences of ignoring or rejecting. As can be seen from the figure, the threats may be distinguished from the offers on the basis of the different position of their alternative consequences in relation to the norm. For instance, the consequences of the rejection of an offer lie on

[18] Robert Nozick, 'Coercion', in Peter Laslett *et al.* (eds.), *Philosophy, Politics and Society*, 4th ser. (Oxford: Blackwell, 1972).
[19] Steiner, 'Individual Liberty', 39.

the norm—this is for Steiner analytical—while the consequences of ignoring a threat are placed below the norm.

Steiner holds that this distinction between offers and threats says nothing about the way or degree in which both sorts of intervention affect practical deliberation. First of all, the *modus operandi* of both kinds of intervention is the same: to ensure a remainder when the degree of desirability appertaining to the consequences of the non-fulfilment (or rejection) is subtracted from that appertaining to the consequences of the fulfilment (or acceptance). Secondly, it is not necessarily true that threats exert a bigger influence than offers, since it is the difference in desirability between fulfilment (or acceptance) and non-fulfilment (or rejection) that determines the ability to affect practical deliberation both of offers and of threats, and it is far from necessary that this difference is larger in the case of threats than in the case of offers. Whilst the distinction between an offer and a threat needs to be established by reference to a norm, both the *modus operandi* of an intervention and its force are determinable without appeal to the norm. Given that there is no difference between the way in which offers and threats respectively affect the practical deliberations of their receivers, and that apparently there is no other way of saying that threats affect personal freedom than that it is through their effect on such deliberations, Steiner concludes that there is no reason for thinking that, if threats in fact affect freedom, they are in this respect different from offers. Of course, since nobody would want to say that offers affect personal freedom, Steiner's argument tends to prove that threats do not do so either.

Although the argument just expounded is at first sight plausible, a simple move will neutralize it. The argument presupposes that, if threats affect freedom, they cannot do so in the same way as preventing somebody by force from doing something, just as it presupposes that there is only one possible way of thinking— albeit mistakenly—that threats affect freedom, namely, by affecting the practical deliberation of the receiver through a change of the desirability of certain alternatives of action. The neutralizing move consists in maintaining that both prevention by force and threats affect freedom in the same and only possible way, while offers are not able to diminish a person's freedom though they may very well influence his behaviour. What is the (only) way in which freedom may be affected? In a pioneering study,[20] Benn and Weinstein claim that the general way in which *P*'s freedom may be affected is by closing or restricting certain options that *P* would otherwise have. This proposal needs to be supplemented by two clarifications. First, to judge whether a proposal increases or decreases the receiver's options one has once again to resort to a standard or norm which in this case, I wish to suggest, is the course that events would normally have followed in the absence of the restriction in question. Secondly, the term 'option' is here meant to denote not only the opportunity to do or forbear from doing a certain thing, but also the possibility to be or remain in a certain condition or state of affairs. Thus, for instance, if my new neighbour has a dog that barks all day long, I may be said to have lost the option of living a quiet life, even though the idea of living a quiet life could not be completely defined in terms of the performance of certain actions.

In accordance with the view under consideration, both physical compulsion and convincing threats cause a loss of the victim's freedom in that they restrict his menu of options in relation to the counterfactual situation in which the compulsion is not present or the threat is not made. By contrast, offers do not affect the receiver's freedom, since they do not restrict, but necessarily increase, his menu of options. For example, 'Use my car whenever you like' does not deprive the receiver of any option he might have had in the absence of the proposal and gives him the additional option of using the car without asking for permission to do so; but 'Your money or your life' certainly deprives the victim of one option, namely, that of living and keeping his money; perhaps too it gives the victim a new option, namely, that of suing me, in the context of a legal system banning threats, but this is not a necessary feature of threats, as it is of offers. The criterion of distinction between threats and offers based on the effects of the two kinds of intervention in the repertoire of options of the receiver[21] suggests two interesting points: first, that

---

[20] S.I. Benn and W.L. Weinstein, 'Being Free to Act, and Being a Free Man', *Mind*, 80 (1971).

[21] This criterion is also adopted in Oppenheim, *Political Concepts*, 62; in J. P. Day, 'Threats, Offers, Law, Opinion and Liberty', *American Philosophical Quarterly*, 14 (1977); and in Matti Häyry and Timo Airaksinen, 'Elements of Constraint', *Analyse & Kritik*, 10 (1988). W.A. Parent criticizes the view of

exerting an influence on the deliberations of a person and attacking his freedom are two completely different things, albeit compatible (e.g. the effect of threats), and, secondly, that it is far better to conceive negative freedom as the non-restriction of options rather than as the absence of physical compulsion.

A natural objection to the exclusion of offers as possible limitations of freedom is encouraged by the problem of the so-called coercive offers, of which Nozick's classic example is that of a master who offers to spare one of his slaves the daily beating if he performs an unpleasant task. The difficulty lies in the fact that the master's proposal does not eliminate any option that the slave would have had in the absence of the proposal but actually adds one, to wit, avoiding a beating by performing the task indicated. And nevertheless this proposal seems to limit the slave's freedom in much the same way as would compelling someone to do a nasty job by threatening him with a thrashing if he does not. One way of explaining coercive offers in terms of the non-restriction of options consists in taking as the norm or baseline in these cases, just as Nozick proposes, the course of events morally required.[22] On the plausible assumption that the course of events morally required excludes slavery and therefore the habit of the daily beating, the proposal involves eliminating (in relation to the baseline adopted) the option of not carrying out the unpleasant task without having to undergo a beating and consequently constitutes a restriction of freedom. A similar point of view is held by Daniel Lyons, who asserts that Q offers B to P coercively in return for A when: (1) P is rationally reluctant to give up A to Q (on any terms, or in particular for this B); and (2) Q could, *should*, and ordinarily would agree to relieve P of his need on more favourable terms.[23] Other writers go further and analyse all the coercive proposals, whether threats or coercive offers, as offences against morality. For instance, David Miller holds that somebody constrains the freedom of another by a proposal

freedom as non-restriction of options, unconvincingly in my opinion, in 'Freedom as the Non-Restriction of Options', *Mind*, 83 (1974); Benn and Weinstein's reply can be found immediately afterwards in 'Freedom as the Non-Restriction of Options: A Rejoinder'.

[22] Nozick, 'Coercion', 115–16.
[23] Daniel Lyons, 'Welcome Threats and Coercive Offers', *Philosophy*, 50 (1975), 429.

decreasing the desirability of any of his alternatives of action when by so doing he violates a moral duty.[24] And Vinit Haksar's opinion is that, in order to distinguish threats from coercive offers, and these from non-coercive proposals, 'it is essential to see what the proposer's declared plan is should his proposal be rejected by the other party'. For Haksar a necessary condition of a coercive threat is that the proposer's declared unilateral plan should be an immoral one, i.e. if the proposer carried out his declared unilateral plan, he would be violating a moral duty. This author also claims that coercive offers are distinguished from non-coercive ones by virtue of the fact that the former, as distinct from the latter, involve an attempt to take an unfair advantage of the recipient's vulnerability.[25]

Those analyses of the coerciveness of threats and coercive offers which underline that these proposals characteristically move away from a moral standard or transgress a moral duty, especially of equity, have the disadvantage of implying the endorsement of a moralized definition of the concept of freedom;[26] when freedom is limited and when it is not comes then to depend on the moral rules one subscribes to, which, by hypothesis, cannot be based upon the value of freedom. An alternative to the strategy mentioned is to advance a purely descriptive explanation of the coerciveness of coercive offers. David Zimmerman has a suggestion to make in this direction: an offer is coercive only if P would prefer to pass from the normally expected pre-proposal situation to the proposal situation, but he would very much prefer to pass from the real pre-proposal situation to an alternative pre-proposal situation in which he does not actually find himself owing to the active intervention of Q.[27] This suggestion supposes adopting a counterfactual norm or baseline. In terms of the approach defended above of coercion as restriction of options, such a norm may be described as a possible situation

---

[24] David Miller, 'Constraints on Freedom', *Ethics*, 94 (1983), sect. 3.

[25] Vinit Haksar, *Civil Disobedience: Threats and Offers* (Delhi: Oxford University Press, 1986), 46–7.

[26] The idea of a 'moralized definition' of freedom is introduced in G.A. Cohen, 'Capitalism, Freedom and the Proletariat', in Alan Ryan (ed.), *The Idea of Freedom: Essays in Honour of Isaiah Berlin* (Oxford: Oxford University Press, 1979), 12.

[27] David Zimmerman, 'Coercive Wage Offers', *Philosophy and Public Affairs*, 10 (1981), 132–3.

which is richer in the matter of options than the actual one and in which the recipient would find himself but for a certain active intervention on the part of the offerer. The objection that has been made to his proposition is that it yields the preposterous implication that *any* offer, either in a capitalist system or in a socialist one—the underlying theme is that of labour offers—is coercive because there is always a strongly preferred pre-proposal situation that the offerer (together with others) actively stops arising, namely, a situation in which the offeree possesses all of the society's wealth.[28]

The negative liberal might reply that this objection exploits a defective formulation of the idea underlying Zimmerman's suggestion. In fact, this suggestion cannot be plausibly interpreted in the sense that any possible course of events which does not materialize owing to a series of actions, including those of the offerer, is a suitable baseline for judging the coerciveness of an offer. I would like to suggest, as I do in detail elsewhere,[29] that the baseline one has to resort to to explain the coerciveness of coercive offers is the course that events would have normally followed in the absence of a previous active intervention of the person who later on is to make the offer. The point is that the salient feature of coercive offers is that the offerer forcibly eliminates some option from the menu of options of the offeree before issuing the offer, an option which the offeree would otherwise have at the moment of receiving the offer. Therefore, although coercive offers do not involve a reduction of the menu of options of the receiver in relation to the course that events would have normally followed but for the issue of the offer, they do involve a contraction of the menu of options of the receiver in relation to the course that events would have normally followed in the absence of the previous active intervention of the offerer. This is to say that to find the coerciveness of a coercive offer one has to go back to a moment prior to the issue of the offer. Coercive offers are coercive precisely because they could not possibly count as offers if it were not for a previous active intervention of the offerer which alters the menu of options that the offeree would

---

[28] Lawrence A. Alexander, 'Zimmerman on Coercive Wage Offers', *Philosophy and Public Affairs*, 12 (1983), 161–2.
[29] Martín Farrell and Horacio Spector, 'Dos tesis sobre amenazas y ofertas', unpublished.

otherwise have. Thus, for instance, if I poison someone and then offer him the antidote in exchange for his house, my proposal may be seen as an offer in relation to the situation the victim finds himself in after his being poisoned, but it would never have been seen as an offer in the absence of my previous intervention. Now, the baseline that is used in the objection to Zimmerman's suggestion (i.e. a situation in which the offeree possesses all the wealth of society) has nothing to do with the baseline I am suggesting here. In fact, it is not the normal continuation of the events that would have taken place in the absence of the previous intervention of the offerer: it is merely one of the very many possible courses of events. Yet, the criterion advanced here for characterizing coercive offers is not free from bewildering questions. Even though the application of this criterion will in practice produce satisfactory results since the coerciveness of coercive offers is due in the vast majority of cases to a previous active intervention of the offerer (i.e. the offeree lacks an option he would have had but for the offerer's conduct), it may well be the case that the coerciveness of such offers is not due to an individual previous intervention of the offerer but to the working of an institutional arrangement depending on the action of a social group which the offerer belongs to. For instance, this would be the case as regards the master's offer in Nozick's example if the example were constructed so that slavery is an institution sustained by collective action. In this case the negative liberal might reply that the coercion involved in the example does not lie in the offer itself but in the institution of slavery. This point is of course controversial and requires further analysis. However, I do not think that the position of the negative liberal is in this respect seriously threatened, since in any case he might defend himself by arguing that, whether through the concept of coercive offer or not, his position does account for the slave's unfreedom: slavery is after all a paradigmatic case of injury to negative freedom.

Actually Desired versus Possibly Desired Actions

As has been said already, there are two well-known positions with regard to the pertinent object of coercion. One position, upheld by Berlin in *Two Concepts of Liberty*, is associated with the conception of freedom as the absence of impediment to those actions which an agent really wants to perform. The other position is associated with freedom as the absence of restriction on possible choices. The former position feeds on the fact that as a rule we do not say that somebody is unfree to make an action that he does not want to make. As Benn and Weinstein put it, there is something paradoxical in saying that a person is free or unfree to starve, cut off his ears, or die.[30] Nevertheless, in line with these authors, the answer might be that the predicate 'is free to do X' implies pragmatically, and not logically, that X is a possible object of a reasonable choice, but not that the subject of the predicate wishes in fact to do X. Thus, though it seems odd to say that one is free to cut off one's ears, it would be quite to the point for an atheist to affirm proudly that in his country he enjoys freedom of worship, and even to demand the granting of it if it should be lacking.

Besides, it is counter-intuitive to maintain, as the first position does, that a necessary condition of our being free or unfree to do an action is that we actually desire it, inasmuch as this implies, as Berlin admits, that we can augment our freedom just by suppressing those desires whose satisfaction is obstructed by the intervention of others. Furthermore, given that, in accordance with this position, only of actions actually desired may it be asked whether one is free or unfree to perform them, the position likewise implies the strange consequence that the freedom of someone may be increased by augmenting the number of cases in which the question whether one is free does not arise.[31]

The second position, propounded among others by Parent,[32] Steiner,[33] and Feinberg,[34] as well as by the later Berlin, admits that interfering with the actual desires of a person may often be enough to curtail his freedom, but not necessarily so. To affect freedom in this conception it suffices to obstruct a possible action, without minding whether it is actually wanted or not. Feinberg calls that sort of freedom involved in this conception 'dispositional freedom', given that it may truly be said of somebody who is unfree in this sense to leave a locked room, for

---

[30] Benn and Weinstein, 'Being Free to Act, and Being a Free Man', 195.
[31] Steiner, 'Individual Liberty', 34.
[32] Parent, 'Some Recent Work on the Concept of Liberty', 151.
[33] Steiner, 'Individual Liberty', 33–6.
[34] Feinberg, *Social Philosophy*, 5–7.

example, that if he (counterfactually) were to choose to leave the room, then he would be blocked and thwarted. This position avoids the counter-intuitive consequences pointed out before. But this comparative advantage is in fact superficial. The profound advantage of a conception of freedom as the absence of restriction on possible choices arises when, as Feinberg presents the situation, a question is posed which might apparently be the introduction of a defence of the first position: Why should we have to value the freedom to perform actions which we might merely come to desire when at any given moment we can do whatever we wish without frustration? Or, to quote Feinberg, 'Why complain that a subject is not free to criticize his Führer when he loves his Führer and agrees with all his policies?'[35]

Feinberg argues convincingly that two different ideals of freedom are involved in each of the positions we have been considering: freedom as the minimization of frustration and freedom as the maximization of genuine alternatives open to a person. In the former sense freedom is nothing other than the satisfaction of desires. We have already seen that this does not appear to be the sense we give the word 'freedom' in everyday language. But beyond this question Feinberg points out that it may be true that dispositional freedom is valuable only as a means of satisfying desires and that, if this is so, there is no reason to prefer freedom when the satisfaction of desires is ensured without it. This view does not imply that freedom is fused with the satisfaction of desires, but it does imply that freedom as the non-restriction of possible actions lacks intrinsic value.

The point I am interested in making is that, whether the negative liberal conceives freedom as the satisfaction of desires or distinguishes it from the satisfaction of desires but considers it only of value in the attainment of this state of affairs, negative liberalism overlaps utilitarianism, which is precisely, by definition, a doctrine that lays down as a central value the satisfaction of desires and implies the instrumental value of anything tending to maximize the satisfaction of desires, including of course dispositional freedom, if such were the case. In this way, if negative liberalism were understood as embracing the first position, it would miss its chance of erecting itself as a distinctive political

---

[35] Ibid. 6.

doctrine. If negative liberalism wishes to be a genuine theoretical alternative, it must inevitably conceive freedom as the absence of restriction on possible courses of action, independently of whether or not these are the object of actual desires, accepting the intrinsic value of freedom so conceived. Furthermore, this seems to be the road negative liberals have chosen, notwithstanding some hesitation or lack of clarity that may have slipped into their writings.

Human Agency and Limitation of Freedom

The third decision that must be taken by the negative liberal concerns, as has been stated above, the general type of human behaviour that is capable of limiting freedom. If we take for granted the approach that the negative liberal would surely find it attractive to uphold as set out in the two previous subsections, the question to be answered now is under what general conditions the behaviour of a person constitutes a restriction on the possible alternatives of action open to another person. We have seen that Berlin's first view was that only a deliberate interfering action may enjoy such a status. But this position seems to fall an easy prey to counter-examples. Parent observes that if Q closes his shop forgetting that P is still inside, and is then asked for an explanation, he will probably say: 'I deprived P temporarily of his freedom, but I did not do so deliberately'.[36] According to Parent, accidental interferences, i.e. obstructions arising unexpectedly from one's own behaviour, should likewise count as injuries to freedom.

It is worth taking a look at Miller's interesting standpoint in this matter inasmuch as it differs both from Berlin's original view and from Parent's.[37] For Miller an impediment to action should be counted as a constraint on freedom when it may be held that a person is morally responsible for its existence, either because he put it there deliberately or negligently or because he failed to remove it in spite of the moral duty incumbent upon him to do so. For instance, Q constrains my freedom if he shuts me in a

[36] Parent, 'Some Recent Work on the Concept of Liberty', 151.
[37] Miller, 'Constraints on Freedom', sects. 1 and 2; and 'Reply to Oppenheim', *Ethics*, 95 (1985), 310–14.

room deliberately or without taking reasonable precautions, as well as if he fails to check the rooms when it is his duty to do so and thus leaves me locked in. But, unlike Parent, Miller does not count as a constraint on my freedom Q's closing the door of my room in the reasonable belief that I am somewhere else. In accordance with this viewpoint, failure to remove an obstacle in the way of an action when there is no moral duty to do so is not to be counted as a limitation on freedom either; as, for example, when a passer-by happens to walk past my room and hears me call for help but is so busy that he does not respond.

This sort of connection between the ideas of moral responsibility and encroachment upon freedom is objected to by Oppenheim, who argues that it yields implications divergent from common usage: for example, granted that the guard who locked the prisoner in his cell is not morally responsible for the prisoner's being in that situation, in accordance with Miller's view he does not constrain his freedom; moreover, if the imprisonment is due to a just sentence, then nobody is morally responsible for the prisoner's being locked up and therefore nobody limits his freedom.[38] In his reply Miller asserts that his view does not imply that all restrictions on freedom are morally unjustified. To be responsible for something is to be answerable for it; it is not necessarily to be blameable. Thus, the prison warder and the judge are responsible for the confinement of the prisoner but are not blameable if they act in accordance with just legal provisions.[39] However, it might be observed that to be morally responsible for something means being prima facie morally blameable and, this being so, Miller's theory does imply that it is a tautological judgement to say that it is prima facie blameable to constrain another.[40] Miller affirms in fact that to say that anyone is morally responsible for a state of affairs is 'to say that he is liable to blame if he fails to provide a justification for his conduct'.[41] Yet I do not think that this observation points to an unsurmountable difficulty. Let me explain. An assumption of Miller's theory is that everybody has a prima facie moral duty not

[38] Felix E. Oppenheim, '"Constraints on Freedom" as a Descriptive Concept', *Ethics*, 95 (1985), 305–6.
[39] Miller, 'Reply to Oppenheim', 313.
[40] Häyry and Airaksinen, 'Elements of Constraint', 35.
[41] Miller, 'Constraints on Freedom', 72.

to place any impediment in the way of another person's behaviour; otherwise it would not be understandable why it is prima
facie morally blameable to perform this action deliberately or
negligently (e.g. the mere fact that I am deliberately writing this
book does not justify my being morally blameable, not even in
prima-facie form, for doing so). But the judgement that it is
prima facie morally impermissible to place an obstacle in the way
of another person's action is not itself analytical. In short, the
observation under consideration only shows that the concept of
'constraints on freedom' has a moral import for Miller, but is
lacking in critical power, inasmuch as it is possible to convey the
moral principles regulating freedom and its protection by means
of the phrase 'placing an obstacle in the way of an action', which
is free of moral content.

The difficulty of Miller's theory lies at a deeper level than that
on which the above critiques move. Miller conflates two kinds of
moral assessment of human behaviour which ought to be distinguished. A first kind is concerned with the rightness or wrongness
of an act or omission considered objectively. The other kind
concerns the moral responsibility of an agent for an act or omission. Although it is true that the judgements corresponding to the
second kind usually make sense only when the act or omission in
question has been pronounced wrong, this is by no means necessary, since it is quite legitimate to wonder about the moral responsibility of an agent for a right act or omission (especially if it
enters the realm of supererogation) with a view to praising him.
Both an act and an omission can take place deliberately, negligently, or accidentally. The moral responsibility of an agent for
a wrong act or omission arises when the wrongdoing was done
deliberately or negligently. By contrast, it seems that an agent
may be judged to be morally responsible for a right act or
omission only if his performance was deliberate. But, at any
rate, the moral assessment of the attitudes or character traits of
an agent cannot be identified with the moral evaluation of his
actions considered objectively. Miller is in the right when he
demands intention or negligence to hold an agent morally responsible for the act of setting an obstacle, but he is wrong not to make
the same demand in the case of failing to remove an obstacle.
Besides, in demanding intention or negligence for it to be accurate to say that somebody has constrained another's freedom, as

distinct from his being morally responsible for having performed such an action, Miller excludes the accidental limitations on freedom from the domain of the constraints on freedom, when, as has been said before, the most reasonable thing is to admit with regard to the constraint of freedom, as with regard to any other action, the possibility of its accidental performance.

What I have just said implies that any positive act, whether deliberate, negligent, or accidental, restricting the alternatives of action of a person counts as a constraint on or injury to freedom, and that it is not necessary, still less convenient, to resort to the idea of moral responsibility in this context, despite the obvious fact that this would be indeed unavoidable in establishing whether an agent must answer morally for having constrained another's freedom. Nor is it necessary to appeal to the idea of moral blame. This last idea is in a certain sense a by-product of the notions of wrongness and responsibility: if an agent committed a wrongdoing and is morally responsible for it, then he is morally to blame. Along these lines the negative liberal may build up a notion of freedom devoid of moral taint.

Nevertheless, the negative liberal has still to answer one of the implications of Miller's analysis, namely, that an omission may possibly curtail freedom if it constitutes a violation of the moral duty to remove an obstacle. In fact, the negative liberal is committed to a conception of freedom incompatible with the possibility that freedom is curtailed by omission. Additionally, as we have seen, if freedom were thought of as depending upon moral principles, it could not fulfil the founding role that the negative liberal attributes to it. Thus, the formulation and defence of the negative liberal's position would be better served if he claimed that no omission can injure freedom. To counter this claim Miller appears to be in a position to proffer only counter-examples like the following: 'I am digging with a companion who is stopped by a fall of rock. If I fail to make reasonable attempts to extricate him, how can I avoid conceding that he is now unfree to escape?'[42] The conclusion that Miller attempts to draw from this case is that the freedom of my companion was affected by my failure to rescue him from the rock. The crucial question in analysing the force of this putative counter-example is in what

---

[42] Ibid 74.

sense my companion is unfree to escape. Notice that, if I actually manage to extricate my companion, with as much right as Miller has in saying that if I refrain from doing so my companion is unfree, we can describe my conduct by saying that I free him. But freeing is here restoring the freedom that my companion had lost. Now, it is doubtless paradoxical to say that to free my companion I must previously have refrained from doing so. The solution of this paradox is that, though it is true that, in the event of my failing to rescue my companion, he is unfree, he is so not on account of my omission but because of the fall of rock. There is a sense of the word 'freedom' in everyday language, correlated with the verb 'free' as I have just used it, according to which, if someone's bodily movements are severely limited by natural obstacles outside his body, he is unfree. The proof of this is that, even if I were not with my companion, it would still be true that my companion would be unfree after being trapped by the rock. Miller misleadingly exploits this possible sense of 'being unfree', distinct from the one of 'being interpersonally unfree', to justify his view that omissions may constrain freedom. But it is clearly the latter notion of unfreedom which we are concerned with here.

To sum up, I have endeavoured to show in this section that the negative liberal may reasonably define the concept of negative freedom in accordance with the following principles: (1) both physical compulsion and threats curtail the negative freedom of the victim, in that they restrict his repertoire of options; (2) the restriction of a possible course of action is sufficient to cause a loss of negative freedom, irrespective of whether or not the said course of action is really desired by the victim, and (3) any act, be it deliberate, negligent, or accidental—but not an omission— may in principle constitute an interference with freedom.

Positive Freedom

According to Berlin, positive freedom is related to the question 'What, or who, is the source of control or interference that can determine someone to do, or be, this rather than that?'[43] For

---

[43] Berlin, *Four Essays on Liberty*, 121–2.

Berlin a person enjoys positive freedom when he is his own master, when his choices and acts are the result of his own rational deliberation and may be explained by reference to the purposes and ideas that intervened in this deliberation.[44] Positive freedom is here conceived as self-mastery or self-control. For Berlin positive freedom likewise comprises participation in the political process, especially in the election of government authorities. It is interesting to note that Berlin asserts that the ideas of being one's own master and of choosing what one wants without interference—i.e. of positive freedom and negative freedom—'seem concepts at no great logical distance from each other—no more than negative and positive ways of saying much the same thing'.[45] Yet, in a somewhat confusing manner he declares that the inquiries about the source of control and the area of control of human behaviour are 'logically distinct' and that in this difference is to be found the big contrast between negative freedom and positive freedom.[46]

But, rather than in the logical field, Berlin places the fundamental difference between the negative and positive notions of freedom in the historical process that each of them underwent. He maintains that the concept of positive freedom, the idea of a man directing himself, carries within it the 'suggestion of a man divided against himself',[47] of a 'true' or superior self face to face with an irrational or inferior self, and that this suggestion as a matter of fact has played an important part in the authoritarian utilization of the ideal of positive freedom, a utilization based on the claim that coercion of the lower self does not restrict (positive) freedom if it is orientated towards a subject's true self becoming manifest in its fullest shape. Berlin's vision of the historical transformation of the ideal of positive freedom into an authoritarian doctrine is indeed subtler than I have sketched it, for he distinguishes between two forms assumed by this ideal: self-abnegation and self-realization. Whereas self-abnegation is the elimination of desires to achieve an ascetic independence, by self-realization Berlin appears to understand something like self-identification, achieved by knowledge and the use of reason, with

---

[44] Ibid. 131.   [45] Ibid.   [46] Ibid. 129–30.   [47] Ibid. 134.

the rational principles that of necessity govern the natural world
and in particular the social world in such a way as to wish 'freely'
or 'liberatedly' for what is possible and to refrain from wishing,
again 'freely', for what is not possible.[48]

Hayek, for his part, distinguishes the concept of negative freedom from three other common notions of freedom. The first is
political freedom, i.e. freedom as 'the participation of men in the
choice of their government, in the process of legislation, and in
the control of administration'.[49] With the label, too, of 'political'
freedom, and again as something distinct from the conception of
freedom that he supports, Hayek analyses national or collective
freedom as belonging to a people as a whole, rather than to
individuals. Hayek rightly notes that the conquest of national
freedom has not always meant an increase of individual freedom.
The second notion is 'inner freedom', which refers to the degree
to which a person's actions are guided by 'his own considered
will, rather than by his temporary emotions or moral or intellectual weakness'.[50] The third notion is of freedom as 'the physical
ability to do what I want, the power to satisfy our wishes, or the
extent of the choice of alternatives open to us'.[51] As can be seen,
Hayek regards the idea of effective power to do whatever one
wishes as being equivalent to the notion of having options or
alternatives of action open to us. Further on I shall examine the
plausibility of this viewpoint. For the time being, suffice it to note
that freedom as the absence of coercion is distinguished from
freedom as power and, what according to Hayek is the same
thing, from freedom as the availability of alternatives of action;
in Hayek's words: 'Whether or not I am my own master and can
follow my own choices [without the interference of others] and
whether the possibilities from which I must choose are many or
few are two entirely different questions.'[52]

It is worth lingering over Macpherson's analysis of positive
freedom.[53] He starts off by distinguishing three different concepts

---

[48] Ibid. 134–44.
[49] Hayek, *The Constitution of Liberty*, 13.
[50] Ibid. 15.
[51] Ibid. 16.
[52] Ibid. 17.
[53] C. B. Macpherson, *Democratic Theory: Essays in Retrieval* (Oxford:
Clarendon Press, 1973), 108–16.

fused in Berlin's idea of positive freedom, which he designates PL^1, PL^2, and PL^3. PL^1, the basic concept, refers to self-direction or self-mastery, that is to say, the ability to live in accordance with one's own conscious purposes. PL^2 is the metaphysical-rationalist transformation of PL^1: freedom in this sense means being coerced by the fully rational, i.e. by those who have attained self-mastery. PL^3 is the democratic concept of liberty as sharing in political decision-making. Macpherson claims that these three concepts are logically independent of each other and that PL^1 is the one that supplies the basic and central content of Berlin's idea of positive freedom.

What grounding does Macpherson offer for the logical independence of PL^1, PL^2, and PL^3? Above all, he regards it as evident that PL^1 and PL^3 are not one and the same thing. With regard to the connection between PL^1 and PL^2, he rejects Berlin's thesis that the transformation of PL^1 into PL^2 springs from the logic of PL^1. Berlin describes two forms of this transformation. The first, already mentioned, concerns the suggestion allegedly involved in PL^1 of a man divided against himself. It is clear that the transformation is fallacious here. The second comes from interpreting the notion of rationality in the expression 'rational self-direction' not as conformity with one's own conscious purposes but as conformity with a pre-ordained cosmic order. Macpherson properly points out that this conception of rationality is in no wise essential to PL^1. But Macpherson anyway concedes that there is a transition of a psychological nature from PL^1 to PL^2, which follows two different paths: the conservative and the radical. The conservatives, inasmuch as they do not perceive that the removal of the impediments to action arising out of the structure of private property of bourgeois society is a necessary condition for the achievement of PL^1, are led to favour its achievement by means of the intervention of an authoritarian élite. The radicals, on the other hand, come to adopt PL^2 as a result of their perception of the importance of the impediments to PL^1 inherent in the existing class structure and of their assumption that all non-authoritarian methods of removing these impediments are blocked, theoretically or practically.

This is not the place to assess Macpherson's highly controversial claims about the psychological transition from PL^1 to PL^2. But I am concerned to point out that Macpherson's analysis arrives at the conclusion that Berlin's notion of positive freedom, i.e. PL^1, is equivalent to what he terms 'developmental powers'. Developmental power is a person's ability to use and develop his capacities.[54] Instead of the notion of positive freedom, Macpherson proposes the concept of 'developmental freedom', which covers PL^1 but excludes PL^2 and, therefore, does not run the risk of falling prey to the idealistic transformation that is Berlin's *bête noire*. It is worth noting that the idea of developmental freedom is similar to the concept of freedom as power which Hayek distinguishes as one of the common notions of non-negative freedom. The tendency to associate the notion of positive freedom with the concept of power is actually very marked in the literature. But if the concept of power is to serve to explain what is understood by positive freedom, it must itself be the object of analysis. Alan Gewirth takes on this task in maintaining that freedom is the effective power to perform or engage in a certain class of actions.[55] Effective power is one of the two types of power he distinguishes, the other being latent power. A person may have latent power to do X in that his doing X is not entirely beyond his capabilities, but it requires that other persons or objects act on him in order to activate his power, so that he then and only then has the effective power to do X. He has the effective power to do X if his doing X depends on his own choice so that, given his choice to do X, he does X.

There is, however, an important difficulty over the identification of freedom with the effective power to do particular actions which does not escape Gewirth, though it apparently does Hayek and Macpherson. Let us suppose that a person P is coerced to do X by another person Q. Since P does X, he has the effective power to do X, which implies the paradoxical consequence that P is free to do X, despite his being coerced to do so. Gewirth offers two answers to this argument. The first is that the effective power to do X which is a sufficient condition of the freedom to do X must include the effective power not to do X. The second is that the power that a person needs to have to be free must be

---

[54] Ibid. 41–2. Macpherson contrasts developmental power with *extractive power*, which consists in the ability to use other people's capacities to benefit from them.

[55] Alan Gewirth, *Human Rights: Essays on Justification and Applications* (Chicago and London: University of Chicago Press, 1982), 311–17.

effective in the sense that its direct exercise depends on his unforced choice. As we saw earlier on, the concept of coercion is best analysed in terms of the forcible elimination of the agent's options. If this line is followed and thus 'unforced choice to do X' is assumed to mean choosing to do X when there is the option not to do X, or when there is the option not to do X and not to suffer thereby the disagreeable consequence involved in a threat, then the two responses that Gewirth distinguishes come to be in fact one and the same.

As has already been pointed out, for Hayek freedom as power is equivalent to freedom as availability of alternatives of action. Lawrence Crocker, on the other hand, defends a positive liberalism based on the maximization of positive freedom, this being understood as the presence of options or opportunities, and not apparently as power—in the vein of Macpherson and Gewirth.[56] The question it is natural to ask at this point is whether these two views of positive freedom really overlap, as Hayek maintains, or whether on the contrary they are to be differentiated. Gewirth's remark about the convenience of understanding the freedom to do X as the effective power to do X or not suggests that positive freedom must be conceived not so much as the effective power to perform a particular action but rather as the effective power to do some action or other on a certain occasion, but no more than one action, belonging to a set of mutually exclusive actions.

This last conception of positive freedom does not differ from the interpretation of positive freedom as availability of alternatives of action. I shall endeavour to clear up this point. Let us assume that on a given occasion a person P finds three different actions, X, Y, and Z, attractive. Obviously, the positive freedom of P to perform these three actions cannot be conceived as the fact of P's having the power to do X or Y or Z. For if P has the power to do any of these three actions, he then has the power to effect the disjunction of the three. The positive freedom of P has to be understood rather as the power to do X and Y and Z, but not more than one of these three actions on one and the same occasion. But an alternative way of describing the power of a person to perform any one of a set of mutually exclusive actions

---

[56] Lawrence Crocker, *Positive Liberty: An Essay in Normative Political Philosophy* (The Hague, Boston, London: Martinus Nijhoff, 1980).

is to say that this person has available to him the options constituted by these actions. Consequently, to have the effective power
to do X and Y and Z, but not more than one of these three
actions at the same time, is tantamount to having X, Y, and Z as
open options or available alternatives of action.

Hayek's thesis that freedom as power is equivalent to freedom
as availability of alternatives of action, interpreted in these terms,
hits the mark. Macpherson, Gewirth, and Crocker embrace then
the same ideal of positive freedom, in spite of the two different
presentations involved. Positive liberalism, defended by these
three writers, maintains as the central pillar of collective action
the maximization of positive freedom, in the conception I have
just sketched. The negative liberal is reluctant to accept the ideal
of positive freedom, which he looks upon as little less than an
excuse to extend the functions of the state. For him negative
freedom, conceived as an ideal alternative to that of positive
freedom, justifies individual rights, and demands, via them, a
minimal state, whose functions are confined to the maintenance
of peace, security, and respect for property.

The Measurement of Negative Freedom

A basic assumption of negative liberalism is that negative freedom can be increased or decreased. Berlin shares this assumption
when he maintains 'the wider the area of non-interference, the
wider my freedom'.[57] Since clearly the negative freedom of each
person living in a society cannot be unlimited—this would lead to
Hobbes's state of nature, in which the negative freedom of many
persons would be severely curtailed—there arises the problem of
determining in what measure it is permissible to restrict freedom
for the sake of freedom itself. The solution to this problem
envisaged by the classical liberals, such as Locke and Mill in
Britain, and Constant and Tocqueville in France, was to claim
that there ought to be a certain minimum area of personal
freedom which must on no account be violated.[58] But if the
basic ideal of negative liberalism is the maximization of negative

---

[57] Berlin, *Four Essays on Liberty*, 123.   [58] Ibid. 124.

freedom, then the evaluation of this suggestion, like that of any other attempt to solve the problem in question, depends on the application of a satisfactory criterion for the measurement of negative freedom.

There are two questions that the negative liberal should answer from the start in this respect. The first is whether he will treat 'free to such an extent' as a comparative or metrical concept. To be sure, there is a great difference between measuring negative freedom in the sense of establishing whether one person is freer than another or whether there is more freedom in one society than in another, and measuring it in the sense of determining the absolute quantity of freedom enjoyed by a person or existing in a society. Now, if the position of the negative liberal is to have any practical force, it clearly requires making interpersonal or even intersocial comparisons of freedom. However, it is not clear in my opinion that it likewise requires the construction of an absolute metrical system. Be that as it may, I shall assume that negative liberalism can be made enough sense of by providing criteria laying down how negative freedom is to be compared. Therefore, all I shall say below should be interpreted as referring to the problem of the comparison of negative freedom, rather than to that of the absolute measurement of it.

The second question the negative liberal should answer is whether negative freedom is to be measured in terms of *actions-token* or *actions-type*. Actions-type constitute a class of properties such that, when ascribed to an agent, at a certain moment, the agent is said to be performing a certain action (e.g. cutting the lawn, running, writing a letter). Actions-token are particular actions performed by an agent at a particular moment (e.g. 'John mowed the lawn an hour ago'). When an agent performs an actions-token he exemplifies some action-type.[59] This distinction is fundamental since the result of the computation of freedom of a person or of the freedom existing in a society will vary in most cases according to whether the calculation is made in terms of actions-token or actions-type. Moreover, these two diverging criteria concerning the basis for the measurement of negative freedom give as a result two different conceptions of the basic

---

[59] See Alvin I. Goldman, *A Theory of Human Action* (New York: Prentice-Hall, 1970), 10.

ideal of negative liberalism. Indeed, the measurement of negative freedom in terms of actions-token leads us to conceive the ideal of maximum negative freedom as the minimum obstruction of the possible actions-token of the members of a society. By contrast, the measurement of negative freedom in terms of actions-type implies conceiving this ideal as the existence of the maximal set of liberties-type, there existing a liberty-type when all the members of the corresponding action-type are not obstructed as a class (e.g. through a prohibitory legal rule). To be precise, given that it is conceptually possible for two liberties-type to exist simultaneously even when it is impossible for some of their respective instantiations to occur concurrently, this last conception of maximum negative freedom must rather be stated as the operation of the maximal set of *co-possible* liberties-type, i.e. of liberties-type such that the exercise of one does not prevent the exercise of another.

What criterion should the negative liberal adopt? Day, for example, propounds the criterion centred on actions-type. For him liberties are differentiated as liberties to do X, to do Y, to do Z, etc., where doing X, doing Y, doing Z, etc. are kinds of action, not particular actions, as, for example, expressing one's own ideas, joining an association, practising some religion, performing economic activities, etc.[60] On the strength of this pattern of individuation of liberties, it seems natural to think, as I pointed out earlier on, that the maximization of negative freedom will reach its zenith with the enforcement of the maximal set of liberties-type compatible among themselves in the sense that the exercise of one shall not make impossible the exercise of another. The Kantian demand for the achievement of maximum equal freedom might be interpreted along this line.

As against this conception of the negative liberal ideal, Onora O'Neill argues that it is not generally possible to specify the maximal set of co-possible liberties-type.[61] The first step in the argument is to hold that, in order to determine the broadest set of co-possible liberties, we cannot select the one with the largest number of members. O'Neill alleges that, given that all liberties

---

[60] J. P. Day, 'Individual Liberty', in A. Phillips Griffiths (ed.), *Of Liberty* (Cambridge: Cambridge University Press, 1983), 23.

[61] Onora O'Neill, 'The Most Extensive Liberty', in *Proceedings of the Aristotelian Society*, NS, 80 (1979–80), 45–52.

are liberties to perform certain actions and that actions can be individuated in different ways, it will always be possible to increase the number of members of a set of co-possible liberties by the simple expedient of using more detailed or specific descriptions when enumerating the actions which are the object of the liberties that the set in question includes. An alternative way would be to identify the maximal set of liberties with the dominant set of co-possible liberties, i.e. with a set including all the co-possible liberties in the other sets. O'Neill holds here that there is reason to think that this way will generally be closed. For if there are two liberties that can be exemplified, to do X and Y, which are not co-possible, there cannot be a dominant set of co-possible liberties, because any set dominating the one including the freedom to do X cannot dominate any other that includes the freedom to do Y (otherwise it would not be a set of *co-possible* liberties).

In lieu of a maximal set of co-possible liberties O'Neill suggests that a liberal might accept as an ideal the largest *core*-set of co-possible liberties, that is to say, the largest subset of every non-dominated set of co-possible liberties. In other words, the negative liberal could look for the attainment of the intersection of all the sets of co-possible liberties. However, she argues that there are no liberties that are members of every non-dominated set of liberties. The argument runs thus: Given any non-dominated set of co-possible liberties, we can make up a counterpart set consisting of those liberties to restrict those actions that people have the freedom to perform according to the first set. Since the counterpart sets do not share any member with the original sets, and there does not seem to be any reason to think that the former comprise non-co-possible liberties, the negative liberal will not be able to find an intersection of all the (non-dominated) sets of co-possible liberties.

The conception of maximum negative freedom as the largest possible number of non-obstructed options involving the performance of actions-token is better suited to the idea of negative freedom as the non-restriction of alternatives of action. Berlin's theory of the measurement of negative freedom, expounded mainly in a footnote to his lecture,[62] follows precisely this con-

---

[62] Berlin, *Four Essays on Liberty*, 130.

ception, though it goes beyond the consideration of the number of alternatives of action that a person has available without the interference of a third party. Allow me to quote the central part of Berlin's note:

The extent of my freedom seems to depend on (*a*) how many possibilities are open to me ... (*b*) how easy or difficult each of these possibilities is to actualize; (*c*) how important in my plan of life, given my character and circumstances, these possibilities are when compared with each other; (*d*) how far they are closed and opened by deliberate human acts; (*e*) what value not merely the agent, but the general sentiment of the society in which he lives, puts on the various possibilities.

This theory obviously raises two problems: (1) the weight of each of the five criteria selected in the total computation of a person's freedom, and (2) the way of comparing the degrees of freedom enjoyed by the different members of a society in order to determine the total amount of freedom existing in that society. Berlin does not solve these two problems; he merely states, with regard to the first, that the conclusion about the quantity of freedom a person enjoys will always be a debatable question; and, as regards the second, that the same problem is faced by utilitarianism when it has to compare the well-being of different people. In the Introduction Berlin accepts that the problem of increasing freedom as a whole, and of distributing it (a point he had not touched on in the lecture), 'can be an agonizing problem, not to be solved by any hard-and-fast rule'.[63]

Instead of analysing these two problems, I shall now concern myself to see whether the negative liberal would have to accept the five factors Berlin advances to measure negative freedom with. To begin with, the negative liberal would have to reformulate factor (*d*) by agreeing, as has been said already, that any act, deliberate, negligent, or accidental, can restrict the negative freedom of a person. Furthermore, (*d*) cannot be regarded as a factor on the same footing as (*a*) to reckon the amount of negative freedom a person enjoys.[64] For (*d*) qualifies the content of (*a*) in such a way as to prevent (*a*) 'positivizing' the computation of negative freedom. Thus (*a*) should read for the negative liberal as follows: (*a'*) '[my freedom depends on] how many possibilities

---

[63] Ibid., pp. xlviii–xlix.   [64] Crocker, *Positive Liberty*, 49–51.

are open to me, where a possibility is open unless I am barred
from it by a human action (whether deliberate, negligent or
accidental)'. Besides, (c) and (e) make the value of each option
affect the amount of freedom. Although it is true that (c) reflects
some of our intuitions in measuring freedom, it is not easy to
visualize the reasons for including (e) in a non-perfectionist liberal theory, i.e. in a liberal theory that does not seek to suit the
conduct of people to objective standards of moral excellence.

In a provisional balance, it may be stated that the negative
liberal has to take into account (a'), (b), and (c) to calculate the
amount of negative freedom a person possesses. There is another
factor that Berlin does not mention and that Crocker[65] considers
of vital importance, to wit, the degree to which each alternative
of action differs from the other alternatives. According to this
factor, the variety of options open to a person redounds to the
amount of freedom he has. The negative liberal might in this
context avail himself of the following formula, proposed by
Crocker:[66]

$$\sum_{i=0}^{n} f_i \cdot v_i \cdot d_i,$$

where i enumerates the alternatives of action open to the agent, f_i
stands for the degree of freedom to do each action (deriving from
the difficulties or costs), v_i is the value of each alternative for the
agent, and d_i is the factor that represents the degree of diversity
of each alternative to the other alternatives open to the agent.

As to the degree of variety of the alternatives, it seems far
from obvious that, for example, if today John has open to him
the options of going to the cinema or the theatre, and tomorrow
of going to the cinema or to a tennis match, *ceteris paribus* John
has less freedom today than tomorrow. We might consider that
this is so if John is not as fond of artistic shows as he is of
sporting events, but if John hates games and sports and loves the
theatre, the greater diversity he will have tomorrow will have a
negative effect on the total measure of his freedom. I mean by
this that the variety of options must be judged in the light of the
worth that each option has for the agent, so that this factor

---

[65] Ibid. 53–5.   [66] Ibid. 53.

cannot be looked upon as independent of the value of each alternative. It might be granted, on the other hand, that, when there is uncertainty about what a person's plan of life is, the variety of options increases the odds that the set of options will in the end be more valuable for the purpose of carrying out the plan of life that the person happens to choose or to be following at that moment.

Let us now consider the factor involving the degree of the cost or difficulty in actualizing an option. It is clear that the cost or difficulty can only have influence over the amount of negative freedom a person enjoys if it is imposed by somebody else's positive act, be that act deliberate, negligent, or accidental; otherwise the negative liberal would be introducing by the back door considerations relating to positive freedom but alien to negative freedom.[67] In fact, as Crocker suggests, if the difficulty that John has in running a kilometre in ten minutes, owing to his being physically unfit, is to have an effect on the amount of freedom he has, then it seems natural to say of Peter, whose physical condition makes it impossible for him to run a kilometre in ten minutes, that he is unfree to run that distance in that time, but this conclusion, of course, is at odds with the negative conception of freedom. In concordance with this line of reasoning, Oppenheim maintains that an objective obstacle imposed by somebody else's positive act against the performance of X may reduce the agent's freedom provided that this obstacle does not become a total impediment to doing X or a punishment inflicted on the agent for doing X, since in these cases the agent is directly unfree to do X.[68]

In opposition to the consideration of the difficulties of doing X arising from positive acts by other persons for the purpose of determining the degree of freedom the agent has to do X, Hillel Steiner holds that we must distinguish the case in which the previous actions the agent has to perform to do X, in consequence of the active intervention of somebody else, are causally necessary conditions to do X, from the case in which the necessity involved is not causal. In the first case, if the agent is unfree to perform these previous actions, then he has lost altogether his

---

[67] Ibid. 50–1.   [68] Oppenheim, *Political Concepts*, 76–7.

freedom to do X; but, in the second case, even though he is unfree to perform these actions, he preserves his freedom to do X (unless, of course, other restraints on its execution have arisen). In this way, says Steiner, the owners of British passports, whom the US government requires to be in possession of a visa to enter the USA are not unfree to enter the USA, since it is not impossible (but impermissible) for them to enter the USA without a visa.[69]

It seems to me that Steiner is moving in the right direction when he criticizes the position of those who, like Crocker and Oppenheim, defend the idea of a degree of freedom to do X, but that he fails in his final purpose of rejecting the importance of the difficulties or costs imposed on a person's actions in the overall computation of his freedom. The relevant effect of the costs or difficulties to do X should be treated, to my mind, in the same way as a threat to the agent not to do X. In leaving aside the costs or difficulties imposed on an agent to measure his freedom, Steiner is consistent with his opinion that threats do not reduce freedom because they do not render impossible the act or omission in question. He is right in supposing that if somebody threatens an agent so that he does not do X or places costs or impediments in the way of X, he does not affect specifically the agent's freedom to do X. Nevertheless we have seen that the threatener does indeed deprive the agent of the option of both doing X and not suffering the harm involved in the threat, and that this unquestionably constitutes an injury to the agent's freedom. By the same token, if anybody imposes on an agent costs or difficulties in doing X that for any reason whatever cannot be characterized as coercion, he does not deprive him of the freedom to do X, nor does he diminish his degree of freedom to do X, but he certainly takes away from him the option of doing X without the costs and difficulties in question. It is true, as Steiner says, that these costs and difficulties should not operate as a factor independent of the number of alternatives of action in reckoning up the agent's freedom, but it is not true that they have no influence on this reckoning; for they exert an influence by diminishing the number of the agent's options. In the example

[69] Hillel Steiner, 'How Free: Computing Personal Liberty', in Phillips Griffiths (ed.), *Of Liberty*, 76–8.

of the owners of British passports, it is reasonable to think that by requiring a visa the US government deprives them of the option of entering the USA without one. Even if we suppose, as Steiner does, that the government does not remove this option from the repertoire of alternatives open to the British because it does not make it impossible for the British, but declares it impermissible for them, to enter the USA without a visa, the US government's policy might equally be regarded as injurious to the freedom of the British inasmuch as it undoubtedly takes away from them the option of entering the USA without a visa and without the risk of undergoing a sanction for an infringement of US immigration laws.

What we have been saying suggests that the negative liberal would have to adopt a less comprehensive list of factors than the one arising out of Crocker's formula to measure the negative freedom of people; this list includes only two factors: the number of alternatives and the worth of each of these alternatives for the agent. The view that the value of a person's non-obstructed options should be regarded as impinging upon the amount of freedom that person enjoys is not accepted only by Berlin. Carritt, for example, affirms: 'To be forcibly deprived of super-abundance or even of conveniences impairs liberty less than to be forcibly prevented from appropriating necessities.'[70] Taylor, for his part, invites us to consider the following defence of Albania. In Albania religious worship has been forbidden, but, since in Tiranë there are fewer traffic-lights per capita than in London, Albania is freer than Britain because the number of curtailed acts is far lower there. Taylor concludes that the significance of the options open to the agent in terms of his basic purposes has decisive weight in the amount of liberty he enjoys.[71] This view, however, is not exempt from difficulties. In the first instance, as Steiner observes, the introduction of what he terms 'valuational magnitudes' in the calculation of freedom leads naturally to a computation of the negative value of those options thus valued by the agent, and this brings with it paradoxical consequences.[72] Let

---

[70] E. F. Carritt, 'Liberty and Equality', in Anthony Quinton (ed.), *Political Philosophy* (Oxford: Oxford University Press, 1967), 139.
[71] Charles Taylor, 'What's Wrong with Negative Liberty?', in Ryan (ed.), *The Idea of Freedom*, 183.
[72] Steiner, 'How Free: Computing Personal Liberty', 79–83.

us suppose that John has in t_1 three non-obstructed options, X, Y, and Z, and that the respective values that John assigns to them are $+10$, $+3$, and -8. In accordance with the above formula, the computation of John's freedom in t_1 is 5. But let us assume now that later on, t_2, the government eliminates the option Z from John's menu of options. We would surely be tempted to say that John's freedom has been reduced by the intervention of the government, but surprisingly the application of the above formula implies that the government has more than doubled the amount of freedom that John enjoyed in t_1; for in t_2 the result of the computation is 13. Besides, as Steiner says, to assign unity to all the acts valued negatively would remove this paradox but would create another, namely, that a fair number of repugnant acts might figure in the calculation of liberty with an overall value equal to or even greater than an act valued positively.

It must be emphasized that confronted with Steiner's argument about the inadmissibility of negative values in the calculation of freedom the negative liberal could not simplify matters by replying that this calculation should exclude all the acts valued negatively by the agent. This move would imply a return to the thesis already discarded that only interferences with the actions that the agent actually desires can count as limitations on freedom. This thesis, as I have already said, rests on some utilitarian ideal and draws away from the ideal of the minimization of interferences peculiar to negative liberalism. This is the point. The inclusion of the value that each non-obstructed option has for the agent in the calculation of freedom means introducing into this calculation utilitarian considerations alien to negative liberalism. Steiner's argument merely places on the *tapis* an extreme case in which this inclusion brings about seriously counterintuitive consequences for a negative liberal, namely, when there are options which have negative utility; but there is no need to go so far to show the tensions that are generated by pushing in through the back door of negative liberalism considerations about the utility of the options open to the agent. It would be absurd, for example, to hold that an individual for whom only a few actions are left open by his government, and these are by chance the very ones he sets the greatest store by, is freer than an individual who is prevented by his government from performing only a few actions he happens to be keen on at the time. What should be said in this case is that the first individual has more opportunities of satisfying his preferences than the second, but this is a comparative judgement of an eminently utilitarian nature. As Oppenheim says: 'we must be careful not to confuse the degree of an actor's freedom with the degree of value he attaches to his freedom. The degree of my freedom is a function of the possibilities left open to me, but does not depend on whether these do or do not include actions I desire to perform.'[73]

It is true that there are examples, like the Albanian one, that appear to orientate the negative liberal in a direction contrary to the one I have been defending. But I think that the negative liberal might treat our intuitions with regard to these examples without detriment to their basic commitment to the minimization of interferences. In the case of Albania we are asked for a comparison of the amount of freedom existing in two societies. As will be recollected, Berlin is sceptical about the possibility of founding these intersocial comparisons of freedom on precise principles. Nevertheless, it seems to me that there is a rule that we are wont to appeal to implicitly when we make such comparisons, namely, that we do not go by the absolute amount of freedom existent in a society but by the degree to which the amount of freedom really existing in a society approaches the possible maximum of freedom that society could attain to, taking into account its particular characteristics and conditions, excluding to be sure those that have anything to do with impairments to freedom peculiar to that society. It is evident that the London traffic-lights increase the freedom of Londoners when compared with a state of things in which there is heavy traffic and no mechanical means for its proper control. If Tiranë had the same traffic problem as London then the absence of traffic-lights would bring about any number of reciprocal obstructions arising spontaneously for the Tiranians. In the circumstances of British society, the presence of traffic-lights does not mean a drawing away from the maximum of freedom possible but an approach to it. On the other hand, in the circumstances of Albanian society, as probably in those of any other society, the lack of freedom of worship means a withdrawal from the possible maximum of

---

[73] Oppenheim, *Political Concepts*, 74.

freedom for that society. The negative liberal might then assert that we think that British society is freer than Albanian society inasmuch as it approaches its own possible maximum of freedom to a greater degree than Albanian society does.

In answer to a suggestion for the computation of freedom that concentrates exclusively on the number of the agent's non-obstructed alternatives of action, the following criticism might be made. Let us assume that in accordance with a fully effective set of rules Doe can go anywhere but cannot criticize whereas Roe cannot leave his house but may say whatever he likes. If anyone asks which of the two is the freer, a sensible reply seems to be that Doe is freer in one respect (movement) and that Roe is freer in another (expression), but, if it is asked which is freer 'on balance', the only interpretation is that what is being asked is which of the two respects is the more important. It is clear, however, that if we are to avoid a vicious circle, the standard of importance has to be independent of 'being conducive to freedom'. The objection under consideration thus concludes that 'since "maximal freedom" (having as much freedom on balance as possible) is a notion that can be made sense of only by the application of independent standards for determining the relative worth or importance of different sorts of interests and areas of activity, it is by itself a merely formal ideal, one that cannot stand on its own feet without the help of other values'.[74] What could the negative liberal have to say to this criticism? It seems to me the negative liberal has at least the following line of reply open to him. It is true that we think that some liberties are more import-ant than others and that this entails that these relative import-ances should be explained in terms of the connection of negative freedom with other values. But it does not follow from this that negative freedom is not intrinsically valuable. This conclusion would follow only if we assumed that it is self-contradictory to affirm of a thing that it is intrinsically valuable and, at the same time, instrumentally valuable. Furthermore, the use of expres-sions like 'freer' or 'greater loss of freedom' in contexts in which

---

[74] Joel Feinberg, *Rights, Justice, and the Bounds of Liberty* (Princeton, NJ: Princeton University Press, 1980), 11. A similar argument may be found in Ronald Dworkin, *Taking Rights Seriously* (London: Duckworth, 1978), 266–78. Joseph Raz calls this criticism 'the revisionist challenge'; see his *The Morality of Freedom* (Oxford: Clarendon Press, 1986), 13.

we mean that the freedom one person lacks is more important than the freedom that another person is short of suggests erroneously that the loss of freedom caused by the curtailment of an important liberty is larger than that caused by the curtailment of a trivial one. But we can get round this suggestion quite easily if we say that the restriction of more important liberties is not a larger restriction of freedom, but a more serious one, this difference of seriousness being attributable to the encroachment upon other values or to the probability that this restriction will generate new transgressions against freedom.[75] The negative liberal could in short argue that the ideal of maximum freedom is indeed self-sufficient when interpreted as the possession of the largest possible number of non-obstructed alternatives of action, and not as the possession of the more important liberties.

The negative liberal has still to face the problem of the individuation of the non-obstructed options of a person. I referred previously to O'Neill's argument against the notion of maximum freedom as a maximal set of liberties to do actions-type, started from the premiss that it is always possible to increase or diminish the number of any set of liberties-type by changing the mode of individuation of the corresponding actions-type. When the computation of freedom is practised in terms of actions-token, is it in a better position with regard to the problem of individuation? I think that the negative liberal might answer this question affirmatively if he makes use of one pattern of individuating actions-token which, like that advanced by Donald Davidson,[76] is centred in the different sequences of bodily movements which make up the different actions-token and in the different space-time occasions associated with each of these actions. By applying this criterion of individuation, the negative liberal considers that all the descriptions of possible actions-token of a given agent referring to the same bodily movements and the same space-time occasion capture only one option for the purpose of calculating freedom. The measurement of freedom in terms of possible

---

[75] I expounded this line of reply to the 'revisionist challenge' in 'Liberalismo, perfeccionismo y comunitarismo', *Cuadernos de Investigación*, 12, Instituto de Investigaciones Jurídicas y Sociales 'Ambrosio L. Gioja' (University of Buenos Aires) (1989), 5–6.

[76] Donald Davidson, 'Agency', in *Essays on Actions and Events* (Oxford: Clarendon Press, 1980).

actions-token not only allows the negative liberal a greater congruity between this aspect of his theory and the ideal of negative freedom as options not obstructed by the active intervention of other persons, but also opens up to him an interesting way of sidestepping the grave problem of 'counting' the components of total freedom. Of course, this way does not prevent the negative liberal from maintaining that the fact that one society respects the freedom to do a particular type of action and another does not proves that there is a conglomeration of options, namely, all the possible particular actions which exemplify the type of action in question, which are open to the members of the first society and closed to those of the second.

2
The Instability of Negative Liberalism

In the previous chapter I tried to delineate a convincing version of negative liberalism. At each step in the construction of this version I attempted to choose the best of the theoretical alternatives lying open to the negative liberal. In this task I was guided by the wish to show negative liberalism as a theory worth criticizing. It would serve no purpose to criticize negative liberalism by pointing out such problems as a determined champion of this theory might overcome with a modicum of philosophical skill. My endeavours produced a theory advancing as a basic ideal the maximization of negative freedom, conceived as the maximization of options made up of possible actions-token, whether or not the object of actual desires or preferences, not obstructed by the active intervention of other persons (deliberate, negligent, or accidental). This theory defends the primacy of the negative conception of freedom over the positive one. Positive freedom may reasonably be seen as consisting in the availability of alternative courses of action, where several courses of action are available for an agent if he can really follow one or other of them. If an agent is unable to perform an action that action does not count for the purpose of determining his positive freedom, irrespective of whether the cause of this inability is the intervention of other persons or another type of event.

As I pointed out in the Introduction, this book is concerned with a liberal justification of libertarianism or, in other words, a liberal defence of the existence of classical individual rights. The goal is to find a plausible argument which takes as a starting-point adherence to a distinctively liberal social value and reaches a conclusion asserting the existence of pre-eminent negative rights. Negative liberalism may be viewed as a type of liberal defence of libertarianism characterized by its selection of negative freedom from among the possible distinctively liberal values. For the negative liberal the observance of pre-eminent negative rights is the means that leads most naturally to the maximization of negative freedom. Indeed, the value of negative freedom clearly implies the disvalue of the active obstructions to the possible choices of people. Negative rights, promoted to a pre-eminent position in moral reasoning and apparently correlated with the impermissibility of such obstructions, thus appear in the light of conceptual analysis as the moral device blocking in the most direct manner possible the emergence of something which is basically disvaluable for the negative liberal. As long as the negative-liberal argument is carried on in these terms, it moves on a purely conceptual level. Although the negative liberal would also have to take into consideration the possibility that the maximization of negative freedom is sometimes best served by the disregard of negative rights, he might reasonably maintain that, as a rule, the limitation of negative freedom involved in the disregard of negative rights is unlikely to contribute to the maximization of negative freedom. Be that as it may be, my examination of negative liberalism will attempt to point to a more fundamental weakness.

An undefended assumption of this negative-liberal argument is that moral rights have as a correlative certain moral duties, which in the case of negative rights would be no more than obligations to refrain from doing certain things. It is therefore assumed that anybody who affirms the existence of libertarian rights defends the moral impermissibility of certain positive acts. Although, as I hinted, the negative liberal in general does not supply an adequate basis for this assumption about the concept of moral rights, I shall not make use of this failure as a weapon against him. I take this decision because I think that the assumption in question is not peculiar to the reasoning of negative liberalism but on the contrary seems common to any liberal defence of libertarianism. Indeed, I shall avail myself of the assumption about the correlation between moral rights and duties later on in this study, and shall put forward reasons supporting its acceptance.

It is important to distinguish this justificatory strategy concerning the existence of classical individual rights from another negative-liberal strategy which defines negative liberty in terms of these rights. The former strategy, which we may call *instrumental*, sees in negative rights the most natural and direct means of keeping watch over negative freedom, whereas the latter, which I propose to term *constitutive*, sees negative rights not as independent of, and conducive to, negative freedom, but as constitutive of it. As far as I know, Locke was the first to make use of the constitutive strategy when he defined freedom in terms of the respect for the natural rights to life, liberty, and property. Though this strategy would seem to be forbidden him by his adherence to the Hobbesian notion of freedom as the absence of impediment in a passage from *The Second Treatise of Government*,[1] it is clear that Locke uses it when immediately after the passage referred to he states:

Freedom is not, as we are told, *a liberty for every Man to do what he lists*: (For who could be free, when every other Man's Humour might domineer over him?); But a *Liberty* to dispose, and order, as he lists, his Person, Actions, Possessions, and his whole Property, within the Allowance of those Laws under which he is; and therein not to be subject to the arbitrary Will of another, but freely follow his own.[2]

Currently, Rothbard follows a similar path when he defines negative freedom as 'the absence of physical interference with an individual's person and property, with his just *property rights* broadly defined'.[3] The definition of freedom in terms of a set of negative moral rights is a type of moralized definition of liberty. As we saw in the previous chapter, one inconvenience of adopting a moralized notion of freedom is that once one has defined freedom in terms of certain moral principles, one cannot erect such principles on the basis of liberty. This being so, we have to suppose that the negative liberal avoids the constitutive strategy.

Here it is useful too to clarify the type of thesis the negative liberal may try to justify by following the instrumental strategy I have already referred to. In this connection we must be careful to distinguish between the basic libertarian thesis and the complete and articulated formulation of a libertarian doctrine. The basic

---

[1] Sect. 57; quoted at the beginning of Ch. 1.

[2] John Locke, *The Second Treatise of Government*, in *Two Treatises of Government*, ed. Peter Laslett (Cambridge: Cambridge University Press, 1970), 324. On the constitutive role of law in Locke's conception of freedom, see James Tully, 'Locke on Liberty', in Zbigniew Pelczynski and John Gray (eds.), *Conceptions of Liberty in Political Philosophy* (London: Athlone Press, 1984), 71.

[3] Murray N. Rothbard, *The Ethics of Liberty* (Atlantic Highlands, NJ: Humanities Press, 1982), 216.

libertarian thesis is the central component of a libertarian doctrine but does not constitute a normative scaffolding capable of providing a moral solution for the problems of political and social organization. A fully developed libertarian doctrine must also include, among other things, a set of rules delimiting as precisely as possible the spheres of non-interference of individuals living together, whose choices and actions may for that very reason come easily into reciprocal conflict. Inasmuch as the negative-liberal argument that is centred on the proposition that classical individual rights are the most natural and direct medium for the maximization of negative liberty moves on a purely conceptual level, it can only claim to justify the basic libertarian thesis. In order to justify a perfectly developed libertarian doctrine, the negative liberal would have to appeal to empirical considerations concerning the general characteristics of human society and perhaps also concerning the peculiar features of the community in which the moral principles established by the doctrine are to operate.

In this chapter I shall try and show that negative liberalism is an inherently unstable position in the sense that its own internal logic leads its supporters ineluctably to embrace some variety of positive liberalism. By positive liberalism, it is almost needless to say, I understand a theory locating positive freedom in the same place in the moral world that the negative liberal wishes to reserve for negative freedom. This weakness of negative liberalism is in itself sufficient to prevent it from being in a position to justify satisfactorily the basic libertarian thesis. When from the beginning of the following chapter I develop an alternative theoretical approach, I shall do so on the understanding that this approach may be successful just where negative liberalism is most basically deficient, i.e. in the justification of the core thesis of libertarianism.

I believe that negative liberalism suffers from two distinguishable forms of instability. The first is a sort of conceptual instability. The justificatory undertaking of the negative liberal requires him to concentrate on negative freedom as something different from positive freedom. However, under careful analysis, the term 'negative freedom' does not turn out to convey a concept totally distinguishable from the one conveyed by the term 'positive freedom'. The second form of instability, which we shall see to be more important than the first, is a kind of value-instability. I am going to argue that the value-assumptions to which the negative liberal commits himself are in one sense very poor and in another too rich for the purpose of taking up a position that does not lose its identity by merging with positive liberalism. In the first sense, the negative liberal cannot justify why he claims that negative freedom is valuable and positive freedom is not equally so. In the second sense, seeing that the negative liberal holds that the proper way to respond to the value of negative freedom is to seek its maximization, he is bound to agree that, if positive freedom is a value, it is in the same fashion imperative to pursue its maximization.

Conceptual Instability

The distinction between negative freedom and positive freedom that the negative liberal subscribes to in the best version of his position may be expressed by affirming that negative freedom is the absence of restrictions derived from the active intervention of other people whereas positive freedom is the power to put into practice a certain alternative of action. Thus, the negative liberal might say, keeping to the usual jargon in political theory, that negative freedom is a *freedom from* certain obstructions and positive freedom a *freedom to* perform actions. As against this view, MacCallum has argued persuasively that freedom is as much a 'freedom from' as a 'freedom to' and that the partisans of negative freedom and those of positive freedom are not favouring different sorts of freedom but making use of the same concept of freedom characterizable in terms of a single triadic relation.[4] The core of MacCallum's argument is that any intelligible statement about freedom answers to the following scheme: 'P is (is not) free from A to do (not to do) X', where the variable P ranges over agents, the variable A ranges over such different preventing conditions as constraints, restrictions, interferences, and barriers, and X ranges over actions. In other words, all freedom belongs to somebody, and is from something and to do something. When a

---

[4] Gerald C. MacCallum, Jr., 'Negative and Positive Freedom', *Philosophical Review*, 76 (1967).

speaker fails to refer to one of the terms of the scheme, this is due to the fact that the context shows clearly what it is or that he wishes to emphasize the terms that he does mention.[5]

It might be thought that MacCallum's argument does not pay attention to the fact that, as Taylor says,[6] negative freedom is an opportunity-concept and positive freedom an exercise-concept. Positive freedom consists from this standpoint in the exercise of control over one's own life, an exercise that manifests itself in doing not whatever we desire but what is conducive to our self-realization; negative freedom, for its part, encompasses what we are able to do, the options we have, whether we do something to actualize them or not. Tom Baldwin has explored a similar line of analysis.[7] For him, the concept of negative freedom does not involve the requirement that an agent shall achieve an end so that he may be said to be completely free to achieve this end; in other words, anyone who has full negative freedom to do something may still not do it if he chooses not to. One the other hand, Baldwin suggests that positive freedom *par excellence* is moral freedom, that is to say, the effective realization of a personal moral ideal. According to the adherents to moral freedom, such as Kant and Green, it is a sort of freedom because it is the achievement of the condition in which we are not only what we should be but what we really are. In this way, the idea of moral freedom presupposes that human nature includes an essential engagement with certain moral ideals. However, it is clear that the negative liberal cannot resort to this manœuvre in defence of his conceptual apparatus. Let me show why. When tracing the distinction between negative freedom and positive freedom in the most plausible version of his position, the negative liberal does not focus on the 'positiveness' of actually executing certain actions, but on the 'positiveness' of having all that is needed to perform them; not on the 'negativeness' of 'not doing something while being able to do so' but on the 'negativeness' of there being no interference with doing so. It is this last point (the 'negative-

[5] Joel Feinberg, *Social Philosophy* (Englewood Cliffs, NJ: Prentice-Hall, 1973), 9–10.

[6] Charles Taylor, 'What's Wrong with Negative Liberty', in Alan Ryan (ed.), *The Idea of Freedom: Essays in Honour of Isaiah Berlin* (Oxford: Oxford University Press, 1979).

[7] Tom Baldwin, 'MacCallum and the Two Concepts of Freedom', *Ratio*, 26 (1984).

ness' of the absence of impediments) that constitutes for the negative liberal the touchstone for determining the negative or positive character of a conception of freedom. Thus, for instance, if you have not enough money to do an action but are not faced by any obstacles due to the active intervention of other people, you enjoy negative freedom from the conceptual viewpoint of negative liberalism, but in terms of a distinction marked out *à la* Taylor or Baldwin you cannot be said to enjoy negative freedom.

In the light of MacCallum's scheme, the dispute between the negative liberal and the positive one such as is suggested by the distinction between negative freedom and positive freedom set out in the previous chapter may be conceived as a dispute about the range of the variable A. Whereas the positive liberal maintains that this variable ranges over any sort of impediment or obstruction in the way of an action, such as lack of economic means, physical disability, or the coercion of other people, the negative liberal only allows this variable to range over restrictions imposed actively by other people. MacCallum's argument is geared towards showing that this dispute has not to be analysed as involving a discrepancy between two concepts of freedom, about what freedom is, or even about two kinds of freedom, but rather as a disagreement about what cases or instances of loss of freedom each of the parties considers basically undesirable and is prepared to avoid by means of recognizably suitable tools to ensure freedom. Assuming this analysis to be correct, the difficulty that seems to emerge for the negative liberal is that he cannot soundly maintain that he is defending negative freedom as something distinct by its very nature from positive freedom. This is valid both for a conception of the nature of negative freedom in terms of constitutive characteristics of a genus or kind as it is for one that includes in this nature those specific features that give rise to a species.

The negative liberal might attempt a defence by alleging that even if he accepts the analysis of the dispute between negative liberalism and positive liberalism associated with MacCallum's scheme, he can still assert that he is engaged with negative freedom as a set of cases or instances of freedom different from the set of cases or instances of freedom which the positive liberal is concerned with. If both sets of cases of freedom were to be independent of each other, the position of the negative liberal would be strategically similar to that of the positive liberal; both should give reasons justifying their concern with one of the sets but not with the other. In this case, the analysis of the disagreement between the negative liberal and the positive liberal would make it necessary for the former to adduce reasons justifying the differential attention he pays to certain instances of freedom, but it would not place him at a strategic disadvantage to the positive liberal. But it is clear that the two sets of instances of freedom alluded to are not independent of each other, since the set of instances on which the positive liberal concentrates comprises the whole set selected by the negative liberal. This being so, the positive liberal does not need to justify his failure to consider the instances of freedom that interest the negative liberal because actually he considers them together with other instances; but the negative liberal must indeed justify his neglecting those cases of freedom which concern the positive liberal but not him.

The instability of the concept of negative freedom generates the need to justify the peculiar importance of those states of things to which the negative liberal attributes a fundamental worth. If the negative liberal could break away from MacCallum's argument by showing that negative freedom is by generic— or at least specific—nature different from positive freedom, it would not then be so urgent for him to justify his denying to positive freedom a fundamental significance: no more urgent than justifying his denying it to other facts or states of things people usually set store by, such as happiness, beauty, or knowledge. It is precisely the identity of genus and species between negative freedom and positive freedom alleged by MacCallum that gives rise to the presumption that positive freedom is also endowed with those characteristics of negative freedom that justify the negative liberal's assigning it a crucial preponderance.

To reject the identity of species or class the negative liberal might argue that the non-equivalence of the scopes of application of two terms is a suitable criterion for deciding that they designate different classes.[8] Specifically, the negative liberal might adduce that the differences in range of the variables of two triadic predicates otherwise possessing the same meaning give rise to

---

[8] Lawrence Crocker, *Positive Liberty: An Essay in Normative Political Philosophy* (The Hague, Boston, London: Martinus Nijhoff, 1980), 6.

differences in their application to particular cases and, consequently, make it reasonable to think that such predicates stand for different classes. But this argument does not in any way improve the negative liberal's position. For one thing, just consider that, according to the criterion of individuation of classes which it presupposes, the difference between the scopes of application of the expressions 'black duck' and 'white duck' would justify the affirmation that black ducks and white ducks constitute two different classes or species of duck. Nevertheless, in order to elude the necessity of justifying his concern for the negative class or species of freedom but not for the positive, the negative liberal would have to show that these two classes are distinguished in important or, rather, fundamental respects. At any rate, and what is more conclusive, it is useless for the negative liberal to endeavour to prove that negative freedom and positive freedom constitute two different classes because, as I said before, the scope of application of negative freedom is included integrally in that of positive freedom, so that negative freedom might be at most no more than a subclass of the positive class of freedom. Thus, the negative liberal would have to explain why he is not concerned with the positive class of freedom but is with a subclass of this class, i.e. negative freedom.

The negative liberal might attempt to embark on the more ambitious enterprise of rejecting the identity of generic nature that MacCallum postulates between negative and positive freedom. The one weapon, however, that he has at his disposal is the affirmation that an argument about the scope of application of the three variables of the relation of freedom is an argument about what triadic relation freedom is.[9] This affirmation is hard to sustain. If one admits that both the positive and the negative liberal deal with one and the same triadic predicate standing for a 'basic relation of non-obstruction',[10] the disagreements about the range of its variables can only be interpreted as empirical disagreements about when this relation arises or, more probably, as value disagreements about which of its instances or examples are significant for each party or worth taking into account, but by no

---

[9] Ibid.
[10] The expression is Baldwin's, 'MacCallum and the Two Concepts of Freedom', 130.

means as differences about the nature of the aforementioned relation. In addition, even if one agrees that these disagreements about the range of the variables do reflect a difference of opinion about a dimension of the nature of freedom, there is certainly consensus about a central dimension of that nature, namely, that freedom is a relation of non-obstruction of the performance of actions. This point suffices to put the negative liberal in need of justifying his fundamentally different assessment of cases that are similar in the said central dimension.

To sum up, the concept of negative freedom is unstable in the sense that it does not stand for a phenomenon of its own nature distinguishable and entirely separable from the phenomenon the concept of positive freedom alludes to. The conceptual instability of negative liberalism tends to make its defenders slip fatally on the ground of positive liberalism, a process that they can only pull up by setting out reasons to justify the evaluative differentiation they draw between phenomena which are not fundamentally different from each other and are even intertwined. In the next section I shall make it my purpose to show that, when the negative liberal launches out on the task of supplying this justification, he finds out that his position is also value-unstable, in the sense that his value-assumptions lead him, this time irremediably, into the field of positive liberalism.

Value-Instability

If the special consideration that the negative liberal wishes to give to the restrictions arising out of the positive acts of other people is well founded, there has to be a set of reasons R such that (1) R justifies the undesirability of this type of restriction, and (2) R is not true of the other restrictions that the positive liberal holds to be equally undesirable. The central thesis of negative liberalism may be generically described as the assertion that there are basic reasons against certain actions which people must bear in mind in their practical deliberations. These actions are, as I said, positive acts which impose interferences or barriers to possible courses of action. Now, the judgement that there are reasons against an action X seems to involve the assumption that the facts or states of affairs that X necessarily produces are disvaluable. Nobody is likely to claim that a judgement about the existence of reasons against an action is valid for every axiologically possible world, that is to say, for a set of worlds that includes worlds different from ours in respect of the value-properties of the facts and states of affairs that take place in it. Let us take, for example, the judgement that there are reasons against killing innocent people. Do we think that such a judgement is valid for an axiologically possible world in which death is good or, perhaps, for one in which it is not good for people to decide about their own affairs? The response to these questions is surely negative. This being so, the existence of basic reasons against positive acts which impose restrictions on the options of people also depends, at least in part, on the undesirability of the facts or states of things deriving necessarily from these acts.

What are the events produced necessarily by those positive acts which the negative liberal judges it reasonable to avoid and whose disvalue provides the justification for such a judgement? The only value-relevant fact that necessarily results from these acts is the contraction of the menu of options of their victims. The justification of the claim that it is wrong to curtail negative freedom must then include the fact that, by attacking somebody's negative freedom, one necessarily reduces his menu of options. Since the contraction of people's repertoires of options seems actually disvaluable, there is in principle no objection to the negative liberal's trying to justify the undesirability of acts implying a loss of negative freedom by appealing to the disvalue of this contraction. However, we should remember that the contraction of somebody's menu of options is likewise by definition a loss of positive freedom. Thus, although the contraction of the menu of options may justify the undesirability of acts causing a loss of negative freedom, it should be borne in mind that this contraction also occurs when there is a limitation of positive freedom. Consequently, if to justify the undesirability of the obstructions imposed by positive acts the negative liberal gives as a reason that they generate a narrowing of the victim's menu of options, he must also judge as equally undesirable those obstructions or restrictions which have an origin different from the one mentioned. But this is as much as to adhere to the value of the existence of options open to people, i.e. to the value of positive freedom, which includes, but is not exhausted in, negative freedom. To conclude, in the effort to attempt to justify the special consideration assigned to the restrictions arising out of positive acts, the negative liberal finds himself led fatally to subscribe to the central thesis of positive liberalism and, as a result, to forsake his original position.

At this point the negative liberal might protest that, although the judgement that there are reasons against the performance of X depends on the value affected by the necessary results of X, it does not follow that this value can justify by itself a practical requirement to promote it by any means whatever. Specifically, this reply of the negative liberal's says: (1) that the value of the existence of options open to people which he implicitly subscribes to does not entail on its own the requirement that we maximize such options by any efficient means and (2) that this requirement is essential to positive liberalism. These statements are right and proper. There are various possible conceptions of practical rationality. One of them, the maximizing, holds that the rationally appropriate manner of responding to any value is to promote its maximization. This conception belongs to the genus of consequentialist conceptions, according to which when making choices the rational agent must evaluate the results of his conduct in terms of the promotion of those events or states of things he recognizes as valuable. It is clear then that the maximizing conception does not exhaust the group of consequentialist conceptions. In addition, there are conceptions of practical rationality which do not allow that the rational way of responding to the value of certain facts is just to promote them.

Now, though theoretically suitable, the move under consideration is not open to the negative liberal. It should be remembered that the negative liberal endorses the ideal of the maximization of negative freedom. It is obvious then that the negative liberal holds the maximizing conception with regard to the value of negative freedom. This being so, why should he have to reject it in respect of positive freedom, once accepted that it is also a value? Furthermore, why should he have to maintain two different conceptions of practical rationality in the face of two phenomena which are not fundamentally different from each other and are even intertwined? Unless the negative liberal can offer some reason why the maximizing conception is true in relation to negative freedom, but false with regard to positive freedom, he cannot consistently deny that, if people's having open options constitutes a value, then practical rationality requires such options to be maximized, just as the positive liberal asserts.

Could the negative liberal have recourse to another value to justify his adherence to the ideal of the maximization of negative freedom and his rejection of the ideal of the maximization of positive freedom? Before answering this question, it will repay us to recall the habitual division of values into non-moral and moral.[11] The non-moral values are facts or states of affairs whose worth does not depend on the validity of any moral code in particular. A theory about non-moral values tries to answer the question 'What things are good?' The main object of moral codes is to lay down what choices moral agents ought to make and what traits of character they should develop. Accordingly, moral theories include a section about moral rightness and a section about moral virtue; whereas the former aims at answering the question 'What choices are the right ones for me to make?', the latter concentrates on the question 'What traits of character are good?'

Let us take a look at the negative liberal's assertions in terms of this division. The negative liberal affirms that negative freedom is an intrinsic good, i.e. one whose value does not lie in its being an instrument for the securing of another good. According to the division of values, this intrinsic good may be accepted as a moral value or as a non-moral one. The former alternative does not seem admissible for the negative liberal. If he thought that the non-existence of positive acts restricting the repertoires of people's options was a moral value, he would have to affirm that it is always morally good for each agent to choose not to carry out one of those acts. But this affirmation is excluded beforehand by the ideal of the maximization of negative freedom which he endorses. For it is empirically possible, and probable into the bargain, that sometimes the performance of one of these positive acts is a means of avoiding the execution of a larger number of acts of the same type (e.g. a policeman handcuffs a criminal just when the latter is about to take five persons

[11] William K. Frankena, *Ethics*, 2nd edn. (Englewood Cliffs, NJ: Prentice-Hall, 1973), 62 and 80–3.

hostage). It might, however, be replied that in such cases the realization of one of these acts turns out to be justified as a means of maximizing the moral good. But this would involve a serious confusion about the nature of the moral good. If a choice is morally bad, I should not make it; if one believes that to make a choice which the content K is justified as a means of avoiding a larger number of choices with the same content, then what one regards as morally bad is not the choices of type K in themselves, but to choose not to minimize them. The ideal of the maximization of negative freedom does not place moral evil specifically in the choices of positive acts restricting people's options but, more generally, in all choices of acts which do not minimize the number of these acts, a choice of an act imposing a restriction being a possible instance of such choices. Whenever the maximizing conception is applied to a value, this value is in itself recognized as a non-moral value. The content of moral goodness results in these cases from the application of the maximizing conception to the non-moral value in question. It may then be concluded that the negative liberal sees in negative freedom a non-moral value and that the content of moral goodness, as he perceives it, stems from the maximizing conception of practical rationality.

What has just been said implies that on the side of moral values the negative liberal cannot invoke any reason that can justify the special treatment he dispenses to negative freedom *vis-à-vis* positive freedom. His maximizing conception is perfectly applicable to positive freedom, and as a matter of fact the positive liberal applies it. As for non-moral values, we have already seen that to place the non-moral value of negative freedom in people's having open options leads the negative liberal to embrace the basic idea of positive liberalism. He might allege that negative freedom is a means of promoting another value, such as well-being, but this would be tantamount to forsaking his initial position that negative freedom is an intrinsic value. The crucial question then is whether the negative liberal could mention some non-moral value independent of the possession of alternatives of action that is essentially associated with negative but not with positive freedom. This does not appear to be possible. Where could the non-moral disvalue attributed by the negative liberal to positive acts imposing restraints lie but precisely in these restraints?

The argument about the instability of negative liberalism that I have been developing may be synthesized in these terms. Since the concept of negative freedom seems unable to select a phenomenon sufficiently distinguishable from positive freedom, the negative liberal finds himself compelled to delve into the possible justification of his commitment to negative freedom *vis-à-vis* positive freedom. But it seems that the negative liberal has no way of justifying the differential attention he pays to the restraints on people's alternatives of action arising out of positive acts, with regard to restraints admitting to another origin. In order to provide this justification, he has to show that there are reasons against acts implying conceptually an encroachment upon negative freedom which are absent in the limitations of people's repertoires of options which do not derive from those acts. It seems to me, however, that the only reason he can adduce is precisely the value of positive freedom. Once he recognizes that positive freedom is the value underlying his position, the negative liberal has no way of stopping the practical force of this recognition in his reasoning, since by hypothesis he accepts the maximizing conception of practical rationality. The very logic of his position makes him slip irremediably on to the ground of positive liberalism.

But positive liberalism cannot supply a justification of the basic libertarian thesis. This is because the same argument negative liberals use to attempt to justify the existence of certain negative rights would lead positive liberals to justify the existence of equally important positive rights. This being so, positive liberalism cannot justify pre-eminent negative rights. Since negative liberalism has an inherent tendency to merge with positive liberalism, it also fails to justify the basic libertarian thesis. In view of the fall of negative liberalism, it seems to me that it is important for political theory to inquire whether there is an alternative liberal defence of the core of classical liberalism. I shall concentrate on this task from the beginning of the next chapter.

3
Bases for a New Approach

We have seen that in the context of a maximizing conception of practical rationality the recognition that positive freedom is a non-moral good leads the negative liberal fatally into the field of positive liberalism. This aspect of negative liberalism not only deprives it of its identity in the face of positive liberalism but disqualifies it from justifying pre-eminent negative rights, at least in the natural and straightforward shape that I expounded at the commencement of the previous chapter. One possible way of saving negative liberalism would be to present an argument purporting to prove that positive freedom is not a value on the same footing as negative freedom. But, since negative and positive freedom do not appear to be significantly distinguishable and negative freedom may even be considered a part of positive freedom, it seems inevitable to think that, if negative freedom and positive freedom are valuable, they are of similar importance. Once one is embarked on the task of justifying libertarianism on the basis of a distinctively liberal value, it seems to me futile to go on insisting that negative freedom, but not positive freedom, is valuable, or that positive freedom is less important than negative freedom.

At this point it is natural to pose the question whether it is possible to find a liberal defence of the basic libertarian thesis superseding the justificatory failure of negative liberalism. I think that the root of this failure lies in the conception of practical rationality that forms part of negative liberalism. In other words, the flaw is not to be sought in the recognition that positive freedom is a value but in the theory that maintains that the rationally appropriate response to any value is the pursuit of its maximization. It must be pointed out very clearly that this theory is a moral conception open to controversy and that the acceptance of it on the part of the negative liberal without any argument turns it into an unsupported dogma. The alternative approach I wish to suggest admits whole-heartedly that positive freedom is an intrinsic value but rejects the maximizing conception of practical rationality in favour, not of a non-maximizing consequentialist conception, but, more radically, of a non-consequentialist conception. To show the initial feasibility of this approach, it is necessary to argue that judgements of the type '*A* is a value' do not entail moral judgements of the type 'We ought to act in such a way as to maximize *A*'. This means admitting that there is a gap between value-judgements and moral judgements. If it is possible to argue persuasively in this direction, then negative liberalism must be seen as a position comprising two principles of a different nature: an axiological principle according to which negative freedom is intrinsically valuable, and a consequentialist moral principle requiring us to act always in such a way as to produce the largest amount of what has intrinsic worth. What I have endeavoured to prove up to now is that the acceptance of the first principle involves the acceptance of a more general axiological principle stating that positive freedom possesses intrinsic worth. The conjunction of this principle and of the consequentialist moral principle is equivalent to positive liberalism. Although the theoretical approach I suggest starts from the acceptance of the axiological principle concerning the intrinsic worth of positive freedom, it strongly rejects the maximizing moral principle. In this way, this approach runs no risk of merging into positive liberalism.

The existence of a gap between axiological principles and practical judgements, especially moral ones, does not seem hard to sustain. Above all there are reasons of a methodological order for recognizing that value-judgements do not *per se* entail moral judgements. In fact, it may be noticed that, on the assumption that values must be taken into account in moral deliberation, the thesis that judgements of the type '*X* is valuable' entail moral judgements of the type '*X* ought to be maximized' would make maximizing consequentialism true just by virtue of the postulated meaning of value-judgements and all the other moral theories false on the same account, i.e. the non-maximizing consequentialist positions and the whole gamut of non-consequentialist positions. This result does not seem acceptable. If maximizing consequentialism is to be accepted, this will be due to an argumentation proving its superiority to rival moral positions and not as a result of an analysis of the word 'valuable'.

On a substantive level of analysis it does not seem to me

difficult to argue in favour of the thesis concerning the logical independence between axiological principles and moral judgements. Thus John Gray affirms that it is far from obvious that anybody accepting an axiological principle thereby undertakes to maximize what according to the principle has intrinsic value; for instance, he might interpret the principle in the sense that it forbids a lessening of the amount of this intrinsic value extant in the world, but not as a principle requiring the amount to be increased, still less maximized. Gray likewise holds that 'the notion of intrinsic value is itself so opaque that no one can with complete confidence elicit practical maxims from axiological principles which state only wherein it consists'.[1] John Finnis subscribes to the same thesis in different terms when he asserts that the principles that express the general ends of human life do not acquire moral force except through a response to the problem of 'practical rationality'. From this conception of Aristotelian origin practical reasonability is a moral value framing our pursuit of goods.[2] It is true that neither Gray nor Finnis put forward any argument in favour of the thesis that the meaning of axiological judgements is not associated with the maximizing conception other than an implicit appeal to our linguistic intuitions. Moreover, it is not easy to visualize what shape such an argument could take. However, it seems to me that the existence of a non-consequentialist moral tradition and the fact that it is hard to deny that intrinsic values have played an important part in the development of this tradition are a clear sign that our perception of intrinsic values does not find in them the requirement of their maximization. In any case, the burden of the proof falls back upon whoever maintains that maximizing consequentialism is true merely by virtue of the meaning of value-judgements.

The working out of the alternative approach I am suggesting to justify the basic libertarian thesis requires defending an anticonsequentialist or deontological theory of practical rationality. This theory will have to specify what the rationally appropriate response is to the fact that positive freedom possesses intrinsic

---

[1] John Gray, *Mill on Liberty: A Defence* (London: Routledge & Kegan Paul, 1983), 23–4.
[2] John Finnis, *Natural Law and Natural Rights* (Oxford: Clarendon Press, 1980), 100–1.

value. The theory I have in mind implies, broadly speaking, that certain negative moral duties that require abstention from acts against positive freedom have priority in our moral reasoning. The combination of the principle establishing the intrinsic value of positive freedom and the deontological theory alluded to will make possible a justification of libertarian rights and of their pre-eminent importance in our moral life. In this chapter I am going to lay the bases of my approach to the justification of the basic libertarian thesis along three different paths. In the first place, I shall try to clarify in what sense the theory of practical rationality which is part and parcel of this viewpoint is deontological. Next I shall endeavour to sustain a necessary assumption both for negative liberalism and for my view, an assumption which, as I said in the previous chapter, is not the object of explicit argumentation in negative-liberal literature. I refer to the assumption that moral rights may be viewed as logically derived from moral duties of particular importance. This assumption will enable us to found the basic libertarian thesis, laid down in terms of the notion of moral rights but not of moral duties, starting from the existence of pre-eminent negative duties to respect everyone's positive freedom. Lastly, I shall indicate in what particular sense positive freedom may be reasonably looked upon as being vested with intrinsic value.

Moral Deontologism

Moral theories may be seen as doctrines about what reasons or considerations proceeding from the moral realm are to occur as premises in the practical reasonings of moral agents. It is natural to think then that moral deontologism may be characterized in contrast with moral consequentialism according to the type of moral considerations it selects as the basis of the moral argumentation. Deontologism and consequentialism appear to be closely linked with two traditions of moral thought of antique dye, one associated with Hebrew culture, the other with Greek culture. In the former the primary moral fact is the fulfilment of certain mandates, of which the Ten Commandments are the most familiar examples; in the latter, morality has its locus in the achievement of good.[3] This fundamental dichotomy of moral thought reappears clearly in modern times in Kant's and utilitarian ethics respectively. While Kantian ethics places morality in the respect of certain moral imperatives like 'Thou shalt not kill an innocent man' or 'We must keep our promises', utilitarianism concentrates on the production of the greatest possible amount of general happiness.

Some characterizations of deontologism suggest that, while from this moral perspective the fact that an agent must do X depends on the kind of action that X is, for consequentialism this fact on the other hand depends on the consequences or results of X. Thus, for example, when characterizing Judaeo-Christian ethics in contrast with what she terms (for the first time) 'consequentialism', G. E. M. Anscombe writes: 'The prohibition of certain things simply in virtue of their description as such-and-such identifiable kinds of action, regardless of any further consequences ... is a noteworthy feature [of Judaeo-Christian ethics]'.[4] John Finnis, for his part, lays down as one of the basic requirements of his deontological theory of practical rationality that one should not choose to do any act which of itself does nothing but damage or impede the realization of a good. Finnis contrasts this requirement with the consequentialist view that an act of this kind is permissible, and even obligatory, if its good consequences outdo the damage caused by the act in itself. Let us consider, for instance, the act of killing an innocent person in order to save the life of some hostages. For Finnis the good to be obtained through the liberation of the hostages would not be produced *as an aspect of killing an innocent person* but as one of the innumerable multitude of consequences of the act of killing.[5] It is evident that Finnis regards the nature of an act, what an act is in itself, as something different from its consequences. Moreover, the characterization of deontologism as a moral perspective

---

[3] A historiographic account of the origins of moral thought in Jewish and Greek cultures may be found in Crane Brinton, *A History of Western Morals* (London: Weidenfeld & Nicolson, 1959), ch. 3.

[4] G. E. M. Anscombe, 'Modern Moral Philosophy', in W. D. Hudson (ed.), *The Is–Ought Question* (London: Macmillan, 1969), 185–6.

[5] Finnis, *Natural Law and Natural Rights*, 118–19. The idea that the moral obligatoriness of a particular act depends on what kind of action it is is also present in the intuitionist theory of Sir David Ross: see *The Right and the Good* (Oxford: Clarendon Press, 1930), ch. 2.

from which the nature of an act is important but not its consequences seems capable of explaining, for example, why the principle 'Thou shalt not kill' is one of the moral principles usually quoted by deontologists. In effect, judging that a particular action X is morally wrong on the ground that it is a case of killing is to make the moral status of X depend on the kind of action X is.

However, the above characterization of deontologism breaks down because it does away with the difference from consequentialism that we want to capture. According to this characterization the obligatoriness of an action X depends for a moral deontological theory on the kind of action X is. But does not X's belonging to one or another kind often depend on the consequences of X? For instance, does not whether X belongs to the kind 'killing actions' depend on one of the results of X's being the death of someone? Obviously the reply is in the affirmative. In this way the difference between deontologism and consequentialism blurs since in all likelihood all the interesting examples of deontological theory are at the same time, according to the characterization under consideration, instances of consequentialist theory.

There is an interesting move that might be made to save the deontologist from being involved in the consideration of consequences in the moral assessment of certain actions: Let us think of Peter's killing John and call this particular action K. According to a familiar deontological view, K appertains to the 'killing' class and is therefore to be condemned morally. But notice that the consequences of that particular action have no place in this condemnation, unless by consequences one understands not only the events connected causally (contingently) with K but also those facts linked to K in a conceptual manner (necessarily). John's death is not a causal effect of Peter's killing John; the causal effects of this action are other (e.g. that John's children cry, that the police are after Peter, etc.). John's death is indeed a logical or conceptual consequence of Peter's killing John. But seeing that it is precisely John's death and not those other, causal, effects that constitute the reason for a standard deontologist to condemn K, it is evidently false that, when with the word 'consequences' we embrace exclusively the causal effects, the deontologist takes his stand on K's consequences in judging it to be morally wrong; he is simply taking his stand on K's nature, and, as just shown, to do so he does not appeal to the consequences of K either.

The plausibility of this move stems from a criterion of individuation of actions different from the one that lies behind the characterization of deontologism as a moral position evaluating actions morally on the ground of their respective natures and not of their consequences. To clear up this point, let us avail ourselves of a well-known example in the theory of action originally proposed by Donald Davidson:[6] I lift my finger, press the switch, turn on the light, light up the room, and, unawares, warn the burglar. According to the criterion of individuation of actions adopted, what I did will be described by saying that I performed five actions or one only. The criteria of individuation of actions in play may be set out as follows:

(C1) Two actions are identical if, and only if, they involve the same set of bodily movements.

(C2) Two actions are identical if, and only if, they involve the same agent, the same property, and the same temporal occasion.[7]

The acceptance of one or the other criterion implies a variation in the meaning of our action-discourse; the word 'action' in particular will have a different meaning according to whether our discourse presupposes one or the other criterion. It is in virtue of this fact that one and the same statement of our action-discourse may express two different ideas according to the view endorsed in the matter of individuation. Furthermore, in order to express one and the same idea we are often compelled to utter different action-statements, likewise by virtue of the criterion of individuation adopted. To distinguish the two concepts of action at stake I propose to speak of 'movement-action' when our discourse presupposes (C1), and 'description-action' when it presupposes (C2).

There are then two distinct versions of the characterization of

---

[6] 'Actions, Reasons, and Causes', in *Essays on Actions and Events* (Oxford: Clarendon Press, 1980), 4.

[7] (C1) is defended, but not formulated, by Davidson in 'Agency' (included in *Essays on Actions and Events*). (C2) is formulated by Alvin I. Goldman in *A Theory of Human Action* (New York: Prentice-Hall, 1970), 10.

deontologism that I am questioning, each of which answers to an action-discourse associated with a divergent criterion of individuation. In the first version deontologism is characterized as a position for which the moral rightness of any movement-action X depends on the kind of action X belongs to, whereas consequentialism is seen as claiming that the moral rightness of any movement-action depends on its consequences or results. This version is the most natural interpretation of the characterization of deontologism under consideration. The objection made to this characterization really refers to its first version. Within the framework of an action-discourse answering to (C1), the objection would run thus: the nature of many movement-actions hinges on their consequences or, alternatively, the description of many movement-actions depends on their consequences. The second version of the characterization called in question says that for the deontologist the moral rightness of any description-action X depends on the kind of action X belongs to, whereas for the consequentialist on the other hand it turns on the consequences or results of this description-action.

In relation to the second version two important points should be made. First, the phrase 'on the kind of action X belongs to' must be read in the following way: on the property that X involves. Thus the moral wrongness of the description-action of Peter's killing John, for example, would depend for a deontologist on this description-action's involving the property of 'killing someone'. Secondly, and more importantly, it is this version that is made use of by the move denying that the deontologist takes into consideration the consequences of the actions by taking into account their respective natures. In effect, what the move really says is that the deontologist who reflects on John's death in morally condemning the description-action of Peter's killing John does not take into consideration one causal effect but rather one logical consequence of this description-action. Clearly, the move could not be made against the background of the first version. To show this let us suppose that Peter kills John by firing his gun. Let us assume, further, that causal contexts are transparent ones. Then, if the move is to respect the Law of the Indiscernibility of Identicals, it may not say that John's death is not a causal effect of the movement-action of Peter's killing John, for John's death is indeed a causal effect of the movement-action of Peter's firing his gun, and these two movement-actions are identical (according to (C1)).

Anyway, the move in question is quite unsatisfactory. The difficulty lies in the fact that the second version, to which the move must appeal, distorts the consequentialist's position. In accordance with this version, the consequentialist must attend to the causal effects of description-actions when uttering a judgement about their moral quality, but must deem irrelevant their logical consequences if he does not wish to be mistaken for a deontologist. Nevertheless, the logic of his position will often drive him to base his judgement not on the causal effects but rather on the logical consequences of description-actions. Let us consider, for instance, in what way a consequentialist for whom the preservation of human life is an intrinsic good would assess morally the description-action of Peter's killing John. For sure the first thing he would want to take into consideration in making his assessment would be John's death; but he may not do so because, in relation to the said description-action, John's death is not a causal effect but a logical consequence. (It is true that whenever Peter does something that may truly be described as the performance of the description-action of killing John, what he does may likewise be truly described in terms of another description-action that has John's death among its causal consequences, so that the supporter of the second version might defend himself by saying that in any case the consequentialist may take John's death into account in order to judge what Peter does as morally wrong when what he does may be truly described as the performance of the description-action of Peter's killing John. But this does not affect my point in the sense that the consequentialist may not attend to John's death in order to judge *the description-action of Peter's killing John* as morally wrong.)

On the other hand, the position of the utilitarian consequentialist is especially preposterous according to the second version. The heart of his ethic demands that he deem morally right the description-action of promoting human happiness. This being so, he is led to the following dilemma: *qua* utilitarian he must base his judgement on the relation of this description-action to the production of human felicity, but *qua* consequentialist he may not take this relation into account since to do so would be to consider the nature of the description-action of promoting human happiness and not its causal effects.

The second version hides what the first one makes clear, namely, that the moral evaluation of human conduct must of necessity take into consideration the causal process it initiates. There exists nothing like the moral assessment of human behaviour regardless of the modifications that this behaviour gives rise to in the agent's external world. The second version conceals this truth, which is almost a commonplace, under the jargon term 'the nature or kind of an action'. This fundamental shortcoming is responsible for the distorted picture of deontologism and consequentialism it offers. It forces the deontologist to consider only those causal effects that are caught by the verb that happens to designate the action whose morality is being assessed; and it forces the consequentialist to consider only those effects that fall outside the set of features linked to the meaning of that verb. As we saw, the second version deforms in particular the position of the consequentialist. All in all, I think we must discard the second version and, as a result of this, reject the move purporting to defend the characterization of deontologism as a moral outlook having no regard to the consequences of human action. Indeed, I have tried to show that, in considering whether an action appertains to one particular class or not, the deontologist takes its consequences into account, and could not do otherwise if he is concerned with its moral assessment. It seems to me then that there are no reasons for maintaining that deontologism assesses actions morally on the strength of their respective natures but not of their consequences.

It may be asked at this point whether the reverse is not also true, i.e. whether, in making use of the consequences of an action as the touchstone for its moral evaluation, the consequentialist is not *eo ipso* taking into account that this action belongs to a certain class. In fact, according to the characterization of consequentialism I have called in question, the obligatoriness of an action X depends for this moral outlook on the effects of X on the production of some state of affairs S. But is not this the same thing as saying that the obligatoriness of X depends on X's nature being 'to produce S'? For example, is it not true that for utilitarianism the obligatoriness of an action X depends on X's belonging to the class of actions 'to promote general happiness'?

Since the responses to these questions seem affirmative, it may also be denied that the consequentialist judges the morality of actions having regard to their consequences but not to their natures.

In view of the preceding discussion, I lay aside explicitly the idea that moral deontologism excludes the consequences of actions of the set of morally relevant considerations. Instead I shall assume that moral deontologism is a moral outlook that denies that the consequences of actions exhaust the set of morally relevant considerations. In other words, I shall assume that the difference between deontologism and consequentialism does not lie in—for the latter but not for the former—the results of an action's being relevant to determine its moral status, since both moral outlooks take into consideration the consequences of human behaviour, but in the circumstance that consequentialism, as opposed to deontologism, takes *exclusively* into consideration the consequences of actions for the purpose of their moral assessment. For the consequentialist the moral status of an action is completely determined by its causal effects. The deontologist, on the other hand, considers other factors as well.[8] If we assume that the nature of an action necessarily includes other factors in addition to its causal contribution to the production of certain events, it may be illuminatingly asserted that deontologism is a moral outlook that has regard to the nature of an action when it says whether it is right or wrong. When assessing an action morally, the deontologist considers not only the modifications in the world that this action helps to bring about but also all those aspects independent of the *causal structure* of the action that may influence its appertaining to one class or another. Some-

---

[8] For this way of characterizing deontological theories (as denying what the consequentialist ones affirm, i.e. denying that the rightness of an action depends *entirely* on its results), see Richard B. Brandt, *Ethical Theory* (Englewood Cliffs, NJ: Prentice-Hall, 1959), 354–5 (instead of 'deontologism' the term 'formalism' is used here); William K. Frankena, *Ethics*, 2nd edn. (Englewood Cliffs, NJ: Prentice-Hall, 1973), 15, and Bonnie Steinbock, Introduction, in Bonnie Steinbock (ed.), *Killing and Letting Die* (Englewood Cliffs, NJ: Prentice-Hall, 1980), 4 (the term 'absolutism' is employed instead of 'deontologism'). However, I think that, in using a negative notion, the writers quoted have in mind the probable non-existence of 'pure' deontologists, i.e. deontologists who in no case grant moral relevance to the consequences of an action, rather than the fact, emphasized in the text, that considering the nature of an action normally involves taking the consequences into account.

times these aspects correspond to what might be called the *subjective structure* of an action, such as the degree of the agent's knowledge, his intentions, the effort needed to perform the action, etc. Other aspects are independent both of the causal structure and of the subjective structure and have more to do with the connection between the behaviour of the agent and the events to which this behaviour contributes. Thus, sometimes deontologists consider it relevant whether the attack on a good is carried out by action or inaction. The deontological moral theory I shall defend precisely assigns special importance to the active or passive form the agent's intervention assumes in bringing about certain events which involve a curtailment of people's positive freedom. I shall embark upon the study of this question in the following chapter.

A second difference that there appears to be between consequentialism and deontologism is concerned with the second-order axiological theories with which these outlooks tend to be associated. It is usual to distinguish between monist and pluralist axiological theories. While the former recognize the existence of only one value in itself, the latter maintain that there are several values in themselves different and reciprocally independent. The better-known consequentialist theories, like hedonism and welfare utilitarianism, are axiologically monist. The advantage of the association between consequentialism and value-monism is obvious: by recognizing a single intrinsic value, the consequentialist considers moral rightness functionally dependent on a single variable, namely, the measure in which an action promotes or reduces this value. However, it is clear that the consequentialist may embrace a pluralist axiological conception (e.g. Moore's utilitarianism). In such a case the consequentialist finds himself up against the difficulty that an action may affect in diverse ways the different values contemplated in his axiological theory. Unless he affords some rule for comparing the different values in play, his criterion of moral rightness will show uncertain results in a large number of cases. In this way, the consequentialist who decides on value-pluralism finds himself led into upholding the commensurability of the intrinsic values whose existence he recognizes. In short, given the structure of its theory of practical rationality consequentialism tends to be associated either with axiological monism or with an axiologically pluralist position that includes the thesis of the commensurability of intrinsic values. By contrast, given that the promotion of intrinsic values does not constitute the only criterion of moral rightness of the deontologist, he does not appear to need to become engaged with value-monism or with the thesis of the commensurability of intrinsic values.

Moral deontologism, as I conceive it in this essay, has a third peculiar feature which must be pointed out. I refer to what it is usual to speak of nowadays as *agent-relativity*.[9] The first feature of deontologism that I mentioned above is connected with the content of the moral reasons it accepts. Agent-relativity has nothing to do with this question but it has with one of an entirely different character: assuming the existence of a reason R for or against a possible action X performed by an agent P, for whom is this reason valid? Agent-relativism holds that R is valid only for P. *Agent-neutralism*, on the other hand, maintains that R is valid for anyone. The moral reasons postulated by consequentialism are agent-neutral. If within the framework of a consequentialist theory it is affirmed that an event E is good, i.e. that there is a reason R in favour of E's happening, then R is valid for any agent, even for those who are not the ones who are likely to bring E about. Let us suppose that a criminal threatens me that he will kill five innocent persons if I do not kill an innocent man (it is unimportant whether this man is or is not among the five whom the criminal threatens to kill). If I were a consequentialist who agrees that it is wrong to kill an innocent person, I should say that the badness of the possible act of killing on the part of the criminal constitutes for me a reason to prevent this act with as much right as the badness of my act in killing an innocent person constitutes a reason for me to avoid this act. Indeed, if the position of this consequentialist were to include as a requirement the minimization of evil, he would then asseverate that I have in the example the moral duty to kill the innocent person. On the other hand, moral deontologism is closely related to an agent-relative point of view. Let us consider how I would apply the principle that forbids the slaying of an innocent person to the

---

[9] The term 'agent-relativity' was introduced by Derek Parfit ('Prudence, Morality, and the Prisoner's Dilemma', *Proceedings of the British Academy*, 65 (1979); *Reasons and Persons* (Oxford: Clarendon Press, 1984), 104.

foregoing example if I were a deontologist. I should think that the badness of the act of slaying five innocent persons on the part of the criminal does not provide me with a reason on a footing with the reason derived from the badness of my act of killing an innocent person and, consequently, I should conclude that I should refrain from executing this act. (Of course, if I were to think that killing is as wrong as letting others die, I might not agree with this conclusion, seeing that the badness of my not preventing the five persons from dying would indeed supply me with a reason for slaying the innocent man in the example under consideration. However, it is of the utmost importance to note that in this case my moral reasoning would not depart from an alleged agent-neutral moral reason against killing but from an alleged agent-relative moral reason against letting die.)

The concept of agent-relativity enables us to catch an important aspect of the libertarian conception of negative rights. For according to this conception the fact that a possible action X of an agent P transgresses a negative right G of someone furnishes P with a reason not to perform the action which is not outweighed by the circumstance that the failure to do X will cause another agent Q to violate the negative rights G of five other people. Robert Nozick has strongly emphasized this aspect of libertarian rights in considering them *side-constraints*. According to Nozick, libertarian rights do not form part of a goal we must contribute to in the greatest possible measure with our actions. If this were so, then the libertarian conception would not imply an absolute prohibition against the violation of negative rights, but the requirement to minimize the violations of negative rights as a whole. This viewpoint would constitute a sort of utilitarianism in which the non-violation of negative rights would take the place of general happiness.[10] It seems to me that Nozick is right in asserting that this 'utilitarianism of rights' does not afford an accurate vision of the way in which negative rights are conceived in the libertarian perspective. Agent-relativity is thus an essential component of any moral theory that claims to serve as a foundation of the basic libertarian thesis. Here is is important to notice that this feature of negative rights constitutes a powerful additional

---

[10] Robert Nozick, *Anarchy, State, and Utopia* (Oxford: Blackwell, 1974), 28–30.

argument for giving up the maximizing conception of practical rationality subscribed to by negative liberalism. For the intrinsic disvalue of obstructing people's possible choices, conceived from the agent-neutral point of view of negative liberalism, cannot satisfactorily justify negative libertarian rights, but rather the 'utilitarianism of rights' studied by Nozick. In Chapter 5 I shall concern myself with the hard task of seeking the rationale of the agent-relativity of negative rights.

To recapitulate, for the purpose of this book I proposed to characterize moral deontologism as a moral outlook possessing the following features: (1) it admits as moral reasons considerations not based upon the results of human conduct but on the nature of the intervention of the agent in bringing about these results or on the nature of the subjective states preceding the action, (2) it does not commit itself either to value-monism or to the thesis of the commensurability of intrinsic values, and (3) it holds that the moral reasons against certain actions are valid only for the authors of these actions. In the remainder of this section I shall endeavour to dismiss an important objection to moral deontologism in general.

The objection to which I refer finds substance in the fact that the descriptions which play a part in deontological moral evaluations refer to only some of the results of the actions assessed; the other results are not included in the description of what someone did but are counted among 'the consequences of what he did'.[11] It might then be supposed that a further distinction between deontologism and consequentialism is that, while for the latter *all* the consequences of an action are important, for the former only a specified series of these consequences is. This alleged characteristic of deontologism might be used in support of a charge of insensibility against it in face of the great variety of consequences that a human action may have. A natural example here would be: in connection with the deontological principle forbidding persons to steal, all that matters is the result 'being deprived of the use of a good of one's own', but other possible consequences do not matter, such as the use of that good to save a human life. It should be noted, however, that, as it is described, the contrast

---

[11] Jonathan Bennett, 'Whatever the Consequences', in Steinbock (ed.), *Killing and Letting Die*, 112.

claimed does not really exist. In fact, it is untrue that for utilitarianism, for example, all the consequences of an action are important. The resulting 'happiness obtained' alone matters. Though this result, being a very broad one, usually embraces a numerous series of consequences of each action, there are always a number of effects that are left out; for example, when assessing the action of an agent who kills someone else with a pistol, the utilitarian normally will not consider the consequence that the weapon was slightly soiled with powder as a result of the deadly shot.

More plausible appears to be an objection to deontologism starting from a consideration of the *principles of selection* of the morally relevant consequences that the consequentialist may adopt *vis-à-vis* the deontologist. The consequentialist, it might be argued, does not lay down the moral obligatoriness of actions on the basis of their bare consequences but taking the consequences considered evaluatively as his starting-point. Sometimes the same idea is expressed by saying that for consequentialism the moral rightness of an action depends on the *goodness* of its results or consequences.[12] In this way, any consequentialist moral theory would incorporate two components: an ethical principle that makes the moral rightness of an action X depend on the impact X has on the attainment of a good, and an axiological thesis that affirms that good is made up of certain facts or states of affairs. Whether a result is good or bad in the eyes of the consequentialist is a sufficient condition for him to take it into account. According to the objection I am considering, the deontologist's position would in this sense be completely different. Apparently he might regard a consequence as good or bad and even so remain blind to it if it happened not to be comprised in the pertinent verb. In this way, although it is not true, as I have already pointed out, that the consequentialist takes into consideration all the consequences of an action when he utters a moral judgement on it, it might be alleged that the consequentialist always considers all the value-relevant consequences. On the other hand, it seems that the position of the deontologist leads him to consider only a portion of the good or bad results of

---

[12] Frankena, for example, writes: 'A teleological theory says that the basic or ultimate criterion or standard of what is morally right, wrong, obligatory, etc., is the nonmoral value that is brought into being' (*Ethics*, 14). Concordantly: Brandt, *Ethical Theory*, 354; Steinbock, 'Introduction', 4.

an action. This apparent insensibility to many value-relevant results of an action is what lies behind the tendency present, for example, in writers like Jonathan Bennett to characterize deontologism as a type of *moral conservatism, absolutism*, or *rigorism*. Bennett assimilates ethical non-consequentialism to conservatism, defined as a position accepting principles of the following kind: 'It would always be wrong to ... whatever the consequences of not doing so',[13] but his conception of conservatism does not seem to be applicable without more ado to ethical deontologism as I have been describing it up to now. It is misleading to say that, once the deontologist admits that there is a moral reason laying down the moral duty to perform an action, he necessarily disregards altogether the consequences of the action that are not caught up by the verb occurring in the moral principle; he might and should take into consideration those consequences if they defined a type of behaviour whose omission either is permissible in his moral system—i.e. constitutes an exception to the moral principle in question—or else is obligatory. These two possibilities are excluded beforehand by Bennett because (1) he explicitly defines conservatism as a position that lays down moral principles without exceptions ('It would always be ...'), and (2) he implicitly discards the possibility of conflicts between duties within the moral systems he terms 'conservative'. In particular this last manœuvre makes his idea of conservatism fail as an accurate representation of moral deontologism. The logical possibility of conflict between moral principles in a deontological moral system cannot be dismissed without an additional argument. It is precisely a deontologist like Sir David Ross who introduced the idea of prima facie moral duties, in order to make the reconstruction of common-sense morality possible as a logically coherent moral system despite the obvious presence of conflicts between its component principles. Although it is true that a deontologist cannot consider the value-relevant consequences that are not contemplated in *any* of the component principles of the moral system he defends, it is not true that he can only take into account the consequences contemplated in one of those principles.

Besides, and more importantly, it is a mistake to hold that

---

[13] Jonathan Bennett, 'Whatever the Consequences', 111.

deontologism is in essence a 'value-short-sighted' moral outlook. Although, in formulating his moral principles, the deontologist may not take into consideration the total number of facts that are value-relevant for a consequentialist, he may well take into account all those facts that are value-relevant for him. As a matter of fact, there is no reason to prevent a deontological moral theory from being sensitive to all human goods. It might be replied, however, that full sensitivity to values is a necessary property of consequentialist theories (conceived as incorporating an axiological thesis and a practical principle demanding the attainment of good), whereas it is no more than a contingent property of deontological moral theories. But, even if this were true, it could not serve as a basis for indiscriminately condemning all deontological moral theories. Still more, if deontological moral theories had by definition a structure analogous to the one attributed to consequentialist theories, then it might be asserted without any trouble that full sensibility to values is also a property necessary to deontological theories. In support of this assertion, deontological theories would have specifically to include an axiological thesis and a practical principle demanding rationally appropriate answers to the fact that certain events possess intrinsic value (where what is rationally appropriate in such answers necessarily depends in part on considerations alien to the causal structure of the action). The deontological theory I shall be developing in the two following chapters has just this structure, and, therefore, is immune to the charge of 'value-short-sightedness'.

Additionally, we should not forget that practical rationality is an intrinsic *moral* value and that consequently a full consideration of all the values involved, both non-moral and moral, may give rise to differences in the moral evaluation that would be inexplicable if one concentrated exclusively on the non-moral values. Accordingly, the differences of content between the moral judgements of a deontologist and a consequentialist have not necessarily to be explained in terms of value-disagreements in the non-moral dimension, let alone differences of sensitivity to values; more often than not these differences will reflect the different conceptions of practical rationality they respectively uphold. Of course, it would be a patent fallacy to accuse deontologism of axiological short-sightedness in the moral dimension for not subscribing to a consequentialist conception of practical rationality.

The Concept of (Negative) Moral Rights

In the first place attention must be called to the fact that the moral rights to which the basic libertarian thesis alludes are not, in the terminology of Hohfeld, privileges or liberties but claim-rights. Allow me to explain this point. In the question of rights to non-interference, '*P* has the right to do *X*' may mean that '*P* does not have the duty not to do *X*' or '*Q* (and everyone else) has the obligation to let *P* do *X*'. In the first place we are dealing with a privilege and in the second with a claim-right.[14] Although it is a moot point whether moral rights involve liberties, that is to say, whether the exercise of a moral right may constitute the transgression of a moral duty,[15] there is wide agreement on moral rights essentially including claim-rights. Accordingly, there is little doubt that negative moral rights have as their central ingredient negative claim-rights. Our main problem is, then, to analyse the concept of claim-rights (from now on, for brevity's sake, I shall speak of rights on the assumption that the reader understands me to be referring to claim-rights).

There is a vast literature devoted to the analysis of the concept of rights. Though a large part of this literature deals with moral as well as legal rights, here we are concerned only with the part referring to the former. A central issue in discussions about the concept of rights is whether rights-statements are equivalent to

---

[14] Joel Feinberg, *Social Philosophy* (Englewood Cliffs, NJ: Prentice-Hall, 1973), 56–9.

[15] Favouring the affirmative: J. L. Mackie, 'Can There Be a Right-Based Moral Theory?', in J. Waldron (ed.), *Theories of Rights* (Oxford: Oxford University Press, 1984), 169–70; Richard Wasserstrom, 'Rights, Human Rights, and Racial Discrimination', *Journal of Philosophy*, 61 (1964), 630; and Claudia Card, 'Utility and the Basis of Moral Rights: A Reply to Professor Brandt', *Canadian Journal of Philosophy*, 14 (1984), 23. Favouring the negative: Joel Feinberg, 'Wasserstrom on Human Rights', *Journal of Philosophy*, 61 (1964), 642; Ronald Dworkin, *Taking Rights Seriously* (London: Duckworth, 1978), 188; Joseph Raz, *The Authority of Law* (Oxford: Clarendon Press, 1979), 274; Jeremy Waldron, 'A Right to Do Wrong', *Ethics*, 92 (1981); and Richard Brandt, 'Comments on Professor Card's Critique', *Canadian Journal of Philosophy*, 14 (1984), 32.

some sort of duties-statements. The doctrine of the logical correlativity of rights and duties contends, in its crudest form, that (1)
all duties entail other people's rights, and that (2) all rights imply
other people's duties.[16] In this version, the doctrine is barely
maintainable. As Feinberg remarks, there are many duties that
are not correlated to rights.[17] Take, for instance, the duty not to
maltreat animals, laid down in some moral codes. It does not
seem that on the assumption of the existence of this duty one
would have to conclude, as a matter of logic, that animals have a
moral right not to be maltreated. Indeed, it is usual to stress that
only duties in the sense of something owed to someone are logically correlated to rights.[18] In a sophisticated version, the doctrine of the logical correlativity of rights and duties underwrites
the following thesis:

(T1) *P* has a right *against* *Q* that *Q* shall do (shall refrain from
     doing) *X*

is equivalent to:

(T2) *Q* has the duty *to P* to do (to refrain from doing) *X*.

Though this thesis is common to all the supporters of the sophisticated version of the doctrine of the logical correlativity of rights
and duties, they are quick to disagree about the analysis of (T2),
i.e. the idea of a duty to someone. For completeness, it is worth
mentioning, however succinctly, the more important suggestions
in this matter:

Benefit theory:[19]
(T3) *Q* has the duty to do (to refrain from doing) *X*, and
     X (not-*X*) favours *P*'s interests.

---

[16] The doctrine appears thus characterized in Joel Feinberg, *Rights, Justice,
and the Bounds of Liberty* (Princeton, NJ: Princeton University Press, 1980), 143.
A defence of the doctrine may be found in S. I. Benn and R. S. Peters, *Social
Principles and the Democratic State* (London: Allen & Unwin, 1959), 89.
[17] Feinberg, *Rights, Justice, and the Bounds of Liberty*, 143–4.
[18] Ibid. and H. L. A. Hart, 'Are There Natural Rights?', in Waldron (ed.),
Theories of Rights, 81–3.
[19] H. L. A. Hart, 'Bentham on Legal Rights', in A. W. B. Simpson (ed.),
Oxford Essays in Jurisprudence, 2nd ser. (Oxford: Oxford University Press,
1973), 171–9.

Choice theory:[20]
(T4) *Q* has the duty to do (to refrain from doing) *X*,
and *P* is in a position to exempt *Q* from the requirement
to do (to refrain from doing) *X*.
Desire theory:[21]
(T5) If *P* desires *X* to be done (not to be done), then *Q* has
the duty to do (to refrain from doing) *X*.
Justificatory benefit theory:[22]
(T6) Some interest on *P*'s part *justifies Q*'s duty to do (to
refrain from doing) *X*.

The theories of the correlativity between rights and duties
sketched out above are an attempt to supply a formal definition
of rights in terms of different duties-statements; all of them
accept the proposition that rights entail duties on the part of
other people, a proposition which actually follows on from
Hohfeld's definition of the concept of claim-rights. By way of
contrast with these theories, the theory of rights as valid claims is
an attempt to elucidate informally the idea of rights by appealing
to the notions of 'claim' and 'making a claim'. Schematically, this
theory, studied chiefly by Joel Feinberg,[23] upholds the following
analysis of (T2):

(T7) *P* is in a position to make a valid claim (in accordance
with a particular system of rules) that *Q* should do
(should refrain from doing) *X* and to make a complaint
if his claim is not satisfied.

It might be thought that the cash value of this theory is a rejection of the proposition that rights entail duties on the part of
other people. Feinberg affirms, for instance, that basic needs give
rise to claims that are not correlated to duties devolving upon

---

[20] Hart, 'Are There Natural Rights?', 81–3.
[21] Michael Tooley, 'Abortion and Infanticide', *Philosophy and Public Affairs*,
2 (1972), 44–5. For a criticism, in my opinion unpersuasive, of this theory, see
Gary E. Jones, 'Rights and Desires', *Ethics*, 92 (1981).
[22] Neil MacCormick, 'Rights in Legislation', in P. M. S. Hacker and J. Raz
(eds.), *Law, Morality, and Society: Essays in Honour of H. L. A. Hart* (Oxford:
Oxford University Press, 1977), and Joseph Raz, 'Right-Based Moralities', in
Waldron (ed.), *Theories of Rights*.
[23] Joel Feinberg, 'Wasserstrom on Human Rights', and *Rights, Justice, and the
Bounds of Liberty*, 130–58.

particular persons.[24] Yet, Feinberg himself discards this interpretation in asserting that he prefers not to identify rights with claims *simpliciter* but with *valid* claims, which are, according to him, 'reasons for other people's duties'.[25] If the statement that someone has a right involves asserting that there are reasons endorsing the existence of certain duties, then it looks as if the statement that there is a right entails that there are those duties. Thus, the theory of rights as valid claims does not appear to be incompatible with the proposition that all rights entail duties. It must, however, be admitted that the theory under examination introduces a novelty in connecting the idea of rights with the idea of being in a position to put forward a claim. On the one hand, in fact, this move ingeniously places the notion of rights on a higher level of generality than the theories of correlativity, since it deliberately omits a precise determination of the criteria laying down when a person is in a position to make a claim, i.e. when a person holds a right. This determination is left to the relevant legal rules, or the moral principles to be applied, as the case may be. The justificatory benefit theory, for example, commits itself to the proposition that a person may demand the discharge of a duty as the holder of the corresponding right only if the existence of this duty is based upon his interest. Thus, this theory seems to be too restrictive. Let us take the case of rights deriving from a contract or unilateral promise. The corresponding duties do not appear to be based upon the interest of the relevant co-contracting party or promisee, but, rather, on the fact that the one upon whom the duty devolved pledged his word; otherwise the interest of the relevant co-contracting party or promisee might justify the existence of the same duty even in the absence of a contract or promise, which is absurd. On the other hand, the upholder of the theory of rights as valid claims may perfectly well account for these rights by saying that to be the recipient of contractual or unilateral promises is one of the several circumstances capable of placing a person in a position to make a valid claim.

Furthermore, the theory of rights as valid claims holds that the notion of making a claim is an essential component of the language of rights. According to the theory, when there is a right, it

---

[24] *Rights, Justice, and the Bounds of Liberty*, 139–41.
[25] Ibid. 152–3.

is not just a question of there being circumstances justifying the existence of certain duties, but of these circumstances justifying someone's making the claim that these duties exist and requiring them to be complied with; by the same token, a person has the duty to do *X to someone else* when the latter is in a position to claim that the former should do *X*.

What general reason can there be for a public morality to allot someone the position of making a claim for the fulfilment of a duty? The response to this question would supply us with a common criterion to explain why a heterogeneous set of circumstances is capable of placing a person in a position to put forward a valid claim. Nevertheless, I do not believe it easy to point to a single reason explaining why certain positions are suitable for claiming the discharge of certain duties. To start with, it seems to me that we need to distinguish in this context two types of rights and correlative duties: rights arising out of contracts and promises, and rights whose origin is not to be sought in a voluntary transaction. As regards the former, the reason why the promisee or the relevant co-contractor is in a position to make a claim is, in my opinion, the fact that his being so forms a constitutive part of two kinds of interpersonal transaction (i.e. promises and contracts) the existence of which in a society is undoubtedly valuable. With respect to the other rights, a possible answer is provided by Richard Wasserstrom's pioneering analysis.[26] On this account rights are seen as 'valuable and distinctive moral commodities' without which the claims of persons otherwise in possession of rights would inevitably be diminished to the level of requests, privileges, and favours. Wasserstrom analyses the treatment meted out to Negroes by White Southerners at the time of writing his article. Many Southerners, he contends, admit that they have certain moral duties in connection with Negroes but deny that Blacks possess correlative moral rights. In this way, if a Southerner fails to do his duty in relation to a Negro, this is merely a question between him and his conscience. As Feinberg puts it, Wasserstrom's idea is that the substitution of a principle of *noblesse oblige* for a recognition of human rights is a serious moral flaw inasmuch as it involves a fierce

---

[26] Wasserstrom, 'Rights, Human Rights, and Racial Discrimination', *passim*.

attack on personal self-esteem.[27] The function of moral rights in our public morality is, in this line of thought, to show respect for the holders of these rights and thereby to enable them to have a sense of their own value and dignity. This role, it is alleged, cannot be played by the idea of moral duties or by any other moral notion.

In opposition to this thesis about the function of moral rights it may be asked, as in fact William Nelson does ask,[28] whether anyone considering others to be bound to fulfil certain duties in connection with him might not complain if those duties were passed over, even though he might not hold himself to possess correlative rights. After all, demanding the discharge of a moral duty is a very different matter from asking a favour or applying for a privilege. According to Nelson, this question may only be answered negatively if one transfers to the moral realm the legal rule that only holders of rights can be claimants, i.e. the rule that the possession of rights is a *conditio sine qua non* of being able to complain *qua* a claimant. It is true that, legally, there are a number of things mainly connected with the action of the courts that a person can do only in his capacity as a claimant, but, observes Nelson, there are a number of others that do not require this condition. For example, even if the complainant lacks many of the powers the civil claimant possesses, he may certainly make a complaint if he is the victim of a criminal offence. Now, given that in the moral realm there are no lawcourts, it is pointless, says Nelson, to draw a firm analogy between the activity of making a claim in that realm—an activity connected with human dignity and self-respect—and the activity of the claimant in the legal field. In other words, there is no reason to assume that the making of a complaint necessarily requires the possession of moral rights: this activity seems closer to that of the complainant, who does not need to possess legal rights. According to Nelson, there are many different conditions that may place one in a position to put forward a complaint, and, although the infringement of a right may be one of them, another is surely that the harmful action of someone involved the failure to comply with a duty.

---

[27] Feinberg, 'Wasserstrom on Human Rights', 642.

[28] William Nelson, 'On the Alleged Importance of Moral Rights', *Ratio*, 18 (1976), 145–55.

Nelson's criticism of the thesis that rights are indispensable moral tools for a morality assuming the value of personal self-respect seems far from easy to refute. Furthermore, this criticism throws serious doubts on the plausibility of establishing a necessary 'two-way' connection between the idea of moral rights and the notion of making a claim and, therefore, on the soundness of the theory of rights as valid claims. If the laying of a claim can be justified by the infringement of a moral duty which does somebody harm, and does not have as a prerequisite the possession of a right, then it is a mistake to define rights in terms of 'being in a position to make a claim'.

There are several other moral functions which, it has been alleged, rights are peculiarly called upon to satisfy. The consideration of these functions might give rise to alternative analyses of the concept of rights. For instance, it has been said (1) that rights characteristically 'trump' moral considerations based on the maximization of social utility or, more generally, that they trump any other kind of moral considerations, (2) that rights create the obligation of compensation or restitution in cases of violation, and (3) that rights distinguish those moral principles that can justly be enforced. Each of these theses is refuted in a brilliant essay by Allen Buchanan.[29] First of all, to say that a certain moral principle—like the ones setting up rights—trumps appeals to social utility (or any other sort of moral consideration) involves not the analysis of the meaning of this principle but the formulation of an external relational statement, a statement about the weighting or priority relation between this principle and other moral principles (like that of utility). The second thesis may be interpreted as a claim about the meaning of 'compensation' or as a claim that rights are necessary conditions for justified compensation. In the first case, Buchanan points out correctly that there is nothing incoherent about the idea of a principle of compensation requiring P to be compensated whenever any of his interests have been encroached upon, but not implying that P has rights against the encroachments in question. In the second, Buchanan points out correctly that even in the legal realm there are compensation duties that do not need to be understood as

---

[29] 'What's so Special about Rights?', in Ellen Franken Paul, Fred D. Miller, Jr., and Jeffrey Paul (eds.), *Liberty and Equality* (Oxford: Blackwell, 1985).

derivatives of the infringement of a right; for example, the duty of compensation arising out of an injury occasioned by unreasonable carelessness or negligence, not to mention the cases of strict liability. Lastly, if the third thesis is taken as the claim that only principles setting up moral rights are enforceable, it looks like a baseless dogma. Buchanan observes that there are principles that, as is widely accepted, lead to the utilization of state force and that they are not principles about rights, namely, those that demand a contribution to certain important public goods.

It should be noted that, although rights do not seem to be necessary conditions for trumping appeals to other moral considerations, for making a claim, for requiring compensation in cases of encroachment upon corresponding interests, or for using state force in the protection of them, it does seem plausible to contend that rights characteristically constitute a sufficient condition for overriding any other kinds of moral reason and providing a prima-facie justification for all the other things I have mentioned. Besides, rights are also apparently connected with an activity of fundamental importance in political terms that has not been accorded the attention it deserves by moral rights theorists, to wit, the self-defence of the interests shielded by rights. Once again, the point is not that rights are necessary conditions for justifiable action in defence of certain interests of one's own, but that they provide a prima-facie justification for this action. All of this naturally does not invalidate the conceptual correlation between rights and duties. When one says that *P* holds a right, one is stating that somebody else has the duty to do certain things, which duty, by the peculiar nature of the value that it is called upon to serve, prevails over any other kinds of moral consideration and justifies prima facie that *P* is in such a moral position that he can validly make a claim or lodge a complaint and act in self-defence, that the possible infringer must compensate him, and that state force may be used to help him, a moral position that would otherwise demand an independent justification.

This explains why, when *X* is the object of a duty allegedly correlated with a right, it is usual to say not just that *X* should be done but that somebody is owed *X*. This manner of speaking is natural in the case of duties arising out of voluntary transactions, like promises or contracts. As I said before, that things contracted or promised not only should be done but are actually owed to someone into the bargain is an essential ingredient of a socially valuable way of creating reliable expectations. It remains to be seen whether the duties associated with libertarian negative rights justify the same way of speaking. One way of contending that they do is to hold that all libertarian rights are of a contractual nature, which is a familiar thesis in contractarian thought. But this manœuvre may be dispensed with. It may very well be argued that the connection goes deeper, i.e. that it is not the case that all libertarian rights are of a contractual nature but that non-contractual libertarian rights are destined to serve in the last instance the same value as the rights originating in voluntary transactions. This is the line of argument I am following in this chapter. I shall suggest that contractual duties and those correlated with non-contractual libertarian rights are based ultimately upon the value of personal autonomy.

It seems clear that the duty to keep one's pledged word is destined to create a compass of predictability in human affairs exceeding the scope of expectations founded upon the fulfilment of non-contractual moral duties and, by this means, to enable every individual to conceive and carry out life plans strategically taking into account the life plans of other individuals. This is to say that the justification of the duty to keep promises and contracts lies ultimately in the value of personal autonomy. Allowing this to be a reasonable assumption, I have still to show that, in preserving positive freedom, duties correlated with the negative rights the basic libertarian thesis refers to protect personal autonomy. This means arguing that positive freedom is inextricably bound up with personal autonomy. It is to this task that the last section of this chapter will be devoted.

Positive Freedom and Personal Autonomy

The idea of autonomy as everybody's ideal capacity is a late development of the human mind. According to Richards, it was hinted at in the late Middle Ages and acquired practical political force in the English Civil War; as a political and social ideal, autonomy found theoretical expression in the writings of Milton and Locke, and received deeper treatment in the works of

Rousseau and Kant.[30] Gerald Dworkin has a different vision of
the historical development of the idea of personal autonomy. He
attributes to St Thomas Aquinas, Luther, and Calvin the great
emphasis placed on the individual acting in accordance with
reason as shaped and perceived by that individual and finds the
modern exposition of the idea of autonomy in the Renaissance
humanists like Pico della Mirandola.[31] Most abstractly understood, autonomy alludes to the condition of a man who, to echo
Rousseau, 'is obedient to a law that he prescribes to himself'.[32]
As I am going to conceive autonomy here, a man is autonomous
when he is the author of his own life, when 'the principles by
which . . . [he] governs his life make his decisions consistent and
intelligible to him as his own, for they *constitute* the personality
he recognises as the one he has made his own'.[33] The choices and
actions of an autonomous man are thus an expression of his own
preferences and aspirations.[34] It is clear that in accordance with
this conception a necessary condition of autonomy is that the
preferences and desires governing the conduct of the individual
be his own. This condition must, of course, receive precise content if the idea of personal autonomy is to emerge from the aura
of obscurity involved in the intuitive explanations I have just
quoted.

I should like, above all, to stress the point that the idea that a
person's preference or aspiration is his own implies much more
than the mere fact that this preference or aspiration exerts a
motivational force over his behaviour; it requires this preference
or aspiration to be congenial to the personality of the person in
question as a whole. It is worth mentioning the chief landmarks
in the analysis of the component of autonomy I am referring to.
In a pioneering article Gerald Dworkin suggested that a person
does X freely if and only if he does X for reasons which he does
not mind acting from; conversely, a person does not act freely in

---

[30] David A. J. Richards, 'Rights and Autonomy', *Ethics*, 92 (1981), 7.
[31] Gerald Dworkin, *The Theory and Practice of Autonomy* (Cambridge: Cambridge University Press, 1988), 13.
[32] S. I. Benn, 'Freedom, Autonomy and the Concept of a Person', *Proceedings
of the Aristotelian Society*, NS., 76 (1975–6), 124.
[33] Ibid. 129.
[34] Robert Young, *Personal Autonomy: Beyond Negative and Positive Liberty*
(London and Sydney: Croom Helm, 1986), 8.

doing X when he does X for reasons he resents having to act
for.[35] Dworkin's starting-point is a rejection of the intuitive thesis
that one always acts in accordance with one's own desires. In
cases of coercion, says Dworkin, the coercer provides the victim
with reasons for acting in the sense of supplying conditions in
which the victim has reasons for acting in the way the coercer
wants which he did not have before; these reasons usually spring
from basic motivations of human beings like self-preservation or
concern for the well-being of loved ones. In Chapter 1 I endeavoured to show that the conditions the coercer brings about are
generically characterizable as the elimination of some option of
the victim's. Dworkin's analysis of the idea of acting freely may
serve as a basis for explicating the related idea of acting autonomously. This analysis presupposes a double vision of human
personality: 'There must be part of the human nature which takes
an "attitude" towards the reasons, desires, and motives which
determine the conduct of the agent.'[36] In contrast with this proposition of the existence of two sides to human personality to
explain the idea of free will, Frankfurt contends that the theory
of human personality that fits in best with the idea that persons
act freely is one that asserts the existence of two or more levels or
orders in the structure of human beings' desires and attitudes.[37]
Frankfurt holds that an essential characteristic of human beings is
the capacity for reflective self-evaluation, manifest in the for-
mation of second-order desires; on this account, people have the
capacity to wish to have or not to have desires and preferences of
the first order. However, more than the mere possession of
second-order desires to have desires of the first order, what for
Frankfurt characterizes a person is the capacity for second-order
volitions, that is to say, the capacity to want a certain desire to
become his own will.

Later, Gerald Dworkin, already concentrating on the concept
of autonomy and following Frankfurt's two-tier view of the
human personality, proposed what he called the authenticity condition of autonomy: for a person to be autonomous his second-
order identifications must be congruent with his first-order

[35] Gerald Dworkin, 'Acting Freely', Noûs, 4 (1970).
[36] Ibid. 378.
[37] Harry Frankfurt, 'Freedom of the Will and the Concept of a Person',
Journal of Philosophy, 68 (1971).

motivations.[38] This means that the autonomous person is identified with the influences motivating his conduct, that he sees himself as the sort of person who wishes to be motivated by these influences. Dworkin now rejects the thesis that autonomy involves the authenticity condition as he had characterized it. His central argument is that the congruence demanded between the second-order identifications and the first-order motivations of a person may take place in situations in which one could not possibly say that this person is autonomous. Dworkin mentions three cases: firstly, a drug addict might want to be motivated by the addiction even though he may not be capable of modifying this first-order motivation; secondly, a person might succeed in identifying himself with motivations that he does not wish to have by changing his second-order desires; and, thirdly, certain manipulations of a person, such as keeping him ignorant or performing a lobotomy on him, do not seem to interfere with his identifications. Therefore Dworkin asserts that what is crucial in the autonomous person is his second-order *capacity* to reflect critically about his first-order preferences and aims and his *capacity* to accept or reject these aims and preferences in conformity with his higher-order preferences and values.[39]

It strikes me that Dworkin's last account does not take due note of the fact that being autonomous, as Young points out, 'is not merely to have capacity, nor the opportunity to exercise a capacity'.[40] The autonomous person is a person who acts autonomously. It is true that, as the case of the drug addict brings out clearly, it is not enough for there to be congruence between a person's second-order preferences and first-order motivations for him to act autonomously. A person acts autonomously when his second-order desires 'authorize' the first-order motivations guiding his conduct, being able to change these motivations if his second-order desires should require him to do so. But, taking the second case mentioned by Dworkin, it does not seem to me obvious that there is something wrong from the point of view of autonomy with the mere fact that the identification of a person with his first-order motivations should come about through a

---

[38] Gerald Dworkin, 'Autonomy and Behavior Control', *Hastings Center Report* (Feb. 1976).
[39] Dworkin, *The Theory and Practice of Autonomy*, 15–20.
[40] Young, *Personal Autonomy*, 49.

change in his second-order preferences. This change might be autonomous if it was due to the influence of higher-order values, the possible existence of which is admitted by Dworkin, or else if it was the fruit of a process of adjustment and balance between the conflicting second-order preferences that a person has. On the other hand, the manipulations resulting in a modification of the second-order preferences and even of the higher-order ones annul a person's capacity to see himself as the result of the natural development of his personality in normal conditions of interaction with the world. This implies that there is a condition of normality implicit in the idea of autonomy that excludes manipulations like lobotomy. To sum up, I believe that autonomy may be reasonably conceived as the condition of someone acting in accordance with first-order motivations critically endorsed by higher-order preferences which he has developed within a framework of normal interaction with the surrounding world.

I should like now to explain what the essential link is that I envisage between personal autonomy and positive freedom. In the first place, I shall make it clear what the type of relationship is that I do *not* regard as essential. It might be thought that positive freedom is a necessary condition of autonomy in the sense that in the absence of positive freedom a person is incapable of moulding his first-order motivations in the corresponding choices and actions. For example, in a society that attaches little importance to theoretical research, anybody devoid of means of his own who is motivated to work in this field cannot obviously make the choices and perform the actions responding to this motivation. So, to possess open options appears to be necessary if a person is to be able to express his own nature in his choices and actions. However, this argument cannot justify the value of possessing the greatest possible number of open options but the value of something different, namely, having open those options involving the choices and actions that are appropriate for giving free rein to a person's actual motivations. According to this line of argument, autonomy would justify having the opportunity of satisfying first-order desires, but not having the broadest repertoire possible of alternatives of action. Still more, if what is in question is a satisfaction of the first-order desires that anybody may actually have, then it might be replied, as Dworkin in fact does reply,[41] that it is not always better to have more choice than less. Dworkin points out that more often than not having choice implies increased costs, as, for example, the costs of looking for the relevant information together with the time and effort needed for taking the decision (the French phrase *embarras de choix* alludes very vividly to this point), the responsibility for the choice, the probability of being liable to social and legal penalties, the possible worsening of the original situation as a result of the aggregate of new options, and the relative decline in well-being in 'prisoner's dilemma' strategic situations. We may conclude then that the worth of a person's positive freedom does not lie in the fact that it is an essential condition for the satisfaction of his first-order desires. Anyhow, though it may be agreed that as a rule greater positive freedom improves the chances of satisfying first-order preferences, this would only prove that positive freedom has instrumental value. But what I need to prove here is that positive freedom has intrinsic value.

There are two arguments that might be used against the attempt to justify positive freedom's having intrinsic value by appealing to its connection with autonomy. The first, put forward by Gerald Dworkin,[42] is directly geared towards proving that positive freedom cannot possess intrinsic worth. Let us suppose that a person P values three things, A, B, and C, in this order of priority. If positive freedom had intrinsic value, then P would rationally rather have the possibility of choosing between B and C than receiving A if the sum of the values of this possibility of choice and of B is superior to the value of A. But Dworkin thinks that it is irrational that in this case P should prefer in the end to receive the second-rank alternative to receiving the one occupying the first position. This argument is patently fallacious. In the first place, even if one accepts the assumption implicit in the argument that P really increases his positive freedom by choosing to have alternative B-or-C, his preference for this alternative could only be deemed irrational if it were to be presupposed that positive freedom lacks intrinsic value. But, as is obvious, this is precisely what is in question. In the second place, the concept of

---

[41] Dworkin, *The Theory and Practice of Autonomy*, 62–81.
[42] Ibid. 80.

'preferring' does not seem intelligible if it is abstracted from the choice contexts. Thus, we should not say that P prefers having the B-or-C alternative to receiving A if he does not have the opportunity of choosing between alternative B-or-C and receiving A. But if P has the opportunity of choosing between having alternative B-or-C and receiving A, then he has from the start three options: A, B, and C. This being so, it is not true that P increases his positive freedom by choosing to have the B-or-C alternative. As a matter of fact, it is preposterous to think that, if P should choose first to have alternative B-or-C instead of receiving A, and should then decide between B and C, he would enjoy a larger number of options than if he were to choose between A, B, and C at one go. Making two choices in two successive steps does not *per se* increase the number of options available. To hold the contrary would imply allowing that any chooser can increase his positive freedom by the simple expedient of adopting a step-by-step method of decision-making. It would imply, moreover, mistaking the number of 'choice-acts' that a person makes in order to select his favourite alternative for his number of options. Consequently, whether P chooses to receive A or to obtain alternative B-or-C and then afterwards opts for B, P has three options. As the amount of his positive freedom remains invariable, the rational choice for P is to receive A.

The second argument runs like this: If autonomy possesses intrinsic value, it is by hypothesis impossible to show that positive freedom has intrinsic value by appealing to a connection between autonomy and positive freedom. For anything that is valuable by virtue of its connection with an intrinsic good can only be claimed to have instrumental worth. This argument takes advantage of a confusion between intrinsic value and what Raz calls value *per se* or in itself. Among intrinsically valuable things Raz distinguishes three different categories: *things valuable in themselves, constituent goods*, and *ultimate goods*. Things valuable in themselves are those whose existence is of value regardless of the existence of anything else. Constituent goods are the elements of what is good in itself that contribute to its worth, i.e. elements without which a thing of value in itself would be less valuable. Ultimate goods are the aspects of one good in itself explaining and justifying the judgement that it is good in itself and whose own value does not need to be justified by reference to other values.[43] Autonomy has intrinsic value in the sense that it is a thing valuable in itself. If positive freedom also had intrinsic value in the sense of being a thing valuable in itself, then certainly this value could not be justified by appealing to an essential connection with autonomy. But what I wish to show is not that positive freedom has intrinsic value in the sense of being a thing valuable in itself but in the different sense of being a constituent good.

I am going to suggest that positive freedom is a constituent good and, therefore, an intrinsically valuable thing, inasmuch as a person's acting autonomously involves his being positively free. My argument is the following. To start with, it must be conceded that a person acts autonomously as long as the first-order motivations governing his conduct properly express his own nature. One case where a first-order motivation fails to express an agent's own nature takes place, as we have seen above, when this motivation does not spring from his second-order or higher-order preferences. But this is not the only possible case. It is quite natural for a person to discard certain first-order motivations as non-expressive of his own nature on account of the reduction of the scope of options in the face of which these motivations have arisen. Let us think, for instance, of the situation of an unemployed man who thus sees himself as 'forced' to rob in order to feed his family, or that of anybody subject to coercion. What happens in such cases is that a person disowns a certain first-order motivation, judging that he is forced to have it given the abnormally narrow compass of options in which he is placed at the time. Although he actually has the motivation he denies, he does not consider it expressive of his own nature but rather as expressive of the situation he happens to be living in. Thus, a person does not see himself as expressing his own nature in acting and, consequently, as acting autonomously if the higher-order preferences out of which the first-order motivations guiding his conduct emerge do not operate in an environment rich in positive freedom.

On the other hand, it is also natural for a person placed in the generic situation described above to claim that his own nature

---

[43] Raz, 'Right-Based Moralities', 188–9.

would be properly expressed by the first-order motivations he would have if he enjoyed a repertoire of options broader than the one he actually has. In the cases that I exemplified above the person typically claims that the first-order motivations expressive of his own nature are those he would have in the face of a repertoire of options like the one he usually has, or the one he had before the occurrence of the 'abnormal' event in question (e.g. dismissal or threat). Sometimes, however, a person may claim that the first-order motivations truly expressive of his own nature are those he would have in the face of a compass of options that he considers 'normal' because it is enjoyed by people like himself, although he has never actually had such a compass of options or in all likelihood ever will have. For example, in a country not making sufficient allowance for research in the humanities, a person may claim that his motivation to work as a lawyer fails to express his own nature because he thinks that, in a country providing him with the option of living as legal philosopher, he would not have that motivation. Leaving aside these minor differences concerning the scope of options which is taken as a norm for the relevant judgements, we may conclude that a person does see himself as expressing *ceteris paribus* his own nature in acting when the first-order motivations regulating his conduct arise in the presence of positive freedom.

What I have tried to show is that it is quite natural for a person to regard certain first-order motivations as giving or not giving proper expression to his own nature in accordance with the greater or lesser scope of options in the face of which such motivations emerge. This means that, in exercising their capacity for reflective self-evaluation, people conceive their own autonomy as involving the possession of first-order motivations resulting from their higher-order values and the presence of positive freedom. It also seems reasonable to think that the greater the number of options available, the more fully a person's first-order motivations express his own nature and, consequently, the more fully he expresses through his conduct his own nature. My point is then that positive freedom is an essential element of the conception of autonomy that a person embraces in trying to assess the extent to which his life is his own work, or an expression rather of the contingencies of the world surrounding him.

As against the thesis that positive freedom is a necessary condition of autonomy, it might be pointed out that at times personal autonomy demands the elimination of some options. Let us take, for example, Ulysses' request to his companions to tie him up so that he would not fall prey to the songs of the Sirens, or the pleasure with which a kleptomaniac receives a prohibition against stealing. Still more important is the case of contracts. I said before that a contract is a kind of interpersonal transaction which is valuable because of its contribution to the autonomy of individuals; but, as is obvious, contracts imply the loss of some options by the parties to them in relation to the pre-contractual situation (together with the appearance of new options). If at times autonomy demands the loss of a portion of positive freedom, then—the argument concludes—positive freedom cannot be a component of autonomy. To answer this objection it seems to be useful to recall the meaning of 'having an option open' in the context of the analysis of the concept of positive freedom. In Chapter 1 I suggested that the idea of positive freedom is connected with what Gewirth terms effective power. We might affirm on the strength of this that a person has open the option of doing X if his doing X depends on his own choice, in such a way that, if he chooses to do X, he does it. Positive freedom is linked with choice in the basic sense that it cannot be said that a person lacks the option to do X if he does not do X because he does not choose to do so. A person's positive freedom can only be affected by barriers or obstructions whose existence is independent of his own choice. This being so, it does not seem reasonable to consider the closing of the options otherwise open to a person by his own free choice and consent as a loss of positive freedom. It is true that, after he is tied up, Ulysses lacks some of the options he enjoyed beforehand, but it does not look as if this lack of options involves a loss of positive freedom seeing that the tying up is an obstruction that Ulysses consents to. The same may be said of the loss of options as result of the making of a contract. The case of the kleptomaniac is different because he cannot be said to have given an explicit consent but at most a tacit one to the loss of the option to steal; however, it is clear that it is only because we assume that the kleptomaniac tacitly consents to the loss of his option of stealing that we think this loss does not affect his autonomy. The eliminations of options invoked by the objection I am considering do not, then, constitute true limitations of positive freedom but rather ways of exercising positive freedom. On this view, positive freedom is linked with the notion of consent[44] since it does not go with the basic sense of positive freedom to consider that the latter may be lost as result of obstructions or interferences chosen and consented to by the agent. Naturally, for the closing of an option to be really consented to by the agent, he must not be misled about, still less kept in ignorance of, the impact that the closing of the option will have on his interests and life plans.[45]

[44] For a defence of the thesis that consent is the basis of the liberal theory of political legitimacy, see Jeremy Waldron, 'Theoretical Foundations of Liberalism', *Philosophical Quarterly*, 37 (1987).

[45] About how deception excludes consent and, consequently, treating another as a person, see Onora O'Neill, 'Between Consenting Adults', *Philosophy and Public Affairs*, 14 (1985).

4
Acts and Omissions

According to the deontological conception of practical rationality there are moral reasons that are not based on the results of human conduct but on the form the intervention of the agent takes in the production of these results. It is clear that in upholding the pre-eminence of negative moral rights one is committed to the thesis that the duty not to actively attack positive freedom prevails over the duty to prevent any injury to positive freedom. This chapter will be devoted precisely to the defence of this thesis, which accounts for one difference or 'asymmetry' present in the common-sense moral evaluation of pairs of actions which, at first sight, are not distinguishable as regards their morally significant results. But before that, in the first section, I am going to reject another possible view for taking account of that difference or 'asymmetry', namely, the view that holds that to injure positive freedom intentionally is not morally equivalent to performing an act which it can be foreseen will produce some injury to positive freedom. Although a large part of the relevant literature for a discussion of these issues is concerned with acts and omissions which contribute in some way to death or to some less serious physical harm, I believe that it is open to reinterpretation in terms of attacks on or injuries to positive freedom. To bring about someone's death is to make an extreme attack on his positive freedom. Something qualitatively similar but less important in degree may be said of physical harms less serious than death. Therefore, whenever in this chapter I use the term 'harm', it is to be understood that I am referring to restraints on positive freedom.

The Intention–Foresight Distinction

The distinction between the effects of an action that are *intended* either as ends or as means to the achievement of those ends and others that are not intended but that are merely *foreseen* is central to the so-called 'doctrine of double effect', upheld by the Roman Catholic Church to justify the permissibility of some therapeutic actions where the cessation of a human life (e.g. a foetus, a terminal patient) is foreseen as a necessary but not desired effect, neither as an end nor as a means. The fact of a result's being intended or merely foreseen, or, as Bentham puts it,[1] of its being *intended directly* or *intended indirectly (obliquely)*, if it counts at all as a moral reason, can only constitute a deontological consideration, since by hypothesis it is not grounded upon the occurrence of certain consequences but presumably on the attitude adopted by the agent in the face of certain consequences. The doctrine of the double effect has as its principal end the justification of differential moral judgements in some pairs of cases that would have to be morally equivalent if only the consequences involved counted. The following are some of these cases:

(1*a*) A patient in her death throes is given a drug to relieve the pain, but her death is accelerated as a result.

(1*b*) A patient in her death throes ceases to feel any pain because she has been given a drug to put an end to her life as the only way of sparing her further suffering.

(2*a*) (*The case of hysterectomy*) A surgeon removes the cancerous uterus of a woman with child in order to save her life, and as a result the foetus dies.

(2*b*) (*The case of craneotomy*) A surgeon crushes the skull of an unborn child as the only way of saving the life of his mother in childbirth (the alternative is that the child may be born alive by means of a *post-mortem* caesarean operation).[2]

---

[1] Jeremy Bentham, *An Introduction to the Principles of Morals and Legislation* (New York: Hafner Press, 1948), 84 (ch. 8).

[2] The examples are given in H. L. A. Hart, 'Intention and Punishment', in *Punishment and Responsibility* (Oxford: Clarendon Press, 1978), 122–3, and Philippa Foot, 'The Problem of Abortion and the Doctrine of the Double Effect', in *Virtues and Vices and Other Essays in Moral Philosophy* (Oxford: Blackwell, 1978), 20–1. The part in brackets in (2*b*) is introduced by Jonathan Bennett, 'Whatever the Consequences', in Bonnie Steinbock (ed.), *Killing and Letting Die* (Englewood Cliffs, NJ: Prentice-Hall, 1980), 109. For Hart's criticism of the standard application of the double effect doctrine to the craneotomy case, see his 'Intention and Punishment', 123–4.

The double effect doctrine implies the ethical permissibility of the (*a*) alternatives and the impermissibility of the (*b*) ones. Since not everyone would agree with this implication, these are not precisely the cases from which the doctrine derives its appeal.

There are a number of examples that seem to imply that the intention–foresight distinction must ineluctably be resorted to in moral contexts where a difference as regards the results of the actions in play is not at first sight involved. It is worth considering these examples in some detail because of their importance not only for the purpose of determining the possible relevance of the intention–foresight asymmetry in common-sense morality but also for the purpose of finding out whether the act–omission asymmetry can play the part assigned by the upholders of the 'double effect' to the intention–foresight distinction. To explain the initial appeal of the doctrine of double effect, Foot presents the following examples:

(3*a*) (*The case of the runaway tram*) A runaway tram comes rushing down the line. There are five people on the line and they will not be able to get off in time because the line is closed in on both sides by steep cliffs. If the tram continues on its way, the five persons will be killed. The driver of the tram cannot stop the downward rush on the sloping gradient but she can switch to another line on which there is only one person. If she does so, she will kill one person instead of five.

(3*b*) (*The case of the threatened judge*) Unless a judge declares guilty and sentences someone for a crime he did not commit, a furious mob will take vengeance on five innocent people.

(4*a*) A doctor has five pills of a rare medicine. She may use them to save the lives of five people, each of whom needs a dose of one pill, or she may use them to save the life of one person who requires a dose of five pills.

(4*b*) A doctor can save five people if (and only if) she kills a sixth person and makes a serum out of his body.

(5*a*) There is a wicked tyrant who tortures people. We can send a rescue squad to save group *A* consisting of five persons or group *B* with only one person (not in group *A*) in it.

(5b) The same wicked tyrant says to us that unless we agree to torture one person, he will torture another five.[3]

Whereas in alternatives (a) the respective bad results are foreseen, it may be alleged that in (b) the same results are desired as means. This difference would justify, in accordance with the double effect doctrine, the favourable moral judgements which the conduct described in the (a) cases would receive, as well as the negative appraisements that would be the lot of the actions in the (b) cases.

There being several examples supporting the moral relevance of the intention–foresight distinction, let us concentrate on possible counter-examples. Consider the following case:

(6a) A group of wicked merchants sells cooking oil knowing it to be poisonous and, as a result, kills a number of innocent people.

(6b) A group of unemployed grave-diggers, desperate for custom, gets hold of the oil and sells it to step up the demand for graves.[4]

The merchants only foresee the death of their customers; they do not intend it as a means; a proof of this is that they would sell the oil all the same even if they supposed that the purchasers on opening the tins would be frightened by the unusual colour and would not consume it. The situation of the grave-diggers is different: if the purchasers of the oil did not consume it, they would not die, and therefore the purpose of the action would be thwarted. Despite the fact that the former is a case of killing with indirect or oblique intention, and the latter of killing with direct intention, we should not agree, says Foot, that there is any moral difference between them. Notwithstanding their initial plausibility, the counter-examples of this type to the double effect doctrine may be at once laid aside because they involve a confusion about the content of this doctrine. In fact, what the doctrine maintains is not that there is always a moral difference between causing an undesirable result with direct intention and causing it

---

[3] Foot, 'The Problem of Abortion and the Doctrine of the Double Effect', 23–5. I follow the presentation of Foot's examples made by Nancy Davis in her 'The Priority of Avoiding Harm', in Steinbock (ed.), *Killing and Letting Die*, 174–5.

[4] Foot, 'The Problem of Abortion and the Doctrine of the Double Effect', 22.

with oblique intention, but that '*sometimes* it makes a difference to the permissibility of an action involving harm to others that this harm, although foreseen, is not part of the agent's direct intention'.[5] A crucial question is exactly *when* the fact mentioned implies a moral difference. Finnis, for example, emphasizes that a usual condition of applying the doctrine is that the desired aspect or effect of the action should be sufficiently good and important in relation to the bad aspect or effect foreseen.[6] The effect desired by the merchants—to make a bigger profit— obviously does not fulfil this requirement.

Other counter-examples could be discarded on similar grounds. In order to show the moral irrelevance of the intention–foresight distinction, when isolated from other possibly important differences, Judith Jarvis Thompson invites us to imagine the following case:

> (7) (*The case of the child missile launchers*) A violent aggressor nation has threatened us with death unless we allow ouselves to be enslaved by it. It has, ready and waiting, a monster missile launcher, which it will use on us unless we surrender. The missile launcher has interior tunnels, each leading to a missile. For technical reasons, the tunnels had to be built very small; for technical reasons also, each missile has to be triggered by a human hand. Midgets are too large. So it was necessary to train a team of very young children, two-year-olds in fact, to crawl through and trigger the missiles.[7]

Here Thompson asks us to imagine two worlds, in each of which there is a different continuation of the case narrated:

> (7a) Their technology being what it is, they were able to build only one missile launcher; it will take at last two years to produce another. (By contrast, training the team of children was easy, indeed, was done in a day.)We are capable of bombing the site. Unfortunately, if we bomb to destroy the launcher to save our lives, we kill the children.
>
> (7b) Their psychology being what it is, they were able to train only one team of children; it will take at least two years to train

---

[5] Ibid.

[6] John Finnis, 'The Rights and Wrongs of Abortion: A Reply to Judith Thompson', *Philosophy and Public Affairs*, 1 (1971), 135.

[7] Judith Jarvis Thompson, 'Rights and Deaths', *Philosophy and Public Affairs*, 2 (1973), 153; name of the example added.

another. (By contrast, building the launcher was easy, indeed, was done in a day.) We are capable of bombing the site. Unfortunately, bombing the site will save our lives only if by bombing we kill the children.

Despite the fact that the intention to kill the children is indirect in (7a) and direct in (7b), we should probably be disposed to admit the moral permissibility of both courses of action. Thompson herself realizes that in this case another of the usual conditions of the application of the double effect doctrine is not fulfilled, to wit, that the victim should be innocent. 'Innocent' is taken here as a term of art: though obviously the children are not to blame for what they would do if the threat is not satisfied, they are not innocent in the relevant sense, it being understood by this something like 'not causing harm' or 'not forming part of the threat'. Notwithstanding her acceptance of this point, Thompson contends that the fact that both in (7a) and in (7b) it is permissible to kill the children, regardless of whether the intention is indirect in one alternative and direct in the other, implies that 'the difference between direct and indirect killing does not have the moral significance which has been claimed for it'.[8] But who has claimed this moral significance for it? It is true that—as Thompson alleges—Finnis makes the mistake of thinking that the innocence of the victim has something to do with the direct or indirect character of the intention;[9] but what cannot be called in question is that the innocence of the victim has something to do—indeed something decisive to do—with the moral reproachability of an act of killing. A double effect theorist might then argue that the intention–foresight distinction is relevant only with regard to the domain of acts which are *morally impermissible by virtue of their objective aspects*; if, on the other hand, an act is permissible by virtue of its objective traits, for example, owing to the fact that it is an act of self-defence, then the problem does not arise whether there is a possibility of moral justification backed up by the indirect character of the intention involved.

But the doctrine of the double effect is not so lucky with other counter-examples that seem to prove beyond doubt that it has

---

[8] Ibid. 155.
[9] Finnis, 'The Rights and Wrongs of Abortion', 137–41.

unreasonable implications or, at least, ones contrary to the judgements clearly deriving from common-sense morality. Foot provides two cases with these characteristics. The following is one of them:

> (8) (*The case of the trapped pot-holer*) A group of people go pot-holing. ... One of them—a fat man—gets stuck in the mouth of the cave and thereby blocks the exit. The cave is flooding rapidly, and all of the pot-holers are bound to be drowned—the fat man is stuck facing *into* the cave—unless the fat man is dynamited out of the exit.[10]

Compare this case with (2*b*). Both the foetus and the fat man are harmed, destroyed as the only means of saving another or other persons (the mother or the rest of the pot-holers). There being direct intention in both cases, common-sense morality would have to condemn both actions according to the double effect doctrine. However, it would seem to many of us unreasonable, as Davis says, that we should have to refrain from causing a death by direct intention, when nothing is gained by doing so, and there is even a loss—of human lives, in the case under consideration.

Even though this case seems to reveal a flaw in the doctrine of double effect, one might still make an attempt to save it by conditioning its application to cases in which the foreseen bad consequences of the action are constituted by an event which would not take place if it were not for the execution of this action; the idea would be that the intention–foresight distinction is morally relevant only in respect of choices where there are conflicting interests, where the action to be judged encroaches upon interests that would not otherwise be affected. Though the possibility of this defence cannot be turned down in advance, it should be borne in mind that the more one restricts the application of a distinction, the less important this distinction becomes. In this particular case, the above defence not only implies that the direct or indirect character of the intention involved in slaying an innocent person has no decisive moral importance, but constitutes into the bargain an *ad hoc* manœuvre so long as it is not accom-

---

[10] Foot, 'The Problem of Abortion and the Doctrine of the Double Effect', 21; the presentation is quoted from Nancy Davis ('The Priority of Avoiding Harm', 197; italics in the original.)

panied by an explanation of why the intention–foresight distinction is relevant in certain cases and not in others, like the one under consideration.

Be that as it may, the other counter-example provided by Foot really does seem to represent a decisive blow to the doctrine:

> (9) (*The case of the lethal fumes*) There are five patients in a hospital whose lives could be saved by the manufacture of a certain gas, but this inevitably releases lethal fumes into the room of another patient whom for some reason we are unable to move.[11]

It goes without saying that in this case the death of the patient from the fumes would be a side-effect, foreseen but not desired as a means—or, of course, as an end—of the action of saving the life of the five patients. This action would be morally permissible according to the doctrine of double effect, and yet common-sense morality requires moral condemnation of making the gas in such a way that it does not in the case of changing the direction of the runaway tram, though in both cases the pertinent intention is merely indirect. It may be concluded, then, that the intention–foresight distinction does not have in common-sense morality the central importance assigned to it by the double effect doctrine.[12]

On the other hand, the above conclusion about the doctrine of double effect converges with the result which may be achieved through an abstract analysis of the propositions in the doctrine. The central proposition asserts that whether an act's bad result is intended as a means or an end by the agent or is merely foreseen

---

[11] Foot, 'The Problem of Abortion and the Doctrine of the Double Effect', 29; name of the example added.

[12] In a later essay ('Morality, Action and Outcome', in Ted Honderich (ed.), *Morality and Objectivity* (London: Routledge & Kegan Paul, 1985)) Foot says that she has modified her position about the distinction between direct and indirect intention being irrelevant to moral judgement; thus she contends that it is morally objectionable to let somebody die deliberately because his death will enable us to save others (p. 25). If Foot is right, it is morally a less serious matter to let somebody die out of apathy than with the purpose of saving others. But it seems to me incredible that the attitude involved in the intention of saving others should be able to worsen the moral condition of an omission in relation to the attitude manifested by someone who apathetically allows somebody else to die. In any case, though Foot's present view may be right, as a matter of fact it does not imply a modification of her previous position understood as the thesis that there is no fundamental moral distinction between commissively harming someone with direct intention and doing so with indirect or oblique intention. This is the thesis I defend in the text.

by him makes a difference as regards the moral standing of the act. To start with, it should be noted that this proposition seems uncontroversial as long as it claims that there is a morally relevant difference between a result's being intended as an end by the agent or merely foreseen by him as a side-effect. The moot point is whether there is a similarly significant difference between a consequence's being intended as a means or merely foreseen as a double effect. What kind of distinction may be drawn between an event's being a means or a 'mere double effect'? One natural answer to this question might be to say that, unlike the means, the side-effect is a causally necessary condition of the end. Yet, this answer is plainly incorrect. Within the context of the double effect doctrine, both the side-effect and the means are causally necessary conditions of the end. If the means followed by the agent were not a causally necessary condition of the end, if—in other words—there were other ways for the agent to attain the end, then the question of whether the goodness of the end pursued justified the bad means would not from the start arise. But it is precisely to this question that the double effect doctrine purports to give an answer, indeed a negative one.

It seems to me then that the distinction between a means and a side-effect, as envisaged by the double effect theorist, could only be based upon the different positions they respectively occupy in the causal structure following the agent's action. This difference may be seen in Figs. 4.1(*a*) and (*b*), which include at most two columns, *A* and *B*, and a series of rows that are numbered starting from the row where the end is placed, which is conventionally indicated by 0. Now the difference searched for seems to show itself in a crystal-clear way: whereas the means occupies the position *A*1, the merely foreseen consequence occupies the position *B*0. (The double effect might also occupy a position below the row 0, but for simplicity's sake I shall ignore this possibility.) This difference in position has two aspects: a column difference and a row difference. Let us focus firstly on the column difference. How would the double effect theorist justify his placing the means on the *A* column and the side-effect on the *B* one? In other words, how would he justify his calling the consequence merely foreseen a *side*-effect, the means and the end being assumed to be *central* events? Clearly, the justification could not be based upon a purely causal reason, for, as said above, both

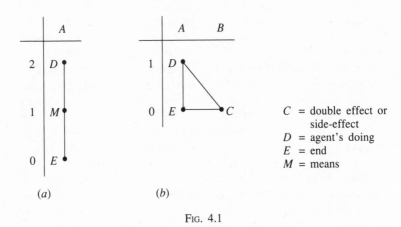

FIG. 4.1

the means and the foreseen consequence are causally necessary conditions of the end. This being so, I think that the double effect theorist can only reply: The difference is that whereas the means is intended (or directly intended), the side-effect is merely foreseen (or indirectly intended). This means that the column difference is for the double effect theorist intentional in nature. According to this view, the *A* column is reserved for events intended (or directly intended), i.e. ends and means, and the *B* column is reserved for merely foreseen events (or events indirectly intended), i.e. side-effects. However, this reply is hardly tenable. Let me show why.[13] The crucial question here is: How might the double effect theorist defend the position that, unlike the means, the side-effect is for the agent an unintended event? The only route open to him is to appeal to a dispositional claim capable of revealing a genuine difference in the attitudes which the agent respectively has towards the means and the side-effect. More specifically, the counterfactual proposition on which the double effect theorist must focus runs like this: If the agent believed that his act would not produce *X*, he would none the less be equally inclined to perform it. He might then contend that this proposition is true when *X* is the side-effect, but false when it is the

[13] My explanation will at this point echo Jonathan Bennett's analysis of the same issue in 'Morality and Consequences', in S. McMurrin (ed.), *The Tanner Lectures on Human Values*, ii (Salt Lake City, Utah: University of Utah Press, 1981), 100–2.

means. Yet, this contention is incorrect. As the agent knows that
the side-effect is a causally necessary condition of the end, if he
believed that his act would not produce the side-effect, he would
also believe that his act would not produce the end and, consequently, would not be equally inclined to perform it. Since, as
already said, both the means and the side-effect are causally
necessary conditions of the end, if the agent believed that his act
would not produce the side-effect, he would be less inclined to
make it, just as he would be if he believed that his act would not
produce the means.

The double effect theorist might, however, protest along the
following lines: What I am claiming is that, if the agent believed
that his act would not produce the side-effect but would nevertheless produce the end, he would be equally inclined to execute
it. Now, it is true that, if the agent believed that his act was
capable of producing the end without the side-effect, he would be
equally inclined to perform it. But when the counterfactual proposition is interpreted in these terms, the difference in attitude
that the double theorist tries to capture does not appear either,
for, if the agent believed that his act was capable of producing
the end without having to bring about first the bad means, he
would also be inclined to perform it, indeed much more inclined.
In short, whichever of the two possible interpretations of the
hypothetical conditions to which the counterfactual proposition
refers is adopted, the agent shows no difference as regards his
inclination to perform the relevant act under such conditions in
the absence either of the means or of the double effect.

I have tried to show that it is not possible to find any real
difference in the attitudes which an agent respectively has towards the means and the double effect: both are regarded as
'prices' to be paid for achieving the end wished for. If the word
'intended' is reserved to denote the condition of an event wished
for as an end by an agent, then both the undesirable double
effect and the undesirable means may be said to be unintended.
We are now in a position to see that it is wrong for the double
effect theorist to place the means on the *A* column, for it is
column *B* which he reserves for the unintended events surrounding his doing. Leaving aside the row corresponding to the agent's
action, when the relevant column correction is introduced
Figs. 4.1(*a*) and (*b*) appear as in Fig. 4.1'.

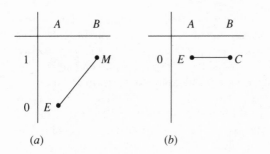

FIG. 4.1′

Let us concentrate now on the row difference. This is obviously a time difference: whereas the event employed as a means takes place before the end, the double effect occurs simultaneously with the event pursued as the end. (The double effect might also occur after the end, but, as hinted above, I shall ignore this possibility for simplicity's sake.) But for this time difference, no distinction could be drawn between the means and the double effect. Suppose, for example, that the agent employs an instantaneous means, i.e. a means which takes no time to achieve the end desired. This possibility is illustrated in Fig. 4.2(a) and (b). In this figure the difference in position between the means and the double effect has completely vanished. But, of course, this is only a hypothetical example. In normal cases the row difference, unlike the column difference, remains. The point is that the distinction between the means and the double effect is based only upon a time difference: whereas the double effect is a side-effect, the means is a side-prerequisite. In most cases, however, this time difference has practical or technical implications, for the normal way of attaining an end is to do things before its occurrence. As is to be expected, these practical implications find expression in common language. So we may say that the agent produced the undesirable prerequisite *in order to* achieve the end, but not that he produced the undesirable effect in order to achieve the end; in the latter case, we would say, rather, that the agent achieved the end *though* this brought about the undesirable effect. But this verbal difference does not reflect any difference in the agent's attitudes or intentions, but merely the time difference already mentioned, together with its practical implications on

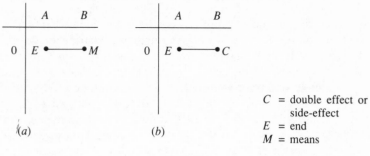

FIG. 4.2

human action. This means that the doctrine of double effect fails on its own terms. For the point of the doctrine—let us recall—is to claim that a certain difference in the *subjective structure* of an action is significant for its moral assessment, as something different from the moral assessment of the agent. But the difference discovered is linked only to relative time positions, that is to say, to certain objective features of the action, and not to its subjective structure. This point aside, the centrally important question is whether, in the absence of intentional or strictly causal differences, a pure time difference may serve as a basis for a moral distinction. With the question put in these terms, I believe that everybody would answer it in the negative without the slightest hesitation. This amounts to a virtual refutation of the double effect doctrine. However, the intuitive moral difference arising in such pairs of cases as (3), (4), and (5), which the doctrine claims to justify, does really exist and remains to be captured. In what follows I shall be arguing that this moral difference is best brought out by a sort of action–inaction distinction.

Priority of the Duty not to Actively Damage Positive Freedom

The thesis that there is an overwhelming duty not to attack positive freedom commissively enjoys all the intuitive support that, as has been observed,[14] is contained in the general principle

---

[14] Foot, 'The Problem of Abortion and the Doctrine of the Double Effect', *passim*.

of the priority of negative duties. This principle can explain satisfactorily our moral intuitions in a series of cases that at first sight are to be dealt with only through the doctrine of double effect. This is what happens with cases (3), (4), and (5). In alternatives (*a*) of these cases the agent has to choose between the fulfilment of a positive duty (mutual aid) and the fulfilment of another positive duty of the same sort (cases (4) and (5)), or between the fulfilment of a negative duty (not to harm) and the fulfilment of another negative duty of the same kind (case (3)); where there is a conflict between two duties of the same type, that duty which shows a more favourable net balance of good takes priority. On the other hand, in alternatives (*b*) the fulfilment of a duty not to harm is opposed to the fulfilment of the duty to help; in these situations the thesis of the priority of negative duties demands the sacrifice of the fulfilment of the positive duty, whatever may be the net balance of good that that implies.

Furthermore, the principle of the priority of the duty not to harm seems to have an advantage over the doctrine of the double effect inasmuch as it explains not only the intuitions the double effect doctrine accounts for but likewise some intuitions that this doctrine cannot explain; such is the case with regard to our intuitions in the case of the lethal fumes (case (9)). In contradiction to what the doctrine of double effect implies, we have the strong intuition that it is not morally permissible to make the gas in question. The thesis of the priority of the duty not to harm agrees with our intuition, since, by any admissible interpretation of 'harming', the manufacture of a gas giving off lethal fumes is a case of harming, and is therefore impermissible according to this thesis even though the manufacture of it is the only possible means of complying with the (positive) duty of helping.

But though the thesis of the priority of the duty not to cause harm, a harm being understood as the curtailment of a person's positive freedom, is plausible, it presents a difficulty we must now face. As Nancy Davis[15] points out, what she calls Foot's Principle of the Priority of Avoiding Harm, formulated in these terms:

> ... the obligation not to harm people is more stringent than the obligation to benefit people

[15] 'The Priority of Avoiding Harm', 178.

admits of different interpretations according to whether it makes use of the distinction between negative and positive duties or the distinction between duties not to harm and duties to benefit. Davis discusses the two following interpretations of the principle:

The negative–positive duty doctrine
(NPD) ... negative duties understood as duties not to perform some positive act which harms are more stringent than positive duties understood as duties to perform some positive act which benefits.

The harm–benefit doctrine
(HBD) ... duties not to harm are more stringent than duties to benefit.

NPD has a different content from HBD if it is assumed that one can harm or benefit not only by doing something but also by forbearing from doing something. In particular, the idea that one can harm by omission has been exploited to justify the so-called economic and social rights and the redistributive measures that their legal enforcement occasions.[16] 'A person may cause evil to others not only by his actions but by his inaction,' said Mill, although he maintained that while 'to make anyone answerable for doing evil to others is the rule, to make him answerable for not preventing evil is, comparatively speaking, the exception'.[17]

It is clear that it might be contended, as Davis observes, that 'there is a conceptual connection between positive acts (or doings) and benefits, or between positive acts and harms, which is such that we *cannot* speak of benefiting or harming unless there is a positive act'. This view, Davis goes on to say, might be grounded on the following reasoning:

To harm someone is to cause him to be worse off (and to benefit someone is to cause him to be better off) than he otherwise would have been. But if we are, in fact, doing nothing, then we cannot be said to have affected the way things would have been at all. To affect someone for the worse (better) is to cause him to be worse (better) off. But if we do nothing, then there is nothing (no event) that is our causing someone

---

[16] See Ted Honderich, *Violence for Equality* (Harmondsworth: Penguin, 1980); C. S. Nino, *Ética y derechos humanos* (Buenos Aires: Paidós, 1984); Joseph Raz, *The Morality of Freedom* (Oxford: Clarendon Press, 1986).
[17] John Stuart Mill, 'On Liberty', in *Utilitarianism. On Liberty. Essay on Bentham*, ed. Mary Warnock (Glasgow: Collins, 1979), 137.

to be worse (better) off. Hence, we cannot harm (benefit) someone by doing nothing.[18]

Davis properly contends that this reasoning is weak. On the one hand, it presupposes a conception of causality according to which negative events cannot constitute causes. But it does not seem possible to take it for granted without a specific argument that no negative event may play a causal role merely on account of its negative nature. On the other hand, it presupposes an arbitrarily narrow conception of 'harming' according to which to harm someone is to cause someone harm; the reasoning under consideration would collapse if we were to agree, à la Hart–Honoré, that to harm someone is not so much to cause that person harm as to be responsible for the fact that he is suffering harm.

Be that as it may, to get entangled in the battle of words over whether all harm is necessarily active or, on the contrary, harm may be done by inaction or omission, will lead us nowhere. Even if we agree that it is possible to harm by omission, no objection follows to the Principle of the Priority of Avoiding Harm always provided this principle is maintained under the interpretation given by NPD, or even according to HBD so long as it is understood that, when this doctrine speaks of 'harming', it is referring to 'actively harming'. Interpreting 'actively harming' as 'actively injuring somebody's positive freedom', the Priority of Avoiding Harm Principle turns into the thesis that there is an overriding duty not to actively injure the positive freedom of people. But what does 'actively injure somebody's positive freedom' mean? Tentatively we may affirm that P actively injures Q's positive freedom if and only if he makes bodily movements that set up a causal process the consequence of which is to restrain Q's positive freedom in such a way as it would not have been restrained if P had not made the aforesaid bodily movements. The thesis that there is an overwhelming duty not to actively injure positive freedom, understood in this form, can explain the case of the lethal fumes (case (9)) but not the case of the trapped pot-holer (case (8)). Dynamiting the fat pot-holer is actively injuring his positive freedom in the sense defined. However, this behaviour might be justified inasmuch as the poor man would anyhow have died from drowning if he had not been blown up.

---

[18] 'The Priority of Avoiding Harm', 180.

We may conclude that the thesis that there is a pre-eminent moral duty not to actively injure positive freedom is quite congenial to our basic moral intuitions. Given that the existence of a negative overriding duty implies the existence of the corresponding pre-eminent negative right provided that this duty protects personal autonomy, and that positive freedom is a component of personal autonomy, it may be claimed that the basic libertarian thesis is firmly rooted in common-sense morality. Now, it may naturally be thought that the thesis that there is an overriding moral duty not to actively injure positive freedom implies the thesis that it is morally more serious to affect positive freedom by action than to do so by inaction. In the next two sections I am going to try and fill out the content of this second thesis.

Forms of Inaction

To begin with, I must make it clear that I am using the term 'inaction' in a deliberately vague manner. It is a label to include, as 'forms of inaction', what is denoted by three phrases used centrally in discussions about the moral significance of the different ways in which an agent may bring about a disvaluable event:

(a) not doing X,
(b) refraining from doing X (forbearing from doing X),
(c) omitting to do X.

The first phrase is the least demanding as regards the conditions which must be met for it to be properly applied. Not doing X at a moment t_1 does not even require that the change involved in doing X should not have taken place at the moment immediately preceding t_1. Moreover, if that change took place at the moment immediately preceding t_1, not doing X at t_1 would be unavoidable. As Wright points out, it is logically true that if a window is closed at t_1, nobody is closing it at t_1.[19] This is a key to understanding why 'bare inaction' lacks interesting descriptive content from the moral point of view. The behaviour of a person is morally interesting when it can be said to have contributed in some way to bringing about some event, particularly a valuable

---

[19] Georg Henrik von Wright, *Norm and Action* (London: Routledge & Kegan Paul, 1963), 45.

or disvaluable event; but it only makes sense to say that a behaviour contributed to the happening of an event E if, at the
moment immediately before the behaviour, E had not taken
place. In this way, it is necessarily true that an indefinitely large
number of the types of behaviour that may be described through
the phrase 'not-doing' do not help to bring about any event, and
therefore any valuable or disvaluable event. Because it has an
excessively comprehensive content, 'not-doing' is not in a condition to capture the morally significant forms of human inaction.

The second phrase is more interesting for our purposes.
Although it is a truism that an agent does not do X when he
refrains from doing X, it seems clear that 'refraining from' is
more restrictive than 'not-doing'. There are four conditions that it
is reasonable to associate with the idea of refraining that are
responsible for its scope of application's being comparatively
more restricted than that of the concept of merely not-doing.
Each of these conditions gives us a conception of refraining that
is logically richer and, consequently, possesses a progressively
smaller field of application. (I shall distinguish each of these four
conceptions of refraining by adding a numerical sub-index to
'refraining from' and to all the members of its family of words.)
The first condition is the most important in the sense that it is
indispensable if refraining from is to be distinguished from bare
inaction. If a window is closed, it is true that one does not close
it, but it is not true that one refrains from doing so. To refrain
from closing the window, it is necessary for the window to be
open. In general terms, an agent refrains from making a change
on a given occasion only if on this occasion the world is open to
the change. The notion of refraining that results from this first
condition may be defined thus: an agent refrains$_1$ from doing
something on a given occasion if, and only if, he does not do this
thing and the world is open to the change involved in doing it.
The second condition is clearly presupposed, just like the first,
in the everyday use of 'refraining from'. This condition runs
as follows: an agent refrains from making a change on a given
occasion only if he has the *capacity* to make this change. For
example, it would be incorrect to say that a doctor refrains from
restoring to life a patient who has just died, despite the fact that
obviously the world is open to this change at the moment of the
possible refraining. We have thus rounded out a second concep-

tion of refraining, definable as follows: an agent refrains$_2$ from doing something on a given occasion if, and only if, he does not do it, the world is open to the change involved in doing this thing, and he has the capacity to do it. The third condition is that the agent should be aware of the opportunity of doing the thing in question, understanding by 'opportunity' both that the world should be open to the change involved and that he should be able to bring about the change. The fourth condition is that the agent should decide not to do the thing (where 'deciding' implies the consideration of reasons). 'Refraining$_3$' and 'refraining$_4$' are defined easily by progressively adding the third and the fourth condition to the definition of 'refraining$_2$'.[20] From now on, whenever I speak of 'refraining', it should be understood that I do so in the sense of the second conception defined above. I make this decision because, as I said in Chapter 1, we should not rule out the possibility of carelessly or even accidentally refraining from doing something.

The last phrase I include in the concept of inaction (phrase (c)) is ambiguous. 'Omitting to do X' may be used with two different meanings. In the first case the expression 'omitting to do X' is equivalent to 'refraining from doing X'. (Though this implies that 'omitting to do X' is liable to the four interpretations I set out above in connection with the conception of refraining, I shall ignore, as already said, the third and the fourth interpretation.) In the second case, the meaning of 'omission' does not coincide with that of 'refraining' but may be elucidated by an appeal to the latter notion. An agent omits to do X in this sense not only when he refrains from doing X but when besides it was expected that he would do X or it was considered that X was the right thing to do or something that should be done, whether for moral reasons or for reasons of another type. 'Daniel failed to help the injured man' and 'Martin (suffering from hypertension) omitted to control his blood pressure' are two clear examples of the use of this notion of omission. Both notions of omission may be found in

---

[20] In this paragraph I have followed Wright's analysis of forbearances (*Norm and Action*, 45–6), with a slight difference: Wright does not distinguish my first conception of refraining (forbearing) because he includes in the idea of being able to do something both the condition that the world should be open to the change involved in doing this something and that the agent should possess the capacity to do it, conditions that in the text are treated separately.

the philosophical literature. Thus, for instance, Foot handles the first notion when, referring to the reason underlying the non-consequentialist asymmetries, she asks: 'Is the operative difference the difference between act and omission, between what someone does and what he refrains from doing?'[21] It is evident that Foot presupposes in this question that the conceptual pair act–omission is equivalent to the doing–refraining-from-doing pair. Bennett makes use of the second notion of omission when he writes: 'you can't properly be said to "omit" to do something unless you prima facie ought to have done it; and so we have a substantial moral taint in the language of act/omission if the latter term is properly used'.[22]

To distinguish the two concepts of omission one might speak in the first case of 'sheer omission', and of 'commissive omission' in the second. This last expression is particularly adequate because it calls attention to the most significant feature of the second concept of omission. So, an omission can be naturally described as a *commission*, as doing something, if the agent was expected in some way to do the corresponding positive act or if this act constituted one of his duties or was in any other way exactable from him, especially on account of the role he was playing. The expression 'commissive omission' underlines the peculiarity of the second class of omissions of admitting as a rule a description in terms of 'doing something'. Let us suppose that a mother does not feed her son and that, on account of this, he dies. This omission may be adequately described by saying that the mother starved her son to death. It is not the same with sheer omissions. If a stranger does not feed a beggar and the beggar dies, we say that the stranger did not feed the beggar, but not that he starved the beggar to death.[23]

Lichtenberg contends that the applicability of the commissive description to a number of omissions is due not only to the presupposition of certain moral beliefs about the agent's obligations but also to the fact that, unlike the case of sheer omissions, in commissive omissions the agent has always done something to

[21] Foot, 'Morality, Action and Outcome', 24.

[22] Bennett, 'Morality and Consequences', 50.

[23] Judith Lichtenberg, 'The Moral Equivalence of Action and Omission', in K. Nielsen and S. C. Patten (eds.), *New Essays in Ethics and Public Policy*, *Canadian Journal of Philosophy*, suppl. vol. 8 (1982), 21.

undertake or commit himself to perform the corresponding positive act. For example, the mother, in addition to not feeding her
son, did certain relevant things, as, for instance, bringing the
child into the world. So Lichtenberg proposes to call sheer omissions 'genuine' or '*ex nihilo*' ones.[24] It seems to me that this
contention is wrong, in fact obviously so. It is clear that, in saying
that the mother starved her son to death, we do not wish to make
any reference at all to the previous act of giving birth to the child.
With the positive description of her omission, we merely imply
that the mother in omitting to do what she should have done
transgressed or *violated* an ethical obligation. Let us suppose that
the boy in question was 4 years old at the time and that up to that
moment he had been plentifully and properly fed. I think that
Lichtenberg would not be prepared to say that the mother had
begun to starve her child four years earlier; or even before that,
from the moment of its conception! Besides, it does not seem
true that, provided on omission admits of a commissive description, there should be involved a previous act on the part of the
agent consisting in committing himself or undertaking to perform
the positive act. If on a dark night *P* knows that *Q*'s next step will
take him over the edge of a precipice, and he fails to utter a
simple word of warning because it does not matter to him or
because he wants *Q* to die, it is natural to describe *P*'s conduct
by saying that he killed *Q*,[25] even though *P* has not undertaken in
any way to see to *Q*'s safety. For the commissive description of
an omission to be adequate it is important, as has been said, that
this omission constitute in itself the violation of some duty, particularly of a moral nature.

The terminology of commissive omissions should not lead one
into the error of thinking that, though a factual difference may
be established between sheer omissions and actions (or commis-
sions), it is not possible to establish a factual difference between
actions and commissive omissions. Commissive omissions consist
not in doing something, but, just like sheer omissions, in not
doing anything. The difference between sheer omissions and
commissive omissions does not lie in the different type of behaviour on the part of the agent, but rather in the different type

[24] Ibid.
[25] The example is from Bennett, 'Whatever the Consequences', 118–19.

of *description* that this behaviour admits by virtue of the special circumstances surrounding it. This becomes quite clear as soon as one reflects on the circumstance that the commissive omission is, by definition, a special case of forbearance and, therefore, of sheer omission. But despite the fact that the concept of commissive omission may also be differentiated from that of action, it is at a fundamental disadvantage in comparison with the notion of forbearance or sheer omission when it comes to be used in the tracing out of basic moral distinctions. Let us remember that the distinction between action and inaction is intended to serve as a basis for justifying moral judgements about the forms of behaviour a person should follow. The notion of commissive omission is not in a position to render this service, from the moment when it has itself to presuppose judgements about people's duties, particularly moral ones. Indeed, the notion of 'commissively omitting *X*' comes to be equivalent, in ethical contexts, to the idea of 'transgressing the moral duty of doing *X*', an idea that evidently cannot be of any use in determining what our moral duties are, precisely because it presupposes this determination. It is as well, then, to dismiss the notion of commissive omission and direct our attention to the concept of forbearance or sheer omission. For reasons of simplicity I shall in the future employ the expression 'omission' when referring to what I have called 'sheer omissions'.

Formulation of the Distinction

Now, those who hold that there is a moral difference between acts and omissions do not want of course to say that any wrong act is morally worse than any wrong omission. This thesis would be obviously false. If Bessie insults Peter, she does not behave, in normal circumstances, worse than if she fails to throw a lifebelt to Martin, who is drowning and cries to Bessie for help. Yet the defenders of the act–omission distinction in the moral realm would surely say that if Bessie kills Daniel, she does something worse than omitting to throw Martin the lifebelt. In speaking of a moral asymmetry between acts and omissions, we are not alluding, then, to an asymmetry between any wrong act and any wrong omission, but between certain wrong acts and their 'corresponding' omissions. Thus, it might be thought that the right way of formulating the thesis of the moral difference between acts and omissions is by saying that doing X—i.e. causing X to happen—and failing to do X—i.e. refraining from causing X to happen—are morally inequivalent. This last proposition, however, bears within it a dangerous confusion.

Let us suppose that we want to compare Bessie's act towards Daniel with her omission with respect to Martin. To this end it would be natural to describe her respective tracts of behaviour by saying 'Bessie killed Daniel' and 'Bessie failed to throw Martin the lifebelt'. Yet, since Bessie's omission to throw Martin the lifebelt is clearly something quite different from Bessie's omission to kill him, we are not comparing Bessie's doing X with her failing to do X. Therefore, the act–omission question is not one concerning doing X and omitting to do X, where X stands for the same thing in both cases.

On the other hand, the phrase 'failing to do X' does not show a logical behaviour exactly symmetrical to that of the phrase 'doing X' as far as the reference to the morally significant dimension of human behaviour is concerned. This point may be explained as follows. It goes without saying that the acts and omissions that are relevant from the moral standpoint are those which in some sense may be said to have 'contributed' to the bringing about of some disvaluable (or valuable) event. However, although 'doing X *simpliciter*' normally has logical implications about the event that the act has helped to produce (the only exception is when the phrase merely denotes bodily movements), 'failing to do X *simpliciter*' normally lacks such implications. So, for instance, 'Bessie killed Daniel' entails 'Daniel died', but 'Bessie failed to throw Martin the lifebelt' does not entail 'Martin died'. I think that it is now easy to understand why the question whether or not there is a moral equivalence between acts and omissions cannot be stated in terms of a moral asymmetry (or symmetry) between doing X and failing to do X *simpliciter* even when the latter X is said to stand for something capable of stopping the event referred to by the former X.

The question is not whether or not doing X is morally different from failing to do X but whether *doing X is morally different from helping to bring about X by omitting to do Y*. One contributes to the production of X by failing to do Y when to do Y is the act of preventing X from happening or, what comes to the same thing, the act of intervening or helping so that X does not take place. The problem is, then, whether 'Bessie killed Daniel' describes a tract of behaviour morally equivalent to that described by 'Bessie failed to prevent Martin from dying'. But it appears that 'Bessie failed to prevent Martin from dying' has the same meaning as 'Bessie *let* Martin *die*'. Hence, the problem of the moral asymmetry between acts and omissions is, as is usually stated, the question whether *doing* X is morally different from *letting* X *happen*.

The thesis that there is an overriding duty not to actively injure positive freedom seems to imply that to restrain X's positive freedom and to allow X's positive freedom to be restrained are morally inequivalent. It is now necessary to establish what the precise meaning is of the claim that doing X and allowing X to happen are morally inequivalent. Frances Myrna Kamm remarks that there are two possible analyses of moral inequivalence.[26] According to the first, to do X and to let X occur are morally inequivalent if there is a property which is conceptually required in cases of the one but not conceptually required in cases of the other, and which makes the cases in which it is present morally different from cases with only the conceptual properties of the other. For the second analysis, doing X and letting X happen are morally inequivalent if there is a property which is conceptually required in the cases of the one but conceptually *excluded* from cases of the other, and which makes the cases in which it is present morally different from the cases with only conceptual properties of the other.

When the thesis of the moral inequivalence of doing X and letting X happen is interpreted through the first analysis, but not when it is in accordance with the second, it admits of the possibility of there being cases in which to do X is as wrong as to let X happen if the property conceptually required by 'doing X' is in such cases 'exported' to allowing X to occur, that is, if the property in question turns out to be contingently true of letting X occur. Let us look at an example. Suppose that a property conceptually required by 'P kills Q' is that Q would live if it were not

---

[26] Frances Myrna Kamm, 'Harming, Not Aiding, and Positive Rights', *Philosophy and Public Affairs*, 15 (1986), 5.

for a causal process that P sets in motion through the performance of certain bodily movements. The thesis of moral inequivalence, interpreted in accordance with the first analysis, would not
have to be considered as refuted by our contention that it is
equally wrong to kill someone by drowning him and to fail to
throw a lifebelt to someone whom one has just pushed into the
water. In general terms, given that the property we supposed to
be conceptually required by 'P kills Q' is 'exported' to all the
cases of 'P lets Q die' in which P has played a causal role in Q's
being in such a position that Q will die unless P comes to his
help, the identity of moral response we have to such cases of
letting die and to all the cases of killing does not impair the truth
of the thesis of moral inequivalence when this thesis is interpreted through the first analysis propounded by Kamm.

The thesis of the moral inequivalence of doing X and letting X
happen is liable to another type of vagueness. As Lichtenberg[27]
rightly observes, it can be upheld in the sense that, given a pair of
cases parallel in every respect except that in one the relevant
disvaluable event is liable to be brought about by positive action
and in the other through mere forbearance, the performance of
the act is morally more serious than the mere forbearance, or else
in the stronger sense that positive action bringing about a disvaluable event in one case is necessarily more serious from the moral
standpoint than mere forbearance contributing to the same event
in another, regardless of whether such cases are parallel in other
respects. Whereas the first reading bestows upon the act–
omission distinction a prima-facie power of moral differentiation,
the second assigns to it a conclusive power. In assessing the thesis
of moral inequivalence it is crucial to bear in mind which of these
two interpretations is adopted. Thus, the thesis of prima facie
moral inequivalence is not refuted by the mere fact that there are
cases of letting X happen that have morally negative properties
(not conceptually required by 'doing X') which raise the moral
gravity of these cases in such a way as to place it very near the
moral gravity of the usual cases of doing X. For example, if
letting someone die stems from the motivation of doing evil,
it might come very near the moral gravity of killing him

---

[27] Lichtenberg, 'The Moral Equivalence of Action and Omission', 22.

knowingly,[28] but this does not mean that killing and letting die
are morally equivalent in the prima-facie sense.

As may be seen, when the thesis of moral inequivalence is
interpreted in accordance with the first analysis propounded by
Kamm and the first reading distinguished by Lichtenberg, it is
immune to a series of obvious counter-examples. Nevertheless, it
should be borne in mind that if the thesis of the absolute priority
of the duty not to actively injure positive freedom implies the
thesis of moral inequivalence, it is reasonable to think that it
implies it in the second reading distinguished by Lichtenberg.
Since the thesis of moral inequivalence seems to be difficult to
uphold when understood in the sense that the act–omission distinction has a conclusive power of moral discrimination, it might
be objected that the thesis of the absolute priority of the duty not
to injure positive freedom actively is equally hard to maintain.
Besides, there is another possible argument against the moral
inequivalence thesis which cannot be discarded by the mere expedient of adopting Lichtenberg's first reading. This argument,
which I shall discuss in the following section, appears to show
that the moral inequivalence thesis can only be defended in a still
more diluted version than the one that comes from adopting
Kamm's first analysis and Lichtenberg's first reading and, consequently, may serve as a basis for a second objection to the
thesis of the absolute priority of the duty not to do any active
injury to positive freedom, always on the assumption that this
thesis entails the moral inequivalence thesis. In the following
section I shall also make a point of neutralizing the two objections to the thesis of the absolute priority of the duty not to
actively injure positive freedom, to which I have just referred,
by arguing that this thesis does not really entail the moral
inequivalence thesis.

The Moral Symmetry Argument

Michael Tooley has forcefully attacked the thesis that there is
a moral difference between doing X and letting X occur. The

---

[28] On this point, see Laurence Thomas, 'Acts, Omissions, and Common Sense
Morality', *Canadian Journal of Philosophy*, suppl. vol. 8 (1982).

principle of moral symmetry suggested by Tooley affirms the following:

Let C be a causal process that normally leads to an outcome E. Let X be an action that initiates process C, and Y be an action that stops process C before outcome E occurs. Assume further that actions X and Y do not have any other morally significant consequences, and that E is the only part or outcome of C which is morally significant in itself. Then there is no moral difference between performing action X, and intentionally refraining from performing action Y ... [29]

To illustrate his principle of moral symmetry Tooley propounds the following pair of cases:

(10*a*) (*The case of the diabolical machine*) One is confronted with a machine that contains a child and a military secret. The machine is so constructed that unless one pushes a button, the child will be tortured and the secret will be destroyed. If one pushes the button, the child will emerge unharmed, but the secret will be transmitted to the enemy. One refrains from pushing the button.

(10*b*) One is confronted with a similar machine. This time, however, it is so constructed that unless one pushes a button, a secret will be transmitted to the enemy, while a child will emerge unharmed. If one pushes the button, the secret will be destroyed, but the child will be tortured. One pushes the button.[30]

These cases bring out the two conditions of application that Tooley explicitly included in the original version of his symmetry principle. To start with, the principle lays down that doing X and letting X happen are morally equivalent always provided the motivation in both forms of behaviour is identical (or at least identical with regard to its morally relevant respects). In the cases presented the motivation for one to refrain from pressing or to press the button of the 'diabolical machine' is the same, namely, to prevent the secret from falling into the hands of the enemy. In the second place, Tooley is concerned to make it clear that the moral inequivalence between doing X and letting X happen may

---

[29] Michael Tooley, 'An Irrelevant Consideration: Killing versus Letting Die', in Steinbock (ed.), *Killing and Letting Die*, 57; see also 'Abortion and Infanticide', *Philosophy and Public Affairs*, 2 (1972), 58.

[30] Tooley, 'An Irrelevant Consideration: Killing versus Letting Die', 58–9; name of the example added.

have its origin not only in the difference of motivation but also in the difference of the effort or sacrifice involved in one or other form of behaviour.[31] Saving the life of a person, for example, generally means a sacrifice in time and energy bigger than refraining from killing somebody. If the sacrifice in question is sufficiently great one can reasonably think that there is no moral obligation to undergo it in order to save somebody else's life; but this, according to Tooley, does not imply that the duty not to kill is stronger than the duty to save somebody's life when one has a chance to do so, but that 'positive actions require effort, and this means that in deciding what to do a person has to take into account his own right to do what he wants with his life, and not only the other person's right to life'.[32] To take this factor into consideration, Tooley contends that the symmetry principle should be applied only to pairs of cases in which 'the positive action involves a minimal effort'.[33] This is precisely the case in the diabolical-machine example.

Now Tooley prefers not to incorporate these two conditions in the formulation of the symmetry principle.[34] He now explains that the point of the principle is to establish that the property of being doing-X and the property of being letting-X-occur are two wrong-making characteristics possessing equal importance or weight. This means that the moral symmetry between doing X and letting X happen is prima facie or 'other morally relevant things being equal'. Understood thus, Tooley's principle contradicts the moral inequivalence thesis in either of the two readings distinguished by Lichtenberg. Among the relevant circumstances that may imply a moral difference between doing X and letting X happen Tooley continues to include the nature of the motivations involved and the degree of effort or sacrifice needed to follow one or other course of action; but given that these two factors do not exhaust the set of morally relevant circumstances that might imply such a difference, he deems it as well not to include them in the formulation of the principle. With regard to the degree of effort, Tooley maintains his former position in the sense that the

---

[31] Ibid.
[32] Tooley, 'Abortion and Infanticide', 60.
[33] Ibid.
[34] Michael Tooley, *Abortion and Infanticide* (Oxford: Clarendon Press, 1985), 184–9.

comparison of cases of doing X and letting X happen whose purpose is to test the principle of moral symmetry should be made between cases involving minimal effort.

It is easy to realize, as Trammell says, that the two limitations to the application of the symmetry principle I have mentioned, that is to say, the one concerning motivation and the one concerning effort, belong to two different types of restriction.[35] The restrictions to the symmetry principle of the first type specify that the act and omission which we compare must be equal in regard to some variable, without any further restriction on that variable. Restrictions of the second type specify that the act and omission must be equal in regard to some variable with a further restriction on the range of that variable. The restriction relative to the motivation is of the first type, since it lays down that the positive action and the forbearance which we compare have to be equal in respect of the motivation, without fixing any requirement relating to the nature of the motivation at stake. On the other hand, the restriction concerning the effort belongs to the second type; indeed, as Trammell rightly points out, at the time of applying the principle of symmetry Tooley requires 'not simply that expenditure of energy be equal, but that it must be "minimal"'.[36]

According to Tooley, the symmetry principle agrees with our moral intuitions when it is applied within the restricted scope of application deriving from the two limitations noted (assuming of course that there are no other morally relevant differences between the cases compared). In proof whereof in connection with the requirement of identical motivation, Tooley proposes the following pair of cases:

> (11a) Jones sees that Smith will be killed by a bomb unless he warns him. Jones's reaction is: 'How lucky, it will save me the trouble of killing Smith myself'. So Jones allows Smith to be killed by the bomb, even though he could easily have warned him.
>
> (11b) Jones wants Smith dead, and therefore shoots him.[37]

Notwithstanding the initial plausibility of Tooley's position with respect to this pair of cases, it is not free from difficulties.

---

[35] Richard Louis Trammell, 'Tooley's Moral Symmetry Principle', *Philosophy and Public Affairs*, 5 (1976), 306.

[36] Ibid. 308.

[37] Tooley, 'Abortion and Infanticide', 59.

On the one hand, Trammell contends that in this pair of cases the violent hatred that Jones feels for Smith, and the former's declared intention of slaying the latter by other means if the bomb should be ineffective, have a kind of 'masking' or 'sledge-hammer' effect. 'The fact', says Trammell, 'that one cannot distinguish the taste of two wines when both are mixed with green persimmon juice does not imply that there is no distinction between the wines.'[38] In support of his position, Trammell constructs a pair of cases in which, though an identical motivation is present, it does not consist in violent hatred:

> (12a) Jones sees that Smith will be killed unless he warns him. But Jones is apathetic. So Smith is killed by the bomb even though Jones could have warned him.
>
> (12b) Jones is practising shooting his gun. Smith accidentally walks in the path and Jones sees Smith; but Jones's reaction is apathy. Jones pulls the trigger and Smith is killed.[39]

In these two cases it no longer appears so obvious that the killing of Smith by Jones is not morally worse than Jones's letting Smith die, despite the fact that the attitude involved remains constant. Tooley replies that our intuitions in this pair of cases may reflect a want of distinction between two different judgements: (1) a judgement on the relative wrongness of the actions in question, and (2) a judgement on the moral undesirability of the traits of character that are probably behind those actions. The moral difference that we seemingly see between the act and the omission of Jones should thus be attributed to the fact that, given the normal conditions of the world, somebody who does not mind killing exhibits a more undesirable feature of character than somebody who does not mind failing to save a life.[40] However, it seems to me very dubious that in (12a) and (12b) Jones shows different traits of character. Rather he seems to display one and the same trait of character whose central content is an attitude of indifference to the death of other people; this feature of character may be shown either by slaying or by failing to save the life of others. At any rate, it is not obvious that our intuitions about the moral difference between these two cases do not bear upon the

[38] Richard Louis Trammell, 'Saving Life and Taking Life', in Steinbock (ed.), *Killing and Letting Die*, 167.
[39] Trammell, 'Tooley's Moral Symmetry Principle', 308.
[40] Tooley, *Abortion and Infanticide*, 218–19.

behaviour of Jones in each case. Of course, Tooley might contend that, given the normal conditions of the world, killing is more undesirable than letting die, but this contention would involve a sort of utilitarian justification of the moral inequivalence of doing X and allowing X to happen, which justification obviously contradicts his position that this inequivalence does not exist.

By contrast, it seems to me more likely that our intuitions about the moral *equivalence* of cases (11a) and (11b) answer to the confusion mentioned by Tooley. As a matter of fact, it might be argued that although there is certainly something equally immoral present in (11a) and in (11b), it does not lie in an aspect of Jones's conduct that contributes (omissively or commissively) to Smith's death but in the fact that in both cases Jones reveals one and the same immoral character trait, to wit, a willingness to bring about in certain circumstances the death of a human being by whatever means. Of course, the way in which Jones reveals the immoral bent in question differs from one case to the other: whereas in case (a) Jones does it indirectly, by announcing his intention of bringing about Smith's death, in case (b) he does so directly, intentionally slaying Smith. The argument would consist in maintaining that, if one could separate the level of the moral evaluation of Jones's character from the level of the moral assessment of his conduct, it would then become clear that our intuitions do not support the conclusion that killing Smith is morally equivalent to letting him die by not warning him about the explosion of the bomb. Anyhow, Trammell's criticism of the requisite of identical motivation does not necessarily imply the falseness of the symmetry principle. This criticism might suggest, on the contrary, that the requirement of identical motivation should be replaced by a requirement of identical motivation saving mere apathy. This requirement would belong, just like that of equal and minimum effort, to the second type of requirement distinguished by Trammell.

The requirement of application of the symmetry principle concerning equal minimum effort is not devoid of difficulties either. Though in general forbearances involve minimal effort, it is not necessary that this should be so; for instance, in a particular situation the only way of refraining from running into a pedestrian might be to smash up one's car. This being so, there is a very good point in comparing the cases of doing X and letting

X happen where the effort involved, though constant, is above minimum. In such cases, as Trammell points out, it is suspicious that the moral symmetry Tooley stands up for does not appear. Trammell propounds the following example:

> (13*a*) Jones sees that Smith, a stranger, will die unless he (Jones) acts to save him. It will cost Jones most of his life savings, $5,000, to save him. Jones has no ill feelings toward Smith, but decides not to make the sacrifice necessary to save him.
>
> (13*b*) Jones sees that if he continues in his present course of action, he will directly kill Smith. It will cost Jones most of his life savings to change his plans and thus avoid killing Smith. Jones has no ill feelings toward Smith, but decides not to make the sacrifice necessary to avoid killing Smith.[41]

Trammell surely is right when he claims that our moral intuitions would consider Jones's behaviour in the second case morally more serious than his behaviour in the first. This might provide the ground for asserting that negative duties are stronger than positive ones, if it were not for the fact that Tooley excludes this pair of cases or others alike from the range of the principle of symmetry in laying down as a condition that the effort in the cases compared shall be equal but minimal. It is interesting to quote what Trammell has to say about this exclusion:

Tooley is wise to exclude [these cases] . . . from the scope of the moral symmetry principle; but he does not thereby strengthen the case against the distinction between negative and positive duties, since the very exclusion of cases involving more than minimal effort is an implicit acknowledgement of the importance of the distinction in such cases. In fact the minimal effort restriction on the moral symmetry principle is suspiciously ad hoc. If negative duties are stronger in cases involving great effort, why not also in cases involving moderate effort or even minimal effort?[42]

Tooley now submits that our moral intuitions as regards (13*a*) and (13*b*) may be explained by the circumstance that it does not become clear to us why the sacrifice of $5,000 to save Smith has to be borne wholly by Jones and invites us to consider a couple of cases in which the circumstances themselves imply that the sacrifice may only be made by Jones:

---

[41] Trammell, 'Tooley's Moral Symmetry Principle', 309.
[42] Ibid. 309–10.

(14) Jones has used his life savings of $5,000 to purchase a railway car, which is now careering down the tracks. The tracks branch, one branch leading to a gorge where Jones's train will be completely destroyed, and the other leading to a siding where the car will come to a stop, but only after killing Smith, who has fallen, unconscious, on the tracks. Jones has no way of removing Smith from the tracks in time, or of stopping the car.

At this point Tooley introduces the following two possibilities.

(14a) The position of the switch is such that the railway car will turn on to the siding, killing Smith, but coming to a stop. Jones can switch it to the other branch, thus saving Smith, but totally destroying his $5,000 railway car. Jones decides to do nothing.

(14b) The position of the switch is such that if Jones does nothing, his car will career into the gorge and be totally destroyed. He decides to flip the switch, saving his car but killing Smith.[43]

Tooley claims that in the face of this pair of cases it would be hard for us to find the moral difference in the conduct of Jones which should exist according to Trammell. His position seems to be that Jones's behaviour is either wrong in both cases or right in both cases. Now, it is true that it is difficult to assert that in the first case Jones does something morally preferable to what he does in the second case. Yet, is it true that Trammell is committed to this assertion? Tooley fails to notice that one of Trammell's theses is that the moral wrongness of not helping someone increases and may even reach the level of the wrong of doing somebody evil when one has played a causal role in respect of the fact that the somebody in question is in a position to need one's help.[44] Obviously, Jones has contributed causally to Smith's

---

[43] Tooley, *Abortion and Infanticide*, 220–1.

[44] Trammell, 'Saving Life and Taking Life', 170. It must be noted here that Bruce Russell has argued that it is not the mere causal contribution of an agent to someone else's need, but rather his moral responsibility for it, that justifies assigning him a greater duty of aid than others similarly situated. Russell invites us to consider a case in which you have quite accidentally pushed into the water someone who does not know how to swim: if both you and somebody else on the scene knowingly allow the person who cannot swim to drown, then it seems pointless to say that you have violated a greater duty than the other ('On the Relative Strictness of Negative and Positive Duties', in Steinbock (ed.), *Killing and Letting Die*, 223). However, I do not find this view convincing. It seems to me that in the case described you indeed have a greater duty to prevent the person from drowning; otherwise, you might be naturally claimed to have caused his death through a path of behaviour which is in part accidental (pushing him into the water) but in part also intentional (failing to save him). This claim, which sounds morally significant, cannot be made of others similarly situated.

being in a position to need his aid; indeed, if Jones had not placed his eccentric train on the unusual lines of Tooley's imagination, Smith would not find himself in the position of needing his help. This being so, the failure on the part of Jones to come to his help is morally worse here than his failure to do so in (13a).

Another way of explaining why it is difficult to claim that Jones's behaviour in alternative (a) is morally better than his behaviour in alternative (b) runs as follows. As I said before, the moral inequivalence thesis interpreted according to Kamm's first analysis allows a property conceptually required by 'doing X' to be 'exported' to a case of 'letting X happen'. Now, Tooley says that in alternative (a) Jones does nothing, but he is wise to forget to say that Jones has already done something, namely, making his railway car career along the track leading to Smith. The truth is that in refraining from switching his car Jones lets himself cause Smith's death. Therefore, it is true of Jones's behaviour in (a), just as it is of his behaviour in (b), that he brings about Smith's death through positive action. Since Jones's 'omission' in (a) has 'imported' a property conceptually required by 'doing X', it is natural for it to share the moral gravity of Jones's action in (b). I contend, then, that the couple of cases proposed by Tooley do not afford a counter-example to the moral inequivalence view.

In addition, it seems reasonable to assume that failing to help someone when one has placed this person in a position of need is morally equivalent to actively causing the same damage as this person will suffer unless he receives help. It also seems reasonable to admit that the relations 'being morally better/worse than' and 'being morally equivalent to' are transitive. On these assumptions, the intuitively plausible thesis that the failure to render help when one has played a causal part in the emergence of the need is morally worse than the failure to help when there was no causal intervention on one's part entails that to bring about a harm actively is morally worse than not preventing this harm from coming about (assuming that one made no causal contribution to the appearance of the need in question).[45]

In conclusion, it may be stated that the restriction of the equal and minimal effort is suspect, just as the restriction of identical motivation would be if it were to exclude the case of mere apathy. Tooley admits now that restrictions of the second type

[45] Russell, 'On the Relative Strictness of Negative and Positive Duties', 223.

are suspect, but he affirms that the new formulation of the symmetry principle in terms of the equal importance of two wrong-making characteristics does not incorporate these restrictions (nor, to be sure, those of the first type). But beyond the fact that the symmetry principle does not explicitly incorporate in its new version these restrictions, the important point is that Tooley admits that doing X is not morally equivalent to letting X happen when the circumstances arise which these restrictions allude to. Let us take a look once again at the restriction concerning minimal effort. Tooley continues to assert that if helping someone involves a big sacrifice, then to let that person suffer the damage that the help is meant to avoid may be morally right. On this point Tooley writes: 'If the potential cost, or risk, is very high, this may outweigh one's prima facie obligation to save someone else.'[46] Now let us assume again, as seems reasonable, that the relations 'being morally preferable to' and 'being morally indifferent to' are transitive. Let us further consider the statements (1) not to endure any sacrifice that exceeds a certain point of seriousness is morally preferable to helping somebody, and (2) not to endure any sacrifice that exceeds this point of gravity is *not* morally preferable to not actively bringing about harm to anyone. These two statements jointly imply that not actively to bring about a harm is morally preferable to helping someone. This means that the admission of statement (1) by Tooley commits him to the moral inequivalence thesis, always provided statement (2) is accepted. The same line of argument may be followed to support the thesis that negative duties are stricter than positive ones. In fact, assuming that the relation of 'being stricter than' is also transitive, the acknowledgement that, whereas positive duties may give way when their fulfilment means a great sacrifice or effort for the agent, negative duties continue to be binding even when their discharge involves a great sacrifice on the part of the doer involves accepting that negative duties are stricter than positive ones.

Tooley is aware of the above argument based upon the transitiveness of the relations of moral preferability and moral indifference but apparently rejects it by denying statement (2).[47] The denial of statement (2) implies that 'if the potential cost, or risk,

---

[46] Tooley, *Abortion and Infanticide*, 188.   [47] Ibid. 221.

is very high, this may outweigh one's prima facie obligation not
to harm someone else'. However, Tooley does not advance this
proposition explicitly. Moreover, at the moment of grounding his
apparent denial of (2), he fails to put forward any argument apart
from appealing to the alleged counter-intuitive character of the
conclusion of the argument, i.e. the inequivalence thesis. For this
purpose he quotes a modified version of the runaway tram case,
in which there is only one person on each branch of the line. This
version is structurally similar to the case of the diabolical machine
(case (10)), so that in the last instance the only point of support
of the moral symmetry argument is this case or others like it.

A crucial question for the evaluation of the case of the diabolical machine is what is meant by the statement that doing X is
morally *worse* (or morally more serious, or more gravely wrong)
than letting X happen, where X is something bad. Both Tooley
and Trammell (and a number of others who have discussed the
question) take for granted that to state that doing X is morally
worse than allowing X to occur is tantamount to affirming that
negative duties are stronger (or stricter, or more important, or
'weightier') than positive ones. Thus, Tooley regards the proof of
the moral equivalence thesis as a proof too of the falsity of the
thesis of the priority of negative duties over positive ones. In fact,
in relation to cases (11*a*) and (11*b*), he remarks:

Is one to say that there is a significant difference between the wrongness
of Jones's behaviour in these two cases? Surely not. This shows the
mistake of drawing a distinction between positive and negative duties
and holding that the latter impose stricter obligations than the former.[48]

For his part, Trammell attempts to show the moral asymmetry of
acts and omissions as a way of demonstrating that negative duties
are stricter than positive ones. However, it is not obvious that the
thesis that doing X is morally worse than letting X occur has the
same content as the thesis that negative duties have priority over
positive ones. The first thesis comes to say something like the
following:

(T1) For every tract of behaviour A, for every tract of be-
        haviour B: if A is a case of doing X and B a case of

---

[48] Tooley, 'Abortion and Infanticide', 59.

letting X occur, then (supposing that X is something bad) A is morally worse than B.

Compare (T1) with the meaning that the second thesis appears to convey:

(T2) For every tract of behaviour A, for every tract of behaviour B: if A is a case of doing X and B a case of letting X happen, and A and B belong to a same set of alternatives of action, then (supposing A and B to be morally impermissible) the duty not to do X prevails over the duty to prevent X from happening.

Unlike (T2), (T1) does not circumscribe the asymmetry to possible options of an agent. This point may be cleared up by resorting to the case of the diabolical machine. Evidently, (10a) and (10b) do not describe two courses of action that figure as mutually exclusive alternatives in a doer's choice problem, but two tracts of conduct in different contexts of choice and action. The thesis of the priority of negative duties over positive ones— i.e. (T2)—lays down as a condition of application that the two stages of conduct compared should belong to the same set of alternatives of action. (If a stage of conduct consisting in doing X and another stage of conduct consisting in allowing X to happen belong to different sets of alternatives of action—as is the case with (10a) and (10b)—the thesis of the priority of negative duties might at most be interpreted as affirming with regard to them that *if they should belong to the same set of alternatives*, then the duty not to do X would prevail over the duty to prevent X from happening.)

Consequently, in order to test the thesis of the priority of negative duties (as distinct from the thesis of the moral inequivalence between doing and allowing), it is a mistake to check the moral intuitions that we have in respect of pairs of tracts of conduct which, like (10a) and (10b), appear in different situations of choice. In fact, it might happen that the moral difference existing between two tracts of conduct such as those described in (10a) and (10b) is so small that it is not reflected in our moral thought when we do not have to choose between them. The right way of testing the thesis of the priority of negative duties is, then, to check these intuitions in connection with pairs of conducts that

figure as options in a particular context. This may be done easily
through a variant of the case of the diabolical machine:

(15) Imagine a machine which contains two children, John and Mary.
If one pushes a button, John will be killed, but Mary will emerge
unharmed. If one does not push the button, John will emerge
unharmed, but Mary will be killed. In the first case one kills
John, while in the second case one merely lets Mary die.[49]

It seems to me that our intuitions in this case do not contradict,
or do not clearly contradict, the thesis of the priority of negative
duties. This is at most a single dubious case and as such, in
accordance with standard methodological rules, cannot be
claimed to refute a thesis well supported by our intuitions in
innumerable cases, here exemplified by cases (3), (4), and (5).
However, it is also clear that the case for the priority of negative
duties would gain strength if one could provide a positive analysis
of case (15) capable of explaining why it seems dubious. Indeed,
I think that this task can be done by acknowledging that two
judgements at first blush mutually incompatible are actually true
of this case. On the one hand, there would probably not be much
point in saying that refraining intentionally from pressing the
button is morally better than pressing it. This seems to support
Tooley's position. But, on the other hand, there would probably
be some point in alleging that in such a case one should opt for
not pressing the button, in so far as pressing the button implies
becoming directly involved in a devilish plot with no chance at all
of producing a moral gain. But this is as much to allege that the
duty not to kill John prevails over the duty to save Mary.
Evidently, both judgements could not be true if the relation
'morally worse/better than' (predicated of tracts of behaviour)
were connected logically with the relation 'stricter than' or 'prevails over' (predicated of duties) by means of the following principle: 'X is morally worse than Y if and only if the duty not to do
X prevails over the duty not to do Y'. But the existence of this
presumed logical connection is utterly controversial. Why should
it be necessary to regard it as out of the question that two

[49] Quoted in Trammell, 'Saving Life and Taking Life', 170–1, from Michael
Tooley, 'Abortion and Infanticide Revisited', paper read at the Meeting of the
American Philosophical Association, Eastern Division, held at Atlanta, G., 27–9
Dec. 1973.

conducts could be morally 'equivalent' in the sense that neither is morally better than the other while the duty not to do one predominates over the duty not to do the other? In other words, there is no apparent reason for ruling out the possibility that the relation 'prevails over' has a greater *ranking power* than the relation 'morally better than'; this would in fact be the case if our threshold of discrimination between the comparative goodness of two acts were higher than that corresponding to the comparative weight of two duties. Now it would be natural for this to be so taking into account that, whereas the lack of discrimination with regard to the comparative weight of a duty may imply that morality does not supply an answer to the question 'What is to be done?' and, therefore, undermine morality's practical force, the lack of discrimination of the comparative goodness of two acts performed in different contexts of choice seems to have an impact restricted to the comparative evaluation of actions already carried out or to the assessment of the moral character of the corresponding agents.

The discussion between Tooley and Trammell in my opinion shows that, the equality of the relevant circumstances notwithstanding, in some cases one is inclined to judge that to do X is morally more serious than to allow X to happen (where X is something disvaluable) and in other cases one is inclined to judge that letting X occur is morally as serious a matter as doing X. Faced with this situation, the moral philosopher may take two equally inadmissible ways. He may first, in Tooley's style, defend the moral symmetry principle by establishing restrictions that, like the requirement of equal and minimal effort, exclude those cases in which one is inclined to judge that to do X is morally a graver matter than allowing X to happen. Secondly, he may, in the vein of Trammell, affirm that some of the circumstances present in the cases in which one is inclined to judge that letting X occur and doing X are equally serious matters, like extreme hatred, mask or prevent us from perceiving the greater moral seriousness of doing X. A third alternative, which is the one I wish to advance here, is that both Tooley and Trammell accept as an unsupported dogma that, if there is a moral difference between doing X and letting X happen, then this difference has a magnitude constant across all the pairs of cases that meet the requirement of equality of morally significant circumstances, whatever these circumstances may be. But, as Michael Philips observes,[50] our comparative judgements about the moral seriousness of actions appear to work in a *contextual* manner, which signifies that the magnitude of the moral difference between doing X and letting X occur may vary in accordance with the circumstances of the context, despite their being equal in two cases compared. Thus the considerable effort (but equal in the pair of cases (13)) which causes Tooley so much trouble and the extreme hatred (but equal in the pair of cases (11)) which upsets Trammell as much are circumstances which, respectively, increase or diminish the magnitude of moral difference between doing X and allowing X to happen. It seems to me that the reason why our comparative evaluation of the moral seriousness of pairs of actions is contextual in the sense explained is that the evaluation of the intentions or attitudes of the agent is in practice inseparable from the assessment of the moral goodness or badness of the actions he performs. The evaluation of the moral character of the agent seems to be always involved, and sometimes decisively involved, in our judgements about the moral gravity of his conduct. On the other hand, our judgements on moral duties are by their very nature independent of the moral assessment of intentions or attitudes. These judgements affirm that people ought to do some things and refrain from doing others, not that they must have certain intentions and attitudes.[51] The moral wrongness of an action, as we tend to evaluate it, depends not only on the weight or importance of the moral duty that has been transgressed, but also, and often crucially, on the attitudes that the agent has shown in committing the transgression. Consequently, the thesis about the contextual character of our judgements concerning the goodness or moral gravity of acts and omissions does not imply that our judgements concerning the comparative weight of different moral duties are likewise of a contextual nature. Thus, in case (15), to state that the duty to refrain from pressing the button predominates over the duty to press it is quite compatible with saying that to press the button is not morally a more serious matter than not to press it.

[50] Michael Philips, 'Weighing Moral Reasons', *Mind*, 96 (1987).
[51] For an analysis of moral duties–judgements, see Aleksander Peczenik and Horacio Spector, 'A Theory of Moral Ought-Sentences', *Archiv für Rechts- und Sozialphilosophie*, 73 (1987).

I have argued that the moral symmetry argument is no obstacle to accepting the thesis of the priority of the duty not to do X over the duty not to allow X to occur, where X is the restriction of somebody else's positive freedom. Furthermore, when one concentrates on the normative or practical dimensions of morality,[52] and leaves aside the assessment of the comparative goodness of actions, there do not seem to be any difficulties about accepting this thesis under the second interpretation distinguished by Lichtenberg, that is to say, as a thesis about the conclusive preeminence, or all things considered, of the duty not to actively injure positive freedom. In the next section I shall analyse some cases which, though they apparently constitute counter-examples to this thesis, properly analysed only reflect the fact that the duty not to actively injure positive freedom has exceptions, which present themselves in the shape of principles concerning the moral permissibility of certain actions.

Distributive Exemption

An attempt might be made to attack the principle of the priority of negative duties through a more detailed analysis in the case of the runaway tram (case (3a)). I have said that according to this principle the driver of the tram—let us call her Joan—can switch to the other line because, whether she does so or not, she will violate a negative duty, and must then opt for the lesser evil. Judith Jarvis Thompson has argued vigorously in two articles that this explanation is wrong.[53] The clue to her argument is a variant of the case of the runaway tram:

(16) (*The case of the passenger on the driverless runaway tram*)
Angela is a passenger on a runaway tram. The driver has

---

[52] Michael Slote has recently argued that morality is not a system of precepts for the guidance of human behaviour but rather a set of standards for the appraisal of that behaviour. See his *Common-Sense Morality and Consequentialism* (London: Routledge & Kegan Paul, 1985), ch. 4. For a criticism of this argument, see Horacio Spector, 'Is Slote's Argument against the Practical Character of Morality Sound?', *Rechtstheorie*, 19 (1988).

[53] Judith Jarvis Thompson, 'Killing, Letting Die, and the Trolley Problem', in *Monist*, 59 (1976); 'The Trolley Problem', in *Rights, Restitution, and Risk: Essays in Moral Theory*, ed. William Parent (Cambridge, Mass. and London: Harvard University Press, 1986).

just shouted that the tram's brakes have failed, and has then died of the shock. Angela has the two options that the driver has in the original version.[54]

Thompson is of the opinion that, although it is true that if Joan does nothing, she will kill the five persons on the line, if Angela does nothing, it cannot be said that she kills these five; at most, she lets the tram kill them, but this means that she lets them die and not that she kills them herself. In the later article Thompson avails herself of a still clearer example of how to characterize the conduct of the progatonist:

(17) (*The case of the bystander at the switch*) Rose happens to be standing near the switch. She takes in the situation at a glance, but, unlike what happens in the original version, the driver has fainted when she realized that the brakes would not work. Rose can throw the switch thereby turning the tram herself.[55]

It becomes crystal-clear that, if Rose does not throw the switch, she does not kill the five people on the line but lets them die. Both Angela and Rose are faced with the dilemma of killing the person who is on one of the lines by turning the tram (by moving the steering lever or throwing the switch) or letting the five people on the other line die. Thompson remarks, correctly in my opinion, that whoever reckons that Joan may change the direction of the vehicle will also reckon that Angela and Rose can change it too. Nevertheless, as is obvious, the principle of the priority of negative duties cannot explain this intuition; on the contrary, it seems at first blush to contradict it, since, in the face of the dilemma of apparently transgressing a negative duty and transgressing a positive one, Angela and Rose would have to decide in accordance with this principle to transgress the positive duty, letting five people die so as not to kill the only person who happens to be on the other line. So that there is a reason still not made explicit why it is permissible for Angela and Rose to change the direction of the tram which is independent of the negative or positive character of the duties at stake. This being so, the principle that when faced by two conflicting negative

[54] 'Killing, Letting Die, and the Trolley Problem', 207.
[55] 'The Trolley Problem', 96.

duties one ought to choose to transgress the one involving the lesser evil also cannot be invoked to explain our intuition about the moral permissibility of Joan's turning the vehicle, since it is reasonable to think that, whatever may be the reason why Joan can change the direction of the tram, it is the same reason why Angela and Rose can do so. But what is the difference, then, between the three versions analysed up to now of the case of the runaway tram and cases (3b) and (4b), a difference that is responsible for it being permissible for Joan, Angela, and Rose to kill one person to save five others but not for the threatened judge and the doctor to do so?[56]

Thompson shows that there are other pairs of cases that are similar to the ones mentioned inasmuch as they present the option of killing or letting die and in respect of which our intuitions are, just as in the versions of the case of the runaway tram, apparently contrary to the principle of the priority of negative duties:

(18a) Harry is President, and has just been told that the Russians have launched an atom bomb towards New York. The only way in which the bomb can be prevented from reaching New York is by deflecting it; but the only deflection path available will take the bomb on to Worcester. Harry can do nothing, letting all of New York die; or he can press a button, deflecting the bomb, killing all of Worcester.

(18b) Irving is President, and has just been told that the Russians have launched an atom bomb towards New York. The only way in which the bomb can be prevented from reaching New York is by dropping one of our own atom bombs on Worcester: the blast of the American bomb will pulverize the Russian bomb. Irving can do nothing, letting all of New York die; or he can press a button, which launches an American bomb on to Worcester, killing all of Worcester.[57]

Thompson's view is that, while for Joan, Angela, Rose, and Harry 'killing' involves diverting a threat from a big group to a small one, for the judge in (3b), the doctor in (4b), and Irving, 'killing' involves bringing a new threat to bear on the smaller group. In other words, Joan, Angela, Rose, and Harry minimize

---

[56] 'Killing, Letting Die, and the Trolley Problem', 207–8; 'The Trolley Problem', 94–8.

[57] 'Killing, Letting Die, and the Trolley Problem', 208.

the number of deaths by making something that is already a threat to many become a threat to a few. Thompson maintains that there is a *distributive exemption* from the duty of doing no harm: while in general it is not morally permissible to kill one in order to save five, it is not morally obligatory to let an evil descend from the sky on five when we can make it come down on only one. The idea that there is an 'exemption' that allows us to make a better distribution of evils whose origin is alien to our will and conduct is indeed appealing. Nevertheless, it is not true that this exemption is good for every case; there are situations in which the unrestricted application of distributive exemption would bring about consequences contrary to our moral convictions. Thompson considers, for instance, the following variant of the case of the runaway tram:

(19) (*The case of the fat woman on the foot-bridge*) Hermione is standing on a foot-bridge over the tram track. She knows all about trams and sees one out of control hurtling towards the foot-bridge. She can also see that the driver has fainted (or died of shock, or whatever the reader cares to imagine). Hermione knows that the only way of stopping a runaway tramcar is to drop something very heavy in its path. But the only very heavy object available is a fat woman who is leaning over the railing, watching the oncoming tram. Hermione can push this fat woman on to the track in the way of the tramcar, killing her, or she can refrain from doing so, and let five people be killed.

Let us suppose that Hermione decides to push the fat woman on to the line, killing her. We should surely not say that it is morally permissible for Hermione to proceed in the way she does; as a matter of fact, we should probably go further: we should say that, in doing so, Hermione is violating a moral duty. Nevertheless, it is true of Hermione, as it would be of Joan, Angela, and Rose if they too chose the positive course of action, that she makes something threatening five people come to bear instead on one. What, then, is the difference between Hermione's case and those of Joan, Angela, and Rose that explains the moral distinction we draw in evaluating them? Thompson points out that the morally significant difference between what Hermione does and what Joan, Angela, and Rose would do if they opted for the positive action in question rests upon the moral status of the means by which they can bring about a better distribution of the menace in the shape of the runaway tram. The means that Joan, Angela, and Rose can use is to move the steering lever of the tram (Joan and Angela) or to throw the switch (Rose); this means is not morally relevant. Instead, the means employed by Hermione is to push the fat woman off the foot-bridge; this is not doing something to a thing (the steering lever or the switch) but to a person. Unlike the means made use of by Joan, Angela, and Rose, the means employed by Hermione constitutes in itself the violation of the fat woman's negative right to the control of her body. In other words, Hermione's act is in itself an active injury to the fat woman's positive freedom which is independent of the potential harm involved in the threat. The point is that the moral wrongness of the means employed by Hermione cancels out the moral permissibility that distributive exemption would otherwise imply.[58]

Thompson's distributive exemption thesis illuminates the moral difference between the behaviour of the judge in (3*b*), the doctor in (4*b*) and of Irving, on the one hand, and the behaviour of Joan, Angela, Rose, and Harry, on the other. Whereas the last four can claim to achieve a positive balance in human lives by modifying the range of a threat, the first three claim to save lives by bringing in a fresh menace. Distributive exemption must be conceived as an exception to the duty not to actively injure positive freedom: it does not imply that a positive duty prevails over a negative one, making it morally obligatory to minimize the number of victims of a threat, but merely permits it. Just as we should not be prepared to deny the priority of the duty not to kill merely on the strength that it incorporates an exception to the cases of self-defence, it would not be reasonable to deny the priority of the duty not to actively injure positive freedom merely because it incorporates distributive exemption.

Acts and Causes

Up to this point I have been arguing that the thesis of the priority of the duty not to do X, where X can be generically characterized

---

[58] 'Killing, Letting Die, and the Trolley Problem', 215–16; 'The Trolley Problem', 109–11.

as a restraint on somebody's positive freedom, with regard to the duty not to allow X to take place, fits in well with our moral intuitions. This means that my case for the priority of negative duties is largely based upon our ethical consciousness, as is revealed by philosophical reflection. But if our ethical consciousness draws a moral distinction between doing and allowing, there should also be a factual difference between doing and allowing, not any factual difference whatever, but rather one which might be intuitively pointed to as the reason for the moral distinction in question. This follows from the general point that moral properties are *supervenient* upon factual ones.[59] What remains for me to show then is that there really is some factual property, intuitively relevant from a moral standpoint, conceptually required by 'P actively injures Q's positive freedom' but not by 'P allows Q's positive freedom to be restricted'. I wish to suggest that this property is denoted by the predicate 'brings about the restriction of Q's positive freedom as an effect of a causal process started by P through the performance of certain bodily movements'.

It might be objected that the notion of cause cannot be appealed to to explain the moral distinction between negative and positive duties by arguing that the concept of cause has itself a moral content. C.S. Nino contends in this connection that the idea of agent-causation is best analysed as follows: an agent P causes an event E by doing X (forbearing from doing X) only if P has the *moral duty* to forbear from doing X (to do X) and X (not-X) in conjunction with the other circumstances of the context is a sufficient condition of E. Nino adds that if causal judgements in the domain of human affairs are not to be subjected to the dictates of conventional morality, then it must be admitted that in this analysis the expression 'moral duty' refers to a duty established by critical or ideal morality.[60] For all the plausibility of this analysis in the cases of forbearing from doing X, I think that Nino's conception of causality is not the only one possible. In fact, there must be a non-moral conception of causality if one wishes to account for causation stemming from acts (as something

---

[59] The *locus classicus* of this point is to my mind Richard Hare, *The Language of Morals* (Oxford: Clarendon Press, 1952), sect. 5.2. For a recent discussion on the concept of supervenience, see Horacio Spector, 'Dale on Supervenience', *Mind*, 96 (1987).

[60] Nino, *Ética y derechos humanos*, 206–7.

distinct from omissions). On the one hand, the application of Nino's analysis to cases of doing X produces counter-intuitive consequences. For example, one would like to say that the executioner who dispatched a convict justly condemned to death caused the death of the convict. Yet, if we assume that the executioner did not have the moral duty to forbear from carrying out the execution, Nino's analysis implies that the executioner did not cause the condemned man's death. On the other hand, it is reasonable to think that critical morality identifies the acts it declares forbidden or obligatory in terms of the causation of certain events (and not merely in terms of the performance of certain bodily movements). But this type of identification would create a vicious circularity if the only possible conception of causality were one establishing a conceptual connection with the principles of critical morality. To conclude, it seems to me that Nino's view does not prevent recourse to a conception of causality free from moral taint in order to explain the thesis of the priority of negative duties.

In answer to the view previously expounded about what morally relevant property is conceptually required by 'P actively injures Q's positive freedom', it might be objected that both the active injury to positive freedom and allowing a restraint upon positive freedom involve basically the same type of contribution to the restriction of somebody's positive freedom. Jonathan Bennett has advanced a thesis in this direction in holding that the propositions 'Barbara did X' and 'Peter let X occur' are distinguished only by their degree of specificness. According to Bennett, the first proposition is true if and only if, of all the ways in which Barbara could have moved, only a small number were such as to lead to the occurrence of X; instead, the second proposition is true if and only if almost all of the ways in which Peter could have moved were such as to lead up to the occurrence of X.[61] In other words, whereas the alternatives to doing X are always very numerous, the alternatives to letting X happen are always a few specific courses of action. Bennett's point is, of course, that this factual distinction cannot serve as a basis for a morally significant distinction. However, this writer seems to point to a property

---

[61] Bennett, 'Whatever the Consequences', 119–22, and 'Morality and Consequences', 47–64.

generally present in doing X, but not a necessary property. This
may be shown by resorting to two counter-examples propounded
by Daniel Dinello.[62] In one an agent shoots somebody who has
taken poison and in any case is bound to die: as most of the
agent's possible movements (save giving the potential suicide an
antidote) are followed by the person's death, Bennett's analysis
erroneously implies that the agent let the person in question die.
In the other counter-example, a woman imprisoned for spying is
tied up in such a way that any movement she may make will
electrocute her mate: if the prisoner moves, according to Bennett
she will have allowed her mate to die. Surely to elude the force of
these counter-examples, Bennett now prefers to use the expressions *'positive instrumentality'* and *'negative instrumentality'*,
instead of 'doing something' and 'letting something happen', to
denote the two kinds of behaviour he distinguishes in accordance
with the criterion of specificness.[63] But this move is evidently *ad
hoc*: 'positive instrumentality' and 'negative instrumentality' are
terms of art and nobody has suggested that a morally significant
distinction can be built by appealing to them. It is hardly important to show that the properties these terms are intended to
denote are irrelevant from the moral point of view.

Notwithstanding the failure of Bennett's analysis, it brings out
an incontrovertible point, to wit, when an agent lets X happen,
he does one of all the things he can possibly do, short, to be sure,
of preventing X from coming about. In this way it might be
objected that the situation of somebody who lets X happen is not
different in the respect I suggested above from that of somebody
who does X, since of both it may be said that they do something
that causes X to happen. To evaluate this objection we must first
decide what the concept of cause involved in this context is. I am
going to take up a proposal of Mackie's and understand by 'cause
of X' an individual exemplification of what he calls an *inus*
condition, i.e. an insufficient but non-redundant part of an un-
necessary but sufficient condition of X.[64] There are two points
that it is worth noticing in connection with this suggestion: first, a
part of a sufficient condition is redundant if without that part this

    [62] Daniel Dinello, 'On Killing and Letting Die', in Steinbock (ed.), *Killing and
Letting Die*, 129.
    [63] Bennett, 'Morality and Consequences', 64–72.
    [64] J. L. Mackie, *The Cement of the Universe* (Oxford: Clarendon Press, 1980),
62.

condition is equally sufficient; second, this analysis of the concept of cause admits that a fact recognizes a plurality of causes. By using this concept of cause, the falseness of the objection I am considering may be shown up. Let us take the first case imagined by Dinello. It is clear that in this case the agent made a bodily movement that is the individual exemplification of an *inus* condition of the suicide's death, namely, pressing the trigger of the pistol. (Something similar applies to the case of the tied-up spy). Let us now take the case of an agent who sees somebody drowning and, instead of throwing him a lifebelt, lights a cigarette. Of this agent you cannot say that he made a bodily movement establishing an individual exemplification of an *inus* condition of the death of the person. Indeed, to light a cigarette is not a non-redundant part of a sufficient condition that another should die by drowning. In general terms, it may be said that a property conceptually required by '*P* does *X*' but not by '*P* lets *X* happen' is that *P* makes bodily movements that establish a cause of *X*, i.e. an individual exemplification of an *inus* condition of *X*.

It might still be replied that of the agent who lets the other person drown it may be said that he did something that caused the death of that person, not in the sense of lighting the cigarette but in that of performing the disjunction of all his possible bodily movements excluding those that would have prevented the person in question from drowning. It is evident, however, that this property of letting *X* happen is distinct from the property that I suggested above as conceptually required by doing *X*. As a matter of fact, to perform the disjunction of all possible bodily movements in the context except those preventing an event from happening is not to do something but to fail to do something, namely, to prevent the event in question from taking place. Yet, the force of this retort might reside in the fact that, if failing to prevent something from happening is an instance of an *inus* condition of the death of a person, then the conduct of the agent in incurring this omission does not significantly differ from that involving his killing the person. To meet this retort I am going to appeal to an argument of Eric Mack's designed to show the wrongness of including the absence of 'preventing' or 'thwarting' events among the causal conditions of an event *A*.[65] It seems to

---

[65] Eric Mack, 'Bad Samaritanism and the Causation of Harm', *Philosophy and Public Affairs*, 9 (1980), 257–9.

me that Mack's argument is best formulated as following two different paths. First, he argues that if an event C is a part of a causally sufficient condition of A, then it is confusing and redundant to include not preventing C from taking place among the causal factors of A. For (1) it is the presence of C and not the fact of C's not having been prevented that plays a causal part in the occurrence of A, and (2) the presence of C entails that C has not been prevented. Secondly, it is a mistake to think that the non-prevention of A is causally linked to the occurrence of A: that nobody has prevented A is not a causal condition of A, but instead a logically necessary condition of A, for the occurrence of an event entails that nobody has prevented the event from occurring. Moreover, since in Mack's opinion the preventing of any event is by necessity the preventing of one of the causal conditions of it, the fact that one of the causal conditions of A has not been prevented is not causally linked to A, since the occurrence of A entails that A has not been prevented, which, in turn, entails that none of its causal conditions has been prevented. In short, there do not seem to be any difficulties about admitting that 'doing X' but not 'letting X happen' conceptually requires the property 'makes bodily movements which constitute a cause of X'. Therefore, it may be reasonably thought that this factual property constitutes the reason why the duty not to do X reveals itself in our ethical consciousness as predominating over the duty to prevent X from occurring, where X generically denotes a curtailment of positive freedom.

I asserted earlier on that one of the tenets of the deontological conception of practical rationality that I am suggesting in this book is that there are moral reasons which are not grounded on the results of human behaviour but on the shape of the agent's intervention in the production of these results. My reason for this assertion is that, at a pre-analytical level, the thesis of the priority of negative duties seems to imply the existence of moral reasons not based on the results of human behaviour. This would indeed be the case if 'result' were defined in such a way that it was true that doing X and letting X occur have by necessity the same results. However, if 'result' is defined in accordance with the conception of causality I have sketched above, then it cannot be affirmed that the thesis of the priority of negative duties implies the existence of moral reasons not based on results. Instead, when it is agreed that doing X has a result that letting X happen does not have, we should affirm that the thesis of the priority of negative duties implies the claim that there are moral reasons which consider it of special importance whether one's conduct causes damage to a value[66] (as something distinct from failing to stop a causal process leading to the damage of a value). It is this claim which, properly speaking, constitutes a basic tenet of the deontological conception of practical rationality here suggested.

[66] By 'causes damage to a value A', or 'damages value A', I mean 'impoverishes, inhibits, or interferes with the realization of A'; for this usage, see John Finnis, *Natural Law and Natural Rights* (Oxford: Clarendon Press, 1980), 120.

5
Personal Separateness

The argument in the last chapter was designed to justify the pre-eminent moral importance of those negative duties which can be generically described as duties not to actively damage positive freedom. However, the deontological conception of practical rationality which I am suggesting here must possess two other features to contribute to the justification of the existence of libertarian rights. The first of them bears upon two different meanings of the expression 'damage to a value'. Let us go back to the familiar example of an agent who has the option of killing a person as a means of saving another five or of not slaying the first and letting the other five die. The thesis proposed in the previous chapter implies that if the agent decides on the first course of action, he performs certain bodily movements which cause the death of the first person, whereas if he chooses the second course of action, he does not causally contribute to the death of the five. But though the first course of action causally contributes to the death of a person, it does also involve a causal contribution to the preservation of the life of another five persons; therefore, it might be claimed that, since the positive freedom of the one person and the positive freedom of each of the other five have the same value in so far as they are parts or instances of one and the same value, the first course of action causes a gain of 5 units of positive freedom besides causing a loss of 1. The claim is then that this course of action does not signify a net loss but a net gain of positive freedom and that, consequently, proceeding in this way, the agent does not damage but promotes positive freedom. Here the two meanings of 'damaging a value' that I have just referred to are clearly manifested. In accordance with the first meaning, which we might call *numerical*, an agent damages a value if and only if he causes a net loss of this value. In accordance with the second meaning, which we might label *material*, an agent damages a value if and only if he causes the loss of an instance of this value, irrespective of whether or not this loss is made up for by the benefits accruing from the creation or conservation of other instances of this value. These two conceptions of damage to a value are correlated with two concepts of loss usual in non-philosophical contexts. On the one hand, it would be misleading to say that a company's countable fiscal year showed a loss if during a certain lapse of time it sold below cost to eliminate a competitor and as a result increased its yearly net profit. It is clear that in uses like this one the numerical concept of loss is involved. On the other hand, there are occasions when the use of the material concept of loss becomes evident. A woman who has just lost her father would say that she had suffered a great bereavement, the loss of a dear one, even though she has just given birth to quintuplets; a beloved one is not replaceable in the way that physical goods are. If a deontological conception of practical rationality is to justify the existence of libertarian rights, as they are habitually conceived, it will have to privilege the material concept of damage to a value.

The second feature that our deontological conception of practical rationality has to have is the analysis of moral duties—especially the duty not to actively damage positive freedom—as agent-relative reasons. Even if we accept the overriding importance of the duty not to actively damage positive freedom in the material sense distinguished above, our conception of practical rationality would be incapable of contributing to the justification of the existence of libertarian rights if it saw in the fulfilment of this moral duty an agent-neutral moral value. Let us suppose than an agent is threatened by a criminal with the slaughter of five persons if he, the agent, does not do away with one. It is true that, if the agent gives in to the threat, he will cause a material injury to positive freedom, but, if he holds out against the threat, an active material damage will be done to positive freedom all the same, only it will be on the criminal's part. If the fulfilment of the duty not to do material damage to positive freedom were an agent-neutral value, the course of reasonable action to follow would be to minimize the number of transgressions of this duty and so to give way to the threat. But this result is obviously at variance with the libertarian conception of the right to life.

In the present chapter I am going to try and defend these two features of the conception of practical rationality integrated in my approach to the justification of the basic libertarian thesis. The peculiarity of the theoretical line I shall be following here is that both features become explicable in the light of a comprehensive theory of personal separateness. I wish to suggest that they are not aspects of our moral thinking due to different motivations or intuitions but reflect one and the same concern for an individualistic conception of people in the sundry parts they are called upon to play in interpersonal relations.

Positive Freedom and Individualism

In Chapter 3 I said that the deontologist who adopts value pluralism does not have therefore to follow the typically consequentialist strategy of combining the various ultimate goods in a single overall value and establish a function that will lay down how this value is to be promoted. One of the central theses of Finnis's deontological theory is precisely that 'reason requires that every basic value be at least respected in each and every action'.[1] The main idea that seems to lie behind this deontological tenet is that basic values are incommensurable, two values A and B being incommensurable when A is neither more valuable than B, nor less, and not of equal value.[2] If basic values are incommensurable, then any analysis of costs and benefits along lines of action capable of affecting different basic values is bound to be arbitrary.[3] It might be thought, then, that my reason for assigning moral significance to the material conception of value-damage, as opposed to the numerical conception, reposes upon the thesis of the incommensurability of values, which is usually present in deontological theories. Still I think that this thesis does not imply, in accordance with a widespread view about the individuation of values, the moral condemnation of material active damage to positive freedom. If the agent in our example chooses to kill somebody in order to save five others, reasoning that in this way he is promoting the value of positive freedom, he is not treating two different values as commensurable, since the profits and

---

[1] John Finnis, *Natural Law and Natural Rights* (Oxford: Clarendon Press, 1980), 120.

[2] On this concept, see Joseph Raz, *The Morality of Freedom* (Oxford: Clarendon Press, 1986), ch. 13, and J. Griffin, *Well-Being* (Oxford: Clarendon Press, 1987), 79.

[3] Finnis, *Natural Law and Natural Rights*, 115.

losses that he reckons up to conclude the net profit of choosing this line of action correspond to the same value, namely, to positive freedom. Neither can it be thought that he is treating as commensurable different dimensions of one and the same value, as, for example, life and the control of certain economic resources in respect of positive freedom. As a matter of fact, in the example at hand there is involved one and the same dimension of positive freedom, namely, life. It may be concluded, then, that the thesis of the incommensurability of values, as usually understood, cannot be the basis of a case for the material conception of value-damage. In what follows I hope to render this conception of value-damage plausible by showing that the appeal of the numerical conception, which permits trade-offs between the gains and losses of positive freedom of distinct persons, derives from two different confusions encouraged by the apparently innocent claim that values are universal.

The first confusion is a rather basic one. The claim that values are universal may be understood as affirming that singular value-judgements (e.g. 'John's happiness is valuable') presuppose universal value-judgements of the form '*A* is valuable', where *A* denotes a universal class of facts or states of affairs (e.g. 'happiness is valuable'). So understood, the claim about the universality of values amounts to the thesis of the universalizability of value-judgements.[4] The claim is quite sensible on this interpretation. However, the tendency sometimes is to understand the claim about the universality of values as the view that values are not individual things but wholes or collective entities integrating individual things as parts or components. This erroneous collectivist view about values seems facilitated by the possibility of substantivating in popular speech the adjective 'valuable' in universal value-judgements. These judgements may be expressed not only in the form '*A* is valuable' but also in the form '*A* is *a value*'. In this way you can see yourself led to believe that the different particular exemplifications of 'a value' are only parts or pieces of the 'universal' value in question, which is accordingly conceived as a whole.

---

[4] On the thesis of the universalizability of value judgements, see R. M. Hare, *Freedom and Reason* (Oxford: Clarendon Press, 1963), ch. 2, and *Moral Thinking* (Oxford: Clarendon Press, 1981), ch. 6.

In order to unmask this error, it seems to me important to recall an elementary distinction between a collective form of predication and a distributive one. As regards universal statements, this distinction may be expounded thus: Whereas in the collective form a property is predicated of the whole of all the instances of the universal name occurring in the subject, in the distributive form the property in question is predicated of each one of those instances. For example, the statement 'Penguins are threatened by extinction' would be naturally understood as involving the collective type of predication, but the statement 'Penguins eat fishes' obviously answers to the distributive type. Now, the imprecision of popular speech might make us think erroneously that the predication in universal value-judgements is of the collective type. So it might be held that if I have to choose between assailing Peter's positive freedom and allowing John's positive freedom to be restrained, there is a single 'universal' value involved, namely, that of positive freedom, of which Peter's positive freedom and John's positive freedom are only component parts. Once it is admitted that Peter's positive freedom and John's positive freedom are mere parts of a 'universal' value, it seems natural to think that they are of equal value, since they cannot be said to make a differential contribution to the value of the whole. However, in view of the distinction recalled above between collective predication and distributive predication it becomes clear that, when we say that positive freedom is valuable, we are saying that each person's positive freedom is valuable. Of course, to infer the proposition that positive freedom as a whole is valuable from the proposition that each person's positive freedom is valuable would involve committing a fallacy of composition. Furthermore, it is also clear that the thesis of the universalizability of value-judgements does not imply that value-predication is of the collective type. This thesis implies that, if an individual thing is valuable, then all the other individual things of the same relevant kind are also valuable, but not that, if an individual thing of a certain kind is valuable, then all the things of that kind are valuable as a whole.

The second sort of confusion is to think that the application of the type–case distinction to the ontological analysis of values somehow shows that it is possible to compare and compensate the gains and losses of different instantiations or exemplifications of the same value.[5] Here the claim that values are universal is understood as affirming that the ontological status of values is that of a universal or type. It is therefore held that values are realized in different exemplifications or cases. All this sounds sensible. However, the problem arises when one tries to infer value-consequences from these acceptable ontological propositions. This may be done in the following way. Let us take, for example, the value of having deep love relations with particular persons. It seems undeniable that the nature of this value is such that the loss of a dear one is irreplaceable. However, the irreplaceability of each case or exemplification of this universal value does not imply that having a deep love relation with one's wife has a distinct value. On the contrary, having a deep love relation with one's wife has not a distinct value since it constitutes only one exemplification or case of a universal value, namely, *having deep love relationships with particular persons*. So, although the exemplifications or cases of having deep love relationships with particular persons are irreplaceable, when a man loses his wife, he may none the less acquire again the same amount of this universal value by remarrying. It seems to me that there is involved here a confusion between two utterly different ideas, namely, *values-sameness* and *equality of worth*. The identity criterion for values implicitly admitted in the above reasoning may be couched as follows: two individual things exemplify or realize the same value when they are valuable by virtue of their belonging to one and the same type of thing. The idea of equality of worth I have in mind has a different content: two individual things are of equal worth or value when it is a matter of indifference whether it is one or the other which exists. If two things are of equal value, then the loss of one of them may be totally compensated by the gain of the other. Now, the fact that two individual things exemplify the *same* value does not mean that those things are of *equal* value or worth. Plainly, the claim that values are, from an ontological viewpoint, types does not imply that different instantiations of the same value have equal worth. Consequently, that claim does not imply either that it is possible for the loss of one instantiation to be compensated by the gain of another.

[5] Griffin, *Well-Being*, 337–8 n. 18.

The above point can be made in a different way. The basic idea in the thesis that values are types is *not* that 'valuable' designates a property of a property, i.e. a second-order property, so that types are in themselves valuable. This idea would be hardly untenable: nobody would take seriously the claim that war does not impair the value of life because it *merely* destroys particular lives but not life as a property or universal. It is true that certain expressions of everyday conversation, like 'Mercy is better than justice', might be interpreted as implying that value is a second-order property. But such expressions are really 'loose ways of saying that all particulars having certain properties also exemplify certain value-properties'.[6] Thus, 'Mercy is better than justice' must be taken as saying that 'merciful acts are better than just acts'. If the claim that values are types is to be plausible, it must be understood as saying that, if a certain individual thing is valuable, it is so because of certain properties it has, i.e. its worthwhileness is supervenient upon certain of its universal factual properties. But it is precisely this idea which, as I have tried to show elsewhere,[7] lies behind the thesis of universalizability of value-judgements. This is to say that the thesis that values are types is the ontological correlative of the logical thesis of the universalizability of value-judgements. But it is evident that the thesis of universalizability of value-judgements does not imply that the different instantiations of one and the same value are of equal value. Let me illustrate this point with regard to the value of positive freedom. As far as this value is concerned, the thesis of universalizability implies that, if the positive freedom of a person P is a value, then the positive freedom of another person Q is also a value, but this does not mean that the positive freedom of P is of equal value to the positive freedom of Q.

I have argued that each one's positive freedom need neither be seen as a part or fragment of a 'collective' value nor as belonging in a class of equally worthwhile exemplifications of one value. On the strength of this I think that there are no visible reasons to treat the positive freedom of any person, P, and the positive freedom of any other person, Q, as things of equal worth. In

[6] Everett W. Hall, *What Is Value?* (New York and London: Humanities Press and Routledge & Kegan Paul, 1961), 16.

[7] Horacio Spector, 'Una nota sobre universalizabilidad', *Análisis Filosófico*, 8 (1988).

other words, though I do not deny that the positive freedom of different persons realizes the same value, I deny that the positive freedom of different persons can be regarded as objects of equal value. Of course, I am not suggesting that the positive freedom of some persons is more valuable than that of others. What I am suggesting is that the positive freedom of each person has distinct worth, which means that the positive freedom of any person is neither of greater nor lesser value than, nor of equal value to, the positive freedom of any other. This implies that the loss in positive freedom of one person cannot be compared with and compensated by the gain in positive freedom of another. Thus, if I have to choose between attacking Peter's positive freedom and allowing John's to be restricted, I must consider that I am in the face of two things possessing distinct and incomparable worth. If I damage Peter's positive freedom, this act cannot be justified by arguing that I do not cause a net damage to positive freedom since John's gain compensates for Peter's loss. On the contrary, since the idea of a 'net or numerical damage' to positive freedom is meaningless on the assumption that the positive freedom of each person is of unique value, if I damage Peter's positive freedom, I simply injure positive freedom in the only possible way, that is to say, in the material sense that I characterized earlier on. In other words, granted that the active impairment of positive freedom is morally disvaluable—which proposition I tried to defend in the foregoing chapter—such an impairment can only be morally disvaluable in the material sense.

The view that each person's positive freedom has distinct worth may throw light upon the otherwise obscure concept of human dignity. If the positive freedom of each person is of unique worth, then it is not possible to justify the maltreatment of a person by appealing to an analysis of interpersonal costs and benefits. Thus, human dignity may be regarded as reflecting the worth-uniqueness of each human being. The same idea may be expressed in a different fashion by affirming that the profound meaning of the Kantian idea that people are 'ends in themselves' is not so much that people are bearers of intrinsic, and not merely instrumental, value, but rather that each one of us is the possessor of distinct worth, which means that what impairs the overall goodness of each person's life makes by necessity a differ-ence to the value of the world. But though the thesis that each person has unique worth justifies the principle that material damage to values is morally wrong and, further, may illuminate the idea of human dignity, it is natural to ask why we should have to accept so bizarre a view about the value of human beings. It seems to me that this view is ineluctable if we wish to conceive human beings as separate persons when they are possible beneficiaries or victims of our actions.

Robert Nozick has made an important contribution to our understanding of individual rights in suggesting that behind what he terms 'side constraints' there lurks the idea that people are separate beings who cannot be sacrificed or used without their consent for the attainment of other ends.[8] The paragraph in which Nozick launches this suggestion is worth quoting:

Side constraints express the inviolability of other persons. But why may not one violate persons for the greater social good? Individually, we each sometimes choose to undergo some pain or sacrifice for a greater benefit or to avoid a greater harm: we go to the dentist to avoid worse suffering later; we do some unpleasant work for its results; some persons diet to improve their health or looks; some save money to support themselves when they are older. In each case, some cost is borne for the sake of the greater overall good. Why not, *similarly*, hold that some persons have to bear some costs that benefit other persons more, for the sake of the overall social good? But there is no *social entity* with a good that undergoes sacrifice for its own good. There are only individual people, different individual people, with their own individual lives. Using one of these people for the benefit of others, uses him and benefits the others. Nothing more. What happens is that something is done to him for the sake of others. Talk of an overall social good covers this up. (Intentionally?) To use a person in this way does not sufficiently respect and take account of *the fact that he is a separate person, that his is the only life he has.*[9]

Nozick's jargon about the 'fact' of our separate existences may lead the reader erroneously to think that we are in the presence of an empirical fact. In this case, and assuming the truth of

---

[8] Robert Nozick, *Anarchy, State, and Utopia* (Oxford: Blackwell, 1974), 31. The thesis of personal separateness, wielded as a criticism of utilitarianism, was first suggested by John Rawls (*A Theory of Justice* (Oxford: Clarendon Press, 1972), 27 ff.).

[9] Ibid. 32–3 (emphasis added in the last sentence).

Hume's principle that values are not derivable from mere facts, the 'fact' of our separate existences could not justify the inviolability of people nor the axiological principle according to which each person's positive freedom is of distinct worth. As Mack says, this 'fact' could be seen as requiring a programme to unify everybody in a great social organism.[10] It is plain that what is at stake here is the value that each person shall lead his own life separately. But, as is obvious, this value is none other than that of personal autonomy. Consequently, the 'fact' of our separate existences reflects the value-truth that personal autonomy is intrinsically valuable. Whence follows one consequence of great interest for the understanding of the foundations of libertarian moral rights. To obtain it we must reason as follows. Inasmuch as the axiological thesis about the distinct worth of each person's positive freedom may be reasonably understood as expressing the idea of personal separateness, this thesis is deeply rooted in the intrinsic value of personal autonomy, of each one's leading his own life. But let us recall that positive freedom is valuable as a component of personal autonomy. This is to say that the thesis about the distinct worth of each person's positive freedom reflects the same intrinsic value which positive freedom is imbued with, namely, personal autonomy. Therefore, the negation of the axiological thesis about the distinct worth of each person's positive freedom would be to the detriment not only of the value we place on personal autonomy but also of the value we place on positive freedom itself. This means that the claim that positive freedom is intrinsically valuable somehow involves that each person's positive freedom is of distinct worth. The consequence I have referred to may be then summed up as follows: if positive freedom is intrinsically valuable, it must be so in the sense that each one's positive freedom is of distinct worth.

What I said above has another consequence of capital interest for our inquiry. To start with, let us notice that the axiological thesis about the distinct worth of each person's positive freedom suggests that each person's being the author of his own life is an object of distinct worth. If positive freedom is valuable as a

---

[10] Eric Mack,'How to Derive Libertarian Rights', in Jeffrey Paul (ed.), *Reading Nozick* (Oxford: Blackwell, 1982), 288.

component of personal autonomy, why should we deny to personal autonomy an axiological status which we attribute to positive freedom? So, the ideal of personal autonomy should be looked upon neither as the fostering of a value that is divided into parts or fragments, nor as that of a value whose exemplifications are equally valuable, but as the respect for an endless set of uniquely valuable facts or states of affairs answering to the schema '*P* is the author of his own life', where *P* is a variable whose range is the universe of individual persons. But the thesis about the distinct worth of each person's positive freedom which leads us to regard each one's personal autonomy as an object of distinct worth derives in its turn from the ideal of autonomy. This shows that, curiously enough, the ideal of autonomy is unique in the sense of itself justifying a second-order axiological view, which lays down what the correct axiological formulation of this ideal is.

The thesis about the distinct worth of each person's positive freedom justifies the principle that materially damaging positive freedom is immoral. Furthermore, as already said, such a thesis conveys the idea of personal separateness. I think that this suggests where lies the strength of the principle about the immorality of materially damaging positive freedom. Since the thesis about the distinct and unique worth of each person's positive freedom conveys the idea that we are separate persons, it does not depend merely on our value-opinions, however well or badly grounded, but constitutes an essential part of the conception we have of ourselves as individual persons. The concept of 'individual person' thus has value-content. When we understand ourselves as individual persons we do not see ourselves just as entities possessing factual properties—such as the ability to reason and to plan lives—but as entities with value-properties, endowed with distinct and unique worth. To reject the axiological truth that our respective positive freedoms are distinctly and uniquely valuable would affect profoundly the conception of ourselves as individual persons and would therefore signify a radical change in our way of seeing ourselves. If there is a sense of 'justification' according to which a belief is justified when its rejection implies heavy costs in terms of our overall system of beliefs, there is nothing for it but to think that the axiological principle imbuing the immorality of materially injuring positive freedom is deeply justified.

Agent-Relativity

The justification of the agent-relativity of moral duties correlated with libertarian rights is an extremely difficult task and at the same time essential for the provision of a grounding for the basic libertarian thesis. Whether one uses the denomination 'side constraints', 'deontological reasons',[11] or 'agent-centred restrictions',[12] the existence of agent-relative negative duties capable of implying the moral impermissibility of producing the best overall result is often regarded with scepticism. Nagel, for example, asks: 'But how can there be relative reasons to respect the claims of others? How can there be a reason not to twist someone's arm which is not equally a reason to prevent his arm from being twisted by someone else?'[13] Furthermore, admitting that deontological restraints form part of common-sense moral thought, Nagel writes: 'Yet their paradoxical flavour tempts one to think that the whole thing is a kind of moral illusion resulting either from innate psychological dispositions or from crude but useful moral indoctrination.'[14] Scheffler expresses the difficulty of justifying deontological restrictions by rejecting generally any explanation in terms of the disvalue of some aspect of the violation of such restrictions, such as Nozick's Kantian explanation that individuals are ends and not merely means and, therefore, cannot be sacrificed for the attainment of other ends. Scheffler properly argues: 'Appeals to the disvalue of violations of *R* [agent-relative restrictions] are powerless to explain why it is wrong to violate *R* when doing so will prevent identical violations of *R*.'[15]

Deontological restrictions do not exhaust agent-relative practical reasons. Bernard Williams's analysis of the idea of personal integrity—one of the pioneering treatments of the theme of

---

[11] Thomas Nagel, *The View from Nowhere* (New York: Oxford University Press, 1986), ch. 9. (This chapter is a revised version of 'The Limits of Objectivity', in S. McMurrin (ed.), *The Tanner Lectures on Human Values*, i (Salt Lake City, Utah: University of Utah Press; Cambridge: Cambridge University Press, 1980).)

[12] Samuel Scheffler, *The Rejection of Consequentialism* (Oxford: Clarendon Press, 1982), ch. 4.

[13] Nagel, *The View from Nowhere*, 178.

[14] Ibid. 179.

[15] Scheffler, *The Rejection of Consequentialism*, 87.

agent-relativity in recent moral theory—far exceeds the field of moral reasons.[16] Williams criticizes utilitarianism for its inability to accommodate concern for personal integrity. But what is personal integrity? To illustrate the failure of utilitarianism to take into account the concern for personal integrity, Williams invites us to consider two examples: in one a brand-new Ph.D. in chemistry, George, finds it difficult to accept a job in a laboratory devoted to research into chemical and biological warfare, notwithstanding the fact that his wife and children will suffer from his unemployment and that anyhow the post will be filled by a colleague if he turns down the offer. In the other example, Jim, an English visitor in a South American town, finds it difficult to accept the 'offer' of the local dictator that he should himself slay a native of the place to prevent the dictator from carrying out his plan to put twenty natives to death as a warning to the rest of the population. Williams holds that utilitarianism cannot explain George's and Jim's objections. The argument runs as follows. The utilitarian must admit that, parallel with the project of maximizing desirable results, people have lower-level plans or designs. Among these there are at least four groups: (1) the desires or wishes for things for oneself and one's family and friends, together with tastes; (2) artistic, intellectual, or cultural interests; (3) support for some cause, such as Zionism or the abolition of chemical and biological warfare; and (4) general dispositions of human conduct and character, such as hatred of injustice, cruelty, and murder. These plans or projects provide the basis or groundwork of utilitarian calculations. The choices that an agent must make according to the utilitarian decision procedure depend on two factors: first, the wishes, plans, and preferences of each person (his own included), and secondly, the causal web in which he acts. Therefore, the choices of a utilitarian agent depend on other people's projects in two different ways: first, other people's projects and desires count as much as his own in order to establish which is the maximally desirable result; secondly, the causal background against which he acts is usually influenced by other people's projects. So—the argument concludes—the utilitarian alienates the moral agent from projects and convictions he is deeply identified with.

---

[16] Bernard Williams, 'A Critique of Utilitarianism', in J. J. C. Smart and Bernard Williams, *Utilitarianism: For and Against* (Cambridge: Cambridge University Press, 1973).

It seems, then, that, as Williams sees it, personal integrity consists in acting in accordance with one's own plans and convictions. If George reasons in the utilitarian manner, he sees himself led to act not in accordance with the cause he has embraced (i.e. to do away with chemical and biological warfare) but with the interests of his wife and children; more paradoxically, since he has to attend to the probable effects of his conduct, he is led to subordinate his own decisions to the disposition or plan of his colleagues to work unscrupulously in any well-paid professional post. As for Jim, if he reasons in a utilitarian manner, he will find himself compelled to leave aside his moral undertaking not to commit murder in order to become a kind of tool or instrument of the dictator's plan. Looked upon thus, the idea of personal integrity is not easily distinguishable from the idea of personal autonomy. This interpretation seems to agree with that of Nagel, who treats a central part of the integrity problem worrying Williams by resorting to the concept of autonomy. According to Nagel, there are three main groups of agent-relative reasons: reasons of autonomy, deontological reasons, and reasons bound up with the obligations we have towards persons to whom we are closely related (like parents, wives, or sons). The reasons of autonomy derive from the wishes, projects, commitments, and personal ties of the individual agent and, as I have said, centrally reflect Williams's preoccupation with personal integrity. These reasons are typically agent-relative. If I have decided to dedicate myself to philosophical research, this project supplies me with reasons for making use, for instance, of a research fellowship in Heidelberg, but by itself the project does not provide my wife with reasons for leaving Buenos Aires. Deontological restrictions do not express the subjective autonomy of the agent, but a concern not to maltreat people in certain ways. Both reasons of autonomy and deontological restrictions form a position of choice that Nagel terms 'the personal point of view'. He believes that, in contrast to the impersonal point of view peculiar to consequentialism, in the personal point of view the agent is especially concerned about what he *does*, as distinct from what *happens* or how things are.[17]

In a brilliant essay[18] Amartya Sen analyses systematically the

[17] Nagel, *The View from Nowhere*, ch. 9, *passim*.
[18] Amartya Sen, 'Rights and Agency', *Philosophy and Public Affairs*, 11 (1982).

three types mentioned of agent-relative reasons. He defines three types of neutrality: (1) Doer-neutrality (DN): a person P may do this act if and only if he has no obligation to prevent Q from doing this act; (2) Viewer-neutrality (VN): a person P may do this act if and only if Q has no obligation to prevent P from doing this act, and (3) Self-evaluation neutrality (SN): a person P may do this act if and only if Q may do this act. Doer-relativity (DR), viewer-relativity (VR), and self-evaluation relativity (SR) are defined as the negations of DN, VN, and SN respectively. Sen shows that any two types of relativity imply jointly the third type of relativity and that, if one type of relativity is satisfied, then at least another type of relativity also is satisfied. Of the several relative values analysed by Sen three seem to me of vital importance: the deontological reasons, those connected with the idea of integrity or autonomy (in the version that Sen calls 'of responsibility for integrity'), and the ends bound up with personal ties.

The deontological reasons obviously possess doer-relativity. In Nagel's example, it is not true that it is permissible for me to twist S's arm if and only if it is permissible for me to let somebody else twist S's arm. They also possess viewer-relativity: it is not true that it is permissible for me to twist S's arm if and only if it is permissible for someone else to let me twist S's arm. Yet, deontological reasons possess self-evaluation neutrality: it is permissible for me to twist somebody's arm if and only if it is permissible for somebody else to twist that same person's arm. This is not at all surprising. Self-evaluation neutrality is implied by the principle of universality of moral reasons: if a reason against my doing a particular act X is universal, then it is also good for anybody else's not doing X. Granted that it must be accepted that deontological reasons, because they are moral reasons, are universal, it is only natural that they should not possess self-evaluation relativity. For their part, the responsibility for integrity corresponds to the reasons of autonomy in Nagel's terminology. According to Sen, the reasons connected with responsibility for integrity have, just like deontological reasons, viewer-relativity and doer-relativity: George should not accept the post even if nobody else had the obligation to prevent him from accepting it, and even if he had not the obligation to prevent anybody else from accepting it. Self-evaluation relativity is not a necessary feature of this type of relative reason. Finally, the ends connected with personal ties involve the concern for promoting differentially the benefit of those persons to whom one is closely related, like parents and children.[19] These reasons may be accompanied by viewer-relativity: I may do something to benefit my children to the detriment of Peter's children, but Peter (if he shares this kind of differential concern) should prevent me from doing so. Yet, doer-relativity may possibly not be involved here, since according to these ends, it is not necessary that the benefits to my children should stem from my own acts.

In what follows I shall examine a number of arguments designed to afford the rationale of the agent-relativity of deontological restrictions, which form the only group of agent-relative reasons I am concerned with in this book. A first argument springs from Williams's analysis of the idea of personal integrity. It should be noted that this analysis embraces moral concerns, as is brought out clearly by the fourth group of projects that Williams distinguishes and the particular example of Jim. This point might be obscured because both Nagel and Sen seem to reduce the scope of the idea of integrity (or autonomy) to non-moral personal projects and commitments. It might then be argued that the agent-relativity of deontological restrictions reflects concern for personal integrity. Furthermore, we might cite as a favourable condition for this argument the fact that Sen's analysis shows that both deontological reasons and those of responsibility for integrity share the same types of relativity. Nevertheless, this argument seems faulty to me. As a matter of fact, concern for personal integrity does not back up the observance of deontological restrictions on the part of all moral agents, but only on the part of those who, like Jim, have committed themselves in advance to moral principles establishing such restrictions. Consequently, to have real force the argument must assume that all moral agents should be committed to respect for deontological restrictions. But in making this assumption the argument begs the question, for what it wishes to prove is precisely the reasonableness of deontological restrictions.

An argument connected with this is that of moral purity. Alan

---

[19] In 'The Limits of Objectivity' Nagel did not deal with the obligations bound up with personal ties as independent of reasons of autonomy; in the new version of this essay, surely under the influence of Sen's article, Nagel includes these obligations in a third group of relative reasons.

Gewirth advances this argument when he suggests that the thesis that there are absolute moral rights is linked to the idea that it is disvaluable for an agent to degrade himself.[20] This argument rests on a kind of moral egoism, on the idea that I should have a care for my moral purity without counting the costs. As Nagel points out[21], the argument presupposes what it sets out to prove. Indeed, the fact—if it is a fact—that an agent sacrifices his moral purity in transgressing a deontological restriction, even though it may be a means of minimizing transgressions of the same type, is due to the existence of moral considerations independent of moral purity that establish the agent-relative nature of the deontological restriction in question; otherwise, why should my moral purity have to be affected if I commit a violation of a deontological restriction and *not* if I let others commit a larger number of violations of the same sort? Moral purity implies doing what is morally right but it cannot serve as a basis for laying down what is morally right. Besides, even if we agree that the transgression of a deontological restriction implies the loss of moral purity, the defender of this argument should explain why an agent ought not himself to transgress a deontological restriction as a way of preventing others from committing various transgressions and, therefore, of minimizing the overall loss of moral purity.

Nagel connects the agent-relative nature of deontological restrictions with the difference between intending a result as an end or as a means, and merely foreseeing it. He thus suggests that the absolute moral prohibition against producing a disvaluable result by a directly intentional action stems from the fact that, when an agent is performing an action of this type, he is pursuing evil, or is being guided by evil, seeing that evil by its very nature should repel and not attract. Nagel makes it clear that this is a proposition to explain the attractiveness of deontological restrictions but hardly a justification. But, even taking the claim as an explanation, one can ask: Why should one have to privilege resistance to the pursuit of evil when the result of it is beneficial in terms of overall good? Nagel's reply is as follows: When I occupy the

[20] Alan Gewirth, 'Are there any Absolute Rights?', in *Human Rights: Essays on Justification and Applications* (Chicago and London: University of Chicago Press, 1982).
[21] Thomas Nagel, 'War and Massacre', in *Mortal Questions* (Cambridge: Cambridge University Press, 1979).

impersonal point of view, when I abstract my will and my choices from my self and look at my possible act from outside, when, in other words, I regard the world from nowhere, then it is reasonable that *this person that I am* should pursue evil in order to follow the impersonally best alternative; but when I take the personal viewpoint, I perceive as something of the utmost seriousness that the content of a certain course of action of mine involves the pursuit of evil. Furthermore, the victim of my possible act cannot protest when he adopts an impersonal viewpoint, since the act will bring about the impersonally best state of affairs, but, when he adopts his personal point of view, he cannot but be indignant when he realizes that his own good is the object of a direct attack by me. Assuming that it is not desirable to suppress the personal point of view, there are reasons according to Nagel for agreeing to find room for deontological restrictions in our practical reasoning.[22] Despite its apparent illuminating force, Nagel's analysis seems to me not to provide an adequate explanation of deontological restrictions. In the first place, as I showed in the previous chapter, the difference between intending a result and just foreseeing it does not manage to provide a satisfactory explanation of our deontological moral intuitions. Deontological restrictions not only block, for instance, directly intentional manslaughter but also indirectly intentional manslaughter. Yet this weakness of the double effect doctrine does not imply that we must reject out of hand Nagel's explanation. Formulated in a general manner, Nagel's thesis is that there is an aspect of acts transgressing deontological restrictions which are the object of special concern when the agent occupies his personal point of view but not when he looks at the world from nowhere. This aspect might well be that such transgressions involve an active and material damage to a value, and not a directly intentional pursuit of evil. But at this point we might legitimately inquire why from the personal viewpoint the fact of my possible act's having a certain feature should be an object of greater concern than the fact of five possible acts of somebody else which I could prevent possessing respectively the same feature. To reply that this is due to the personal viewpoint's implying by its own essence this major concern would be tantamount to affirming that

---

[22] Nagel, *The View from Nowhere*, 181–5.

the concept of a personal viewpoint implies considering practical reasons as agent-relative ones. But this begs the question. To describe the consideration of agent-relative moral reasons as 'occupying the personal point of view' can hardly be looked upon as an explanation, still less a justification, of agent-relativity in the moral realm.

An interesting argument might arise out of Sen's analysis of a possible consequentialist moral system incorporating the feature of 'evaluator-relativity'. The central idea is that actions should not be evaluated equally by each agent irrespective of the position he takes up in respect of these actions and of the beneficiaries from them and of the victims; more precisely, if the evaluator of a disvaluable action is himself the author of the action, then the measure of disvalue that he must reasonably attribute to it is as a rule bigger than that any other evaluator must assign to it (e.g. I must allot more disvalue to the act of twisting a child's arm when I am myself the performer of the action). A difficulty Sen has to face is that it appears to be undeniable that, if a moral theory includes contrary evaluative judgements about *one and the same state of affairs*, then it is self-contradictory. To side-step this difficulty, Sen offers a positional interpretation of evaluative judgements, according to which these judgements may be formulated 'from a certain position'. Sen holds that evaluative judgements in the moral field are not analogous to aesthetic judgements of the type 'Mount Everest is beautiful' but to those of the type 'From here, Mount Everest is beautiful'. It is evident that, although the affirmation and denial of the first statement involve a contradiction, this does not necessarily happen with the affirmation and denial of the second.[23]

As against Sen's analysis it may be noted that the judgement 'From here, Mount Everest is beautiful' expresses an aesthetic opinion about the appearance of Mount Everest from the place to which 'here' refers in the context.[24] So one person may declare 'From here, Mount Everest is beautiful' and another 'From here, Mount Everest is not beautiful' because they are predicating 'beautiful' of different things, to wit, the different aspects or appearances of Mount Everest from the different places the

---

[23] Sen, 'Rights and Agency', 29–38.
[24] Donald H. Regan, 'Against Evaluator Relativity: A Response to Sen', *Philosophy and Public Affairs*, 12 (1983), 97–8.

speakers are standing in. But if somebody says 'From here, action X is bad' and somebody else declares 'From here, action X is not bad', it cannot be thought that the speakers are referring to different 'appearances' of the action; instead, they are manifesting a genuine moral disagreement. In other words, the statement 'From here, Mount Everest is beautiful' should be analysed as 'The-Mount-Everest-from-here is beautiful', but the statement 'From here, action X is bad' should be analysed instead as 'Action X is bad-from-here'. Even though the analogy Sen endeavours to make between evaluative judgements in the moral field and aesthetic ones from a certain position is unfortunate, positional evaluative judgements may be used to convey the content of statements about agent-relative reasons. In fact, one may say that the positional evaluative judgement 'Any action X is bad-for-its-author, whoever he is' *means* that there are agent-relative moral reasons against doing X or, less technically, that each person should abstain from doing X. The point is that the formulation of positional evaluative judgements of this type in the context of a moral theory does not make it contradictory when such judgements are understood as statements about the existence of agent-relative moral reasons or simply as duties-statements. But the weakness that the argument of evaluator-relativity now exposes is that positional evaluative judgements, understood as I have just suggested, constitute only an alternative *façon de parler* about deontological restrictions and, therefore, cannot serve as a basis for the provision of a justification of such restrictions.

A more promising justificatory strategy derives from Anselm Müller's criticism of utilitarianism for its 'eventistic' nature, that is to say, for locating the criterion for right and wrong behaviour in the quality of states of affairs.[25] Müller argues that utilitarianism makes nonsense of traditional moral principles like Democritus' maxim 'It is better to suffer wrong than to do wrong'. At first sight, he says, there do not appear to be difficulties about interpreting moral principles in terms of evaluative judgements about certain states of affairs. Thus, the following two judgements seem equivalent:

[25] Anselm Müller, 'Radical Subjectivity: Morality versus Utilitarianism', *Ratio*, 18 (1976).

(1) It is bad to lie.

(2) It is bad that anyone should lie.[26]

It might be thought then that, generically, statements of the type:

(3) It is true of every person P that P should follow the rule 'I ought not to do X'.

are equivalent to propositions of the type:

(4) It is true of every person P that it is bad that P should do X.

Yet Müller shows that this equivalence cannot be maintained in respect of Democritus' maxim. This maxim may be naturally formulated through the following proposition:

(5) It is true of every person P that P should follow the rule: 'I ought to suffer wrong rather than do wrong'.

Following the rule establishing the equivalence between (3) and (4), the utilitarian should be able to translate (5) to:

(6) It is true of every person P that the state of affairs which is P suffering wrong is better than the state of affairs which is P doing wrong.

But, says Müller, (6), unlike (5), carries within it a contradiction. (6) implies:

(7) It is true of any persons P, Q, R, that the state of affairs which is P suffering wrong from Q is better than the state of affairs which is P doing wrong to R.

(7), in its turn, implies the two following propositions:

(8) The state of affairs which is P suffering wrong from Q is better than the state of affairs which is P doing wrong to Q.

(9) The state of affairs which is Q suffering wrong from P is better than the state of affairs which is Q doing wrong to P.

---

[26] This precept means 'It is wrong for anyone to lie', and not 'There is somebody for whom lying is wrong'.

But the state of affairs which is *P* suffering wrong from *Q* is the same as the state of affairs which is *Q* doing wrong to *P*, and the state of affairs which is *Q* suffering wrong from *P* is the same as the state of affairs which is *P* doing wrong to *Q*. Consequently, (8) and (9) imply the following self-contradictory proposition:

(10) The state of affairs which is *P* doing wrong to *Q* is better and at the same time worse than the state of affairs which is *Q* doing wrong to *P*.

By means of his argument Müller intends to support the thesis that propositions of the type 'It is bad that anyone should lie' are not equivalent to statements of the type 'It is bad to lie'. Given that according to Müller utilitarianism is committed to a translation of all moral principles to evaluative judgements about states of affairs or events, such as, 'It is bad that anyone should lie', it cannot avoid falling into a serious distortion of such principles. As far as I know, only one objection has been formulated to the soundness of Müller's argument.[27] The objection runs thus. Let us suppose that *E1* is Jill's doing wrong to Jack and that *E2* is Jack's doing wrong to Jill. In accordance with (6)—and consequently with (7)—this supposition implies: (*a*) inasmuch as *E1* is a case of 'Jack's suffering wrong from Jill', *E1* is better than *E2*, inasmuch as *E2* is a case of 'Jack's doing wrong to Jill', and (*b*) inasmuch as *E1* is a case of 'Jill's doing wrong to Jack', *E1* is worse than *E2*, inasmuch as *E2* is a case of 'Jill's suffering wrong from Jack'. These two evaluative judgements—says the objection—are not self-contradictory since they are formulated in a prime-facie sense and not *all things considered*. The objection assumes then that (6) should be interpreted as a prima facie evaluative judgement.

I believe that this objection misses the target. Even admitting that (6), (7), (8), (9), and (10) are prima facie evaluative judgements, the self-contradiction denounced by Müller is still present. It is certainly possible that a state of affairs is good under aspect (*a*) and bad under aspect (*b*), always provided (*a*) is not the same

---

[27] Lecture by Joseph Raz on 18 November 1986, in his course 'Reasons and Consequences' (Balliol College, Oxford). (John Finnis admits the validity of Müller's argument in *Fundamentals of Ethics* (Oxford: Clarendon Press, 1985), 114–15.)

aspect as (*b*). The point is then that, while *E1* can be better than *E2* under one aspect and worse than *E2* under another aspect, *E1* cannot be better and worse than *E2* under the same aspect. But the aspect 'Jill does wrong to Jack' and the aspect 'Jack suffers wrong from Jill' are one and the same aspect. (The same may be said of the aspect 'Jack does wrong to Jill' and of the aspect 'Jill suffers wrong from Jack'.) Indeed, 'Jill does wrong to Jack' and 'Jack suffers wrong from Jill' constitute virtually the active and passive form of the same proposition. Consequently, the application of (6) and (7) to *E1* and *E2*, even under the prima-facie interpretation, entails under a certain aspect *E1*'s being better and worse than *E2*. This is undoubtedly a contradiction. Of course, a similar analysis applies to the general proposition (10).

As I have already said, Müller tries to support the thesis that propositions of the type 'It is bad that anyone should lie' are not equivalent to propositions of the type 'It is bad to lie'. But, since evidently, when I cause a certain harm to somebody, I do not bring about a worse state of affairs than when somebody does the same harm to me, Müller wonders why we should have to accept Democritus' maxim instead of rejecting it as irrational. His answer is that, in observing this maxim and others of the type 'It is wrong or bad to do such a thing' (or 'I ought not to do such a thing',) one takes decisions from a radically subjective point of view, which involves a different evaluative criterion from that which is appropriate for the comparative assessment of alternatives in the eyes of God, that is to say, from an objective point of view that takes the choosing subject as part of the state of affairs to be assessed. This reply does not differ substantially from Nagel's theory of the subjective point of view and, therefore, suffers from its same weakness. However, if we leave aside the obscure concept of radical subjectivity, Müller's analysis shows, satisfactorily in my opinion, that common-sense moral principles presuppose an essentially agent-relative pattern of practical rationality. In fact, the conversion of judgements of the type 'It is wrong to lie' to the corresponding ones of the type 'It is bad that anyone should lie' leads in the case of Democritus' maxim, as we saw above, to a contradiction and, as regards other moral principles, to a decision-making procedure at variance with the standard way in which such principles serve as a basis in every-day moral deliberation.

Although the agent-relativity of duties connected with individual rights is through Müller's analysis vindicated by its congruence with our intuitions about the rules governing moral reasoning, it seems to me necessary to provide a justification going beyond an appeal to common-sense morality. The first step in this order of things must be a rejection of the idea that deontological restrictions are surrounded by an air of paradox or irrationality. This idea is often invoked by adherents to the consequentialist conception of practical rationality as a criticism of the deontological conception. Specifically, the charge is that it is paradoxical or irrational for it to be morally objectionable to act in such a way as to minimize objectionable acts of exactly the same type: 'If it is a bad state of affairs in which one of these actions is done it will presumably be a worse state of affairs in which several are. And must it not be irrational to prefer the worse to the better state of affairs?'[28]

I believe that it is easy to show that this consequentialist criticism of deontological restrictions begs the question. Indeed, the criticism might be seen as the second famous question-begging argument in the moral philosophy of this century, the first being Moore's argument about the naturalistic fallacy. As will be remembered, the error of Moore's argument is that naturalistic reasoning turns out to involve a fallacy only if we assume beforehand the falseness of ethical naturalism. In a similar fashion, the decision-making procedure that moral agents should follow in conformity with an ethics establishing deontological restrictions becomes paradoxical or irrational only if we assume beforehand the falsity of the deontological theory of practical rationality. On the other hand, it must be borne in mind that non-moral values do not exhaust the axiological universe. There are moral values which have to do with the rationality of our response as choosers and agents to the presence of non-moral worth in certain events and states of affairs. This fact is often overlooked by the consequentialist, who does not realize that his moral theory includes an approach to practical rationality that must compete with alternative approaches, like those that can be constructed in a deontological style. The consequentialist theory of practical rationality, needless to say, is not 'naturally' true. The practical rationality

[28] Philippa Foot, 'Utilitarianism and the Virtues', *Mind*, 94 (1985), 198.

approach I have been working out implies precisely that choosing not to transgress a deontological restriction, even when the transgression is a means of minimizing transgressions of this type by other agents, is in the vast majority of cases practically *rational*. It is unwise to attack this choice rule as paradoxical or irrational by surreptitiously taking a stand on an antagonistic theory of practical rationality. In the context of the practical rationality approach suggested here it is quite legitimate to contend that, computing the moral values at stake, the state of affairs in which an agent chooses not to violate a deontological restriction, even if the violation is a means of preventing others from incurring similar moral violations, is not worse but better than the state of affairs in which this same agent elects to violate the deontological restriction as a means of achieving the end mentioned.

However, the congruence of agent-relative restrictions with our moral intuitions and the non-existence of a halo of irrationality around such restrictions do not suffice to give shape to a theory accounting for their underlying motivation. There is a natural inclination to think that agent-relative restrictions express in the moral realm a certain basic and essential aspect of human nature. For instance, the argument from personal integrity already examined maintains that agent-relative moral restrictions express the fact that a person is a being who by his very nature conceives and pursues projects, undertakes commitments, engages in personal relationships, and embraces ideals, that is to say, a being who creates and develops his own concerns and to whom such concerns matter in a vital and dramatic way. The inclination to look for the rationale of deontological restrictions in some basic aspect of the human personality seems to be a step in the right direction. The difficulty rather resides in the specific aspect of the human personality picked out in this connection by the argument from personal integrity and others constructed in a similar vein. It is indeed difficult to show how the fact that each agent has his own personal perspective, independent of other people's points of view, can explain and justify an agent-relative consideration of the moral reasons involved in the so-called deontological restrictions.

Scheffler's endeavours in this matter are suggestive. He argues that the independence of the personal point of view is a fact that morality can and should take into account by freeing people from the requirement that their actions should always be optimal from the impersonal standpoint, thus enabling them to devote differential attention to their projects and preoccupations. Scheffler even thinks that this 'agent-centred prerogative', as he terms it, captures whatever value there is in Nozick's reminder that with regard to any individual 'his is the only life he has'.[29] Nevertheless, Scheffler does not believe that the independence of the personal point of view can motivate deontological restrictions as it motivates the agent-centred prerogative. It seems to me that the chief reason for his scepticism is that, while the agent-centred prerogative *permits* each individual to concern himself preferably with his own projects and commitments, deontological restrictions do not merely permit but actually *oblige* each individual to shun certain paths of action, irrespective of whether he is personally committed to shunning them. How could this requirement be a rational response to the independence of the personal point of view? It is clear that this rhetorical question is out of place in the measure in which it merely points to the deontic modality involved in deontological restrictions *vis-à-vis* that involved in the agent-centred prerogative. In fact, we are not discussing here whether it is reasonable for deontological restrictions to prohibit certain sorts of action, like torturing or killing. It is supposed that there are moral reasons against commissively injuring positive freedom. What is sought is an explanation of the agent-relative character of such reasons, not of their prohibitory nature. The question formulated above must then be interpreted as directed at the point of possible connection between the agent-relativity of deontological restrictions and the fact that each individual has his personal and independent point of view. So understood, the question does point to a real and probably unsurmountable difficulty.

I think that the agent-relativity of deontological restrictions is a way of giving weight in the field of practical rationality not to the fact of the independence of the personal point of view but rather to the fact that persons not only are separate individuals when they occupy the role of possible beneficiaries or victims of the actions of others but also when they occupy that of beings choosing and acting. If each of us were no more than a part in a

---

[29] Scheffler, *The Rejection of Consequentialism*, 62 n. 30.

gigantic agent organism, then it would be natural and reasonable for me to transgress a deontological restriction in order to minimize the number of transgressions of the organism I form part of. But this agent organism simply does not exist. We are separate persons too in the crucial sense that we are separate agents. When I kill one person to prevent others from slaying several, I do not kill in the least possible measure in the given circumstances: I kill, no more. My possible act of killing is an action of mine in a sense in which the possible acts of killing of others are not. If I choose not to kill in such circumstances, it is true that in some sense it may be said that I let somebody die; but this is a different question and here obviously beside the point. The moral equivalence or inequivalence between killing and letting die was dealt with in the previous chapter, and is independent of the problem of the agent-relative or agent-neutral character of moral reasons. Assuming that there are pre-eminent moral reasons against killing, for instance, what I am saying is that these reasons have to be agent-relative if we take seriously the fact that, when we choose and act, we are separate persons. The fact of personal separateness not only leads us not to treat others like pieces of a living organism but also not to treat ourselves as pieces of a deliberative and acting organism. Thus, what Nozick should have said to explain the agent-relative nature of the duties bound up with libertarian rights is that with respect to any individual 'his is the only conduct he has'.

Let me summarize. Personal separateness has two facets: our separateness as moral agents and our separateness as possible beneficiaries or victims of the behaviour of others. Each of these facets has a different manifestation in our moral thinking. Just as our separateness as possible beneficiaries or victims of the behaviour of others is reflected in the thesis about the distinct and unique worth of each individual's positive freedom, our separateness as moral agents is reflected in the agent-relativity of deontological restrictions. The idea that we are separate persons both when being patients and when being agents constitutes, in its turn, an essential part of the conception we have of ourselves as individual persons. To put it in a word, when we understand ourselves as individual beings, we see ourselves as separate persons in the most comprehensive sense. Agent-relativity is but a manifestation of this truth about human nature.

Conclusion

I said before that the purpose of this book is to present a correct argument which, taking as a starting-point the adherence to a distinctively liberal value, shows as a conclusion the basic libertarian thesis. The central idea animating the discussion developed in the previous chapters is that this argument ought not to be centred in the maximization of negative freedom but in the deontological protection of positive freedom as a component of personal autonomy. I contended in Chapter 2 that the negative-liberal argument suffers from the defect that I termed 'instability'. Negative liberalism is unstable owing to the fact that negative freedom is not susceptible of being conceived or valued independently of positive freedom. So it seems that the value of negative freedom presupposes the value of positive freedom. Granted that the negative liberal is committed to the maximizing pattern of practical rationality, once he agrees that the value of negative freedom presupposes the value of positive freedom, he has no way of eluding the application of this pattern to positive freedom. Obviously, advocating the maximization of positive freedom implies forsaking negative liberalism in favour of positive liberalism. But positive liberalism is incapable of justifying the basic libertarian thesis in the natural and direct way envisaged by the negative liberal, since the same line of argument which the positive liberal might follow to justify the existence of negative rights leads inexorably to the justification of the existence of equally important positive ones.

Although in Chapters 3, 4, and 5 I traced the main lines of the new argument I wish to put forward in justification of the basic libertarian thesis, only now am I in a position to present it in a complete and articulate form. The starting-point of this argument is the whole-hearted recognition that positive freedom is an intrinsic value. In fact, I argued in Chapter 3 that the concept of positive freedom is central to the idea of reflective self-evaluation, which, in its turn, nestles deep down in the ideal of personal autonomy. However, from the fact that positive free-dom is intrinsically valuable it does not follow that one has to proceed to its maximization. This consequence would follow only if we were to agree that the search for maximization of positive freedom is the rationally appropriate response to the fact that positive freedom is valuable. But, as we already know, it is far from being self-evident that maximization is the rationally appropriate answer to the fact of its possessing non-moral value. The maximization requirement of non-moral values stems from a particular theory of practical rationality that can and must be questioned. In fact, in Chapters 4 and 5 I have suggested a deontological theory of practical rationality that involves the fol-lowing three principles: (1) the duty not to commissively damage positive freedom predominates over the duty to prevent the em-ergence of a detriment to this same value, (2) each person's positive freedom has distinct and unique worth, and (3) the requirement not to attack each person's positive freedom is agent-relative. These principles might be formulated more gener-ally as applying to all non-moral human goods, but the examina-tion of this general formulation is beyond the scope of this book.

I have endeavoured to show that the theory of practical rationality suggested is congruent with common-sense moral in-tuitions. The analysis of examples and counter-examples and the examination of Müller's argument served this purpose. Besides, I have attempted to offer a plausible basis for the acceptance of the principles mentioned. This attempt concentrated on the ideas of causation and personal separateness. Specifically, I have suggested that principle (1) stems from the fact that when one damages a value commissively, one causes the corresponding restriction of this value. As regards principles (2) and (3) I have argued that both constitute an essential part of the understanding we have of ourselves as individual persons both when we are possible beneficiaries or victims of others' actions and when we are the authors of actions that may benefit or harm others.

The deontological theory of practical rationality that I have outlined implies that the respect for positive liberty requires an overwhelming observation of the agent-relative restriction not to injure it actively and materially. As is obvious, as far as the non-moral axiological dimension is concerned, the overriding duty not to damage positive freedom actively and materially is based upon the value of positive freedom. But, as I said before, positive freedom has intrinsic value as a component of personal autonomy. Therefore, it may be agreed that, as regards the non-moral axiological dimension, the prioritary duty not to injure positive freedom actively and materially finds its ultimate support in the value of personal autonomy. At the same time, it should be remembered that the analysis of the concept of moral rights which I propounded in Chapter 3 implies that if a moral duty finds sustenance in the protection of personal autonomy, then it is true that the correlative moral right exists. Seeing that, as I have said, the overriding duty not to damage positive freedom actively and materially serves in the last instance the value of personal autonomy, it is reasonable to hold that each person has a pre-eminent moral right correlated with the agent-relative requirement concerning everybody else not to injure his positive freedom actively and materially. But to affirm as much is tantamount to affirming the basic libertarian thesis.

Unlike the negative-liberal argument, my argument in justification of the basic libertarian thesis does not fall prey to the defect of instability since it does not allot any special role to the ideal of negative freedom. Though this argument agrees that positive freedom possesses intrinsic value, it incorporates a deontological theory of practical rationality that blocks the slide towards positive liberalism. The essential idea of my argument is not the maximization of positive freedom but the deontological protection of positive freedom.

In answer to the claim that my argument is not centred in negative freedom it might be objected that 'negative freedom' is no more than a label for the deontological protection of positive freedom and that, inasmuch as my argument is centred in the deontological protection of positive freedom, it does embrace the ideal of negative freedom. This criticism might infer from this two consequences which are contrary to my argument. First, it might allege that, since my justificatory approach embraces the ideal of negative freedom, it must be as unstable as negative liberalism. Secondly, it might allege that, since my argument departs from negative freedom, it is precisely the argument that all those have in mind who attempt to justify the basic libertarian thesis starting from the ideal of negative freedom. When the objection pursues this objective, it does not aim at showing a fault in the justificatory approach that I have suggested but at undermining its theoretical value by denying its distinctiveness with regard to negative liberalism defined as an argumentative strategy centred in negative freedom.

The basic tenet of the above criticism is that my approach cannot be distinguished from negative liberalism. But it should be clear that my approach does differ from the standard version of negative liberalism, developed in Chapter 1. Although the talk about negative freedom may sometimes be an inherently confused form of referring to the deontological protection of positive freedom, it may be shown that the concept of negative freedom in the standard version of negative liberalism differs strikingly from the notion of deontological protection of positive freedom. Consequently, though the idea of deontological protection of positive freedom may capture a possible meaning of the expression 'negative freedom', it does not follow therefrom that the justification of the basic libertarian thesis based upon the deontological protection of positive freedom is unstable as is the negative-liberal justification developed in Chapter 1. Obviously, it is not the mere use of the label 'negative freedom' that is responsible for the defect of instability but its use in the sense that the negative liberal attributes to it. Furthermore, even though my justificatory approach might be described as one 'conception' of negative liberalism, since this 'conception' is different from the standard version developed in Chapter 1, the theoretical value of the work undertaken in Chapters 3, 4, and 5 would anyhow lie in showing how negative liberalism must be conceived if it is to stand a chance of affording a justification of the basic libertarian thesis.

Now, it is not difficult to show that the concept of negative freedom in the standard version of negative liberalism is not equivalent to the notion of deontological protection of positive freedom. First, in the standard version negative freedom is conceived as an alternative to positive freedom. It is clear that this conception of negative freedom would not be possible if negative freedom were by definition a form of protection of positive freedom.

Secondly, if negative freedom were the deontological protection of positive freedom, then the principle of maximization of negative freedom, central to the standard version of negative liberalism, would have to be equivalent to the principle of maximization of the deontological protection of positive freedom. But if we understand by 'deontological protection' the consideration in the practical deliberation of the three principles of practical rationality mentioned earlier, it is plain that the principle of maximization of the deontological protection of positive freedom is untenable, indefensible in a way that the maximization principle of negative freedom is not. In fact, the exigency of maximizing acts that respect positive freedom deontologically will frequently come into collision with the agent-relative consideration that must be given to injuries to positive freedom. For example, if five criminals threaten that each of them will reduce the positive freedom of a different person if I do not reduce the positive freedom of another person, the requirement of maximizing the acts respecting positive freedom deontologically would advise me to give way to the threat, but the principle of respecting the agent-relative restriction not to damage positive freedom commissively and materially would instead require me to hold out against the threat. In other words, if 'negative freedom' means the protection of positive freedom in accordance with the theory of practical rationality that I have outlined in this book, then the notion of maximization of negative freedom is normatively inconsistent. (Yet the principle of maximizing the deontological protection of positive freedom would be normatively consistent if it were to be understood in the sense of minimizing the commissive and material injuries to positive freedom, leaving aside the agent-relative treatment of the immorality of such injuries. This principle would lead to a sort of 'utilitarianism of rights', like the one discussed by Nozick, demanding the minimization of the violation of negative rights.)

Thirdly, and more importantly, the idea of maximization of the deontological protection of positive freedom embodies an internal tension which the idea of maximization of negative freedom is free from. In fact, if the maximizing view is good as a rationally appropriate response to the moral value of the deontological protection of positive freedom, why is this view not good in the first place as a rationally appropriate response to the non-moral value of positive freedom? Conversely, if the deontological view of practical rationality is good as regards the value of positive freedom, why is it necessary to introduce the maximizing view as

regards the moral value of the deontological protection of positive freedom? It should be noticed that this internal tension is
also present in the idea of maximization of the deontological
protection of positive freedom even if we divorce agent-relativity
from the concept of deontological protection. This shows that the
concept of negative freedom in the standard version of negative
liberalism and the notion of deontological protection of positive
freedom, even leaving aside agent-relativity, are different in
nature.

In short, it may be concluded that the theoretical work carried
out in Chapters 3, 4, and 5 provides either an alternative liberal
argument capable of justifying satisfactorily the basic libertarian
thesis, or else a reconstruction of negative liberalism superseding, as far as the justification of the basic libertarian thesis is
concerned, the standard version developed in Chapter 1 and
criticized in Chapter 2.

References

ALBERT, HANS, *Traktat über rationale Praxis* (Tübingen: J. C. B. Mohr (Paul Siebeck), 1978).

ALEXANDER, LAWRENCE A., 'Zimmerman on Coercive Wage Offers', *Philosophy and Public Affairs*, 12 (1983).

ANSCOMBE, G. E. M., 'Modern Moral Philosophy', in W. D. Hudson (ed.), *The Is–Ought Question* (London: Macmillan, 1969).

BALDWIN, TOM, 'MacCallum and the Two Concepts of Freedom', *Ratio*, 26 (1984).

BARRY, CLARKE, 'Essentially Contested Concepts', *British Journal of Political Science*, 9 (1979).

BENN, S. I., 'Freedom, Autonomy and the Concept of a Person', *Proceedings of the Aristotelian Society*, NS., 76 (1975–6).

—— and PETERS, R. S., *Social Principles and the Democratic State* (London: Allen & Unwin, 1959).

—— and WEINSTEIN, W. L., 'Being Free to Act, and Being a Free Man', *Mind*, 80 (1971).

—— 'Freedom as the Non-Restriction of Options: A Rejoinder', *Mind*, 83 (1974).

BENNETT, JONATHAN, 'Morality and Consequences', in S. McMurrin (ed.), *The Tanner Lectures on Human Values*, ii (Salt Lake City, Utah: University of Utah Press, 1981).

—— 'Whatever the Consequences', in Bonnie Steinbock (ed.), *Killing and Letting Die* (Englewood Cliffs, NJ: Prentice-Hall, 1980).

BENTHAM, JEREMY, *An Introduction to the Principles of Morals and Legislation* (New York: Hafner Press, 1948).

BERLIN, ISAIAH, *Four Essays on Liberty* (Oxford: Oxford University Press, 1969).

BRANDT, RICHARD B., 'Comments on Professor Card's Critique', *Canadian Journal of Philosophy*, 14 (1984).

—— *Ethical Theory* (Englewood Cliffs, NJ: Prentice-Hall, 1959).

BRINTON, CRANE, *A History of Western Morals* (London: Weidenfeld & Nicolson, 1959).

BUCHANAN, ALLEN, 'What's so Special about Rights?', in Ellen Franken Paul, Fred D. Miller, Jr., and Jeffrey Paul (eds.), *Liberty and Equality* (Oxford: Blackwell, 1985).

CARD, CLAUDIA, 'Utility and the Basis of Moral Rights: A Reply to Professor Brandt', *Canadian Journal of Philosophy*, 14 (1984).

CARRITT, E. F., 'Liberty and Equality', in Anthony Quinton (ed.), *Political Philosophy* (Oxford: Oxford University Press, 1967).

CASSINELLI, C. W., *Free Activities and Interpersonal Relations* (The Hague: Martinus Nijhoff, 1966).

COHEN, G. A., 'Capitalism, Freedom and the Proletariat', in Alan Ryan (ed.), *The Idea of Freedom: Essays in Honour of Isaiah Berlin* (Oxford: Oxford University Press, 1979).

CROCKER, LAWRENCE, *Positive Liberty: An Essay in Normative Political Philosophy* (The Hague, Boston, London: Martinus Nijhoff, 1980).

DAVIDSON, DONALD, *Essays on Actions and Events* (Oxford: Clarendon Press, 1980).

DAVIS, NANCY, 'The Priority of Avoiding Harm', in Bonnie Steinbock (ed.), *Killing and Letting Die* (Englewood Cliffs, NJ: Prentice-Hall, 1980).

DAY, J. P., 'Individual Liberty', in A. Phillips Griffiths (ed.), *Of Liberty* (Cambridge: Cambridge University Press, 1983).

—— 'Threats, Offers, Law, Opinion and Liberty', *American Philosophical Quarterly*, 14 (1977).

DINELLO, DANIEL, 'On Killing and Letting Die', in Bonnie Steinbock (ed.), *Killing and Letting Die* (Englewood Cliffs, NJ: Prentice-Hall, 1980).

DWORKIN, GERALD, 'Acting Freely', *Noûs*, 4 (1970).

—— 'Autonomy and Behavior Control', *Hastings Center Report* (Feb. 1976).

—— *The Theory and Practice of Autonomy* (Cambridge: Cambridge University Press, 1988).

DWORKIN, RONALD, *Law's Empire* (London: Fontana, 1986).

—— *Taking Rights Seriously* (London: Duckworth, 1978).

FARRELL, MARTÍN, and SPECTOR, HORACIO, 'Dos tesis sobre amenazas y ofertas', unpublished.

FEINBERG, JOEL, *Rights, Justice, and the Bounds of Liberty* (Princeton, NJ: Princeton University Press, 1980).

—— *Social Philosophy* (Englewood Cliffs, NJ: Prentice-Hall, 1973).

—— 'Wasserstrom on Human Rights', *Journal of Philosophy*, 61 (1964).

FINNIS, JOHN, *Fundamentals of Ethics* (Oxford: Clarendon Press, 1985).

—— *Natural Law and Natural Rights* (Oxford: Clarendon Press, 1980).

—— 'The Rights and Wrongs of Abortion: A Reply to Judith Thompson', *Philosophy and Public Affairs*, 1 (1971).

FOOT, PHILIPPA, 'Morality, Action and Outcome', in Ted Honderich (ed.), *Morality and Objectivity* (London: Routledge & Kegan Paul, 1985).

—— 'The Problem of Abortion and the Doctrine of the Double Effect', in Philippa Foot (ed.), *Virtues and Vices and Other Essays in Moral Philosophy* (Oxford: Blackwell, 1978).

—— 'Utilitarianism and the Virtues', *Mind*, 94 (1985).

FRANKENA, WILLIAM K., *Ethics*, 2nd edn. (Englewood Cliffs, NJ: Prentice-Hall, 1973).

FRANKFURT, HARRY, 'Freedom of the Will and the Concept of a Person', *Journal of Philosophy*, 68 (1971).

GALLIE, W. B., 'Essentially Contested Concepts', *Proceedings of the Aristotelian Society*, 56 (1955–6).

GEWIRTH, ALAN, *Human Rights: Essays on Justification and Applications* (Chicago and London: University of Chicago Press, 1982).

GOLDMAN, ALVIN I., *A Theory of Human Action* (New York: Prentice-Hall, 1970).

GRAY, JOHN, *Mill on Liberty: A Defence* (London: Routledge & Kegan Paul, 1983).

—— 'On Liberty, Liberalism and Essential Contestability', *British Journal of Political Science*, 8 (1978).

—— 'Public Goods and the Limits of Liberty', communication to the 1986 General Meeting of the Mont Pélerin Society, St Vincent, Italy.

GRIFFIN, J., *Well-Being* (Oxford: Clarendon Press, 1987).

HAKSAR, VINIT, *Civil Disobedience: Threats and Offers* (Delhi: Oxford University Press, 1986).

HALL, EVERETT W., *What Is Value?* (New York and London: Humanities Press and Routledge & Kegan Paul, 1961).

HARE, R. M., *Freedom and Reason* (Oxford: Clarendon Press, 1963).

—— *The Language of Morals* (Oxford: Clarendon Press, 1952).

—— *Moral Thinking* (Oxford: Clarendon Press, 1981).

HART, H. L. A., 'Are There Natural Rights?', in J. Waldron (ed.), *Theories of Rights* (Oxford: Oxford University Press, 1984).

—— 'Bentham on Legal Rights', in A. W. B. Simpson (ed.), *Oxford Essays in Jurisprudence*, 2nd ser. (Oxford: Oxford University Press, 1973).

—— 'Between Utility and Rights', in Alan Ryan (ed.), *The Idea of Freedom: Essays in Honour of Isaiah Berlin* (Oxford: Oxford University Press, 1979).

—— 'Intention and Punishment', in H. L. A. Hart (ed.), *Punishment and Responsibility* (Oxford: Clarendon Press, 1978).

HAYEK, F. A., *The Constitution of Liberty* (London and Henley: Routledge & Kegan Paul, 1960).

HÄYRY, MATTI, and AIRAKSINEN, TIMO, 'Elements of Constraint', *Analyse & Kritik*, 10 (1988).

HONDERICH, TED, *Violence for Equality* (Harmondsworth: Penguin, 1980).

HUMBOLDT, WILHELM VON, 'Ideen zu einem Versuch, die Gränzen der Wirksamkeit des Staates zu bestimmen', in *Werke*, 5 vols., i (Stuttgart: Cotta, 1960).

JONES, GARY E., 'Rights and Desires', *Ethics*, 92 (1981).

KAMM, FRANCES MYRNA, 'Harming, Not Aiding, and Positive Rights', *Philosophy and Public Affairs*, 15 (1986).

KANT, IMMANUEL, 'Idee zu einer allgemeinen Geschichte in weltbürgerlicher Absicht', in *Kant's Gesammelte Schriften*, ed. Königlich Preussischen Akademie der Wissenschaften, viii (Berlin: Georg Reimer, 1912).

LEVIN, MICHAEL, 'Negative Liberty', in Ellen Franken Paul, Fred D. Miller, Jr., and Jeffrey Paul (eds.), *Liberty and Equality* (Oxford: Blackwell, 1985).

LICHTENBERG, JUDITH, 'The Moral Equivalence of Action and Omission', in K. Nielsen and S. C. Patten (eds.), *New Essays in Ethics and Public Policy, Canadian Journal of Philosophy*, suppl. vol. 8 (1982).

LOCKE, JOHN, *The Second Treatise of Government*, in *Two Treatises of Government*, ed. Peter Laslett (Cambridge: Cambridge University Press, 1970).

LOMASKY, LOREN E., *Persons, Rights, and the Moral Community* (New York: Oxford University Press, 1987).

LUKES, STEVEN, *Power: A Radical View* (London: Macmillan, 1974).

LYONS, DANIEL, 'Welcome Threats and Coercive Offers', *Philosophy*, 50 (1975).

MACCALLUM, GERALD C., Jr., 'Negative and Positive Freedom', *Philosophical Review*, 76 (1967).

MACCORMICK, NEIL, 'Rights in Legislation', in P. M. S. Hacker and J. Raz (eds.), *Law, Morality, and Society: Essays in Honour of H. L. A. Hart* (Oxford: Oxford University Press, 1977).

MACK, ERIC, 'Bad Samaritanism and the Causation of Harm', *Philosophy and Public Affairs*, 9 (1980).

—— 'How to Derive Libertarian Rights', in Jeffrey Paul (ed.), *Reading Nozick* (Oxford: Blackwell, 1982).

MACKIE, J. L., 'Can There Be a Right-Based Moral Theory?', in J. Waldron (ed.), *Theories of Rights* (Oxford: Oxford University Press, 1984).

—— *The Cement of the Universe* (Oxford: Clarendon Press, 1980).

MACPHERSON, C. B., *Democratic Theory: Essays in Retrieval* (Oxford: Clarendon Press, 1973).

MILL, JOHN STUART, 'On Liberty', in *Utilitarianism. On Liberty. Essay on Bentham*, ed. Mary Warnock (Glasgow: Collins, 1979).

—— 'Principles of Political Economy with Some of their Applications to Social Philosophy', in *Collected Works of John Stuart Mill*, iii, ed. J. M. Robson (Toronto: University of Toronto Press; London: Routledge & Kegan Paul, 1965).

MILLER, DAVID, 'Constraints on Freedom', *Ethics*, 94 (1983).

—— 'Reply to Oppenheim', *Ethics*, 95 (1985).

MÜLLER, ANSELM, 'Radical Subjectivity: Morality versus Utilitarianism', *Ratio*, 18 (1976).

NAGEL, THOMAS, 'The Limits of Objectivity', in S. McMurrin (ed.), *The Tanner Lectures on Human Values*, i (Salt Lake City, Utah: University of Utah Press; Cambridge: Cambridge University Press, 1980).

—— 'War and Massacre', in *Mortal Questions* (Cambridge: Cambridge University Press, 1979).

—— *The View from Nowhere* (New York: Oxford University Press, 1986).

NARVESON, JAN, 'Equality vs. Liberty: Advantage, Liberty', in Ellen Franken Paul, Fred D. Miller, Jr., and Jeffrey Paul (eds.), *Liberty and Equality* (Oxford: Blackwell, 1985).

—— *The Libertarian Idea* (Philadelphia, Pa.: Temple University Press, 1988).

NELSON, WILLIAM, 'On the Alleged Importance of Moral Rights', *Ratio*, 18 (1976).

NINO, C. S., *Ética y derechos humanos* (Buenos Aires: Paidós, 1984).

NOZICK, ROBERT, *Anarchy, State, and Utopia* (Oxford: Blackwell, 1974).

—— 'Coercion', in Peter Laslett, W. G. Runciman, and Quentin Skinner (eds.), *Philosophy, Politics and Society*, 4th ser. (Oxford: Blackwell, 1972).

OLSON, MANCUR, *The Logic of Collective Action* (Cambridge, Mass.: Harvard University Press, 1971).

O'NEILL, ONORA, 'Between Consenting Adults', *Philosophy and Public Affairs*, 14 (1985).

—— 'The Most Extensive Liberty', in *Proceedings of the Aristotelian Society*, NS, 80 (1979–80).

OPPENHEIM, FELIX E., '"Constraints on Freedom" as a Descriptive Concept', *Ethics*, 95 (1985).

—— *Political Concepts: A Reconstruction* (Oxford: Blackwell, 1981).

PARENT, WILLIAM A., 'Freedom as the Non-Restriction of Options', *Mind*, 83 (1974).

—— 'Some Recent Work on the Concept of Liberty', *American Philosophical Quarterly*, 11 (1974).

PARFIT, DEREK, 'Prudence, Morality, and the Prisoner's Dilemma', *Proceedings of the British Academy*, 65 (1979).

—— *Reasons and Persons* (Oxford: Clarendon Press, 1984).

PATON, H. J., *The Moral Law* (London: Hutchinson's University Library, 1947).

PAUL, ELLEN FRANKEN, '*Laissez-Faire* in Nineteenth Century Britain: Myth or Reality?', *Literature of Liberty*, 3 (4) (1980).

PECZENIK, ALEKSANDER, and SPECTOR, HORACIO, 'A Theory of Moral Ought-Sentences', *Archiv für Rechts- und Sozialphilosophie*, 73 (1987).

PHILIPS, MICHAEL, 'Weighing Moral Reasons', *Mind*, 96 (1987).

RAWLS, JOHN, *A Theory of Justice* (Oxford: Clarendon Press, 1972).

RAZ, JOSEPH, *The Authority of Law* (Oxford: Clarendon Press, 1979).
—— *The Morality of Freedom* (Oxford: Clarendon Press, 1986).
—— 'Right-Based Moralities', in J. Waldron (ed.), *Theories of Rights* (Oxford: Oxford University Press, 1984).
REGAN, DONALD H., 'Against Evaluator Relativity: A Response to Sen', *Philosophy and Public Affairs*, 12 (1983).
RICHARDS, DAVID A. J., 'Rights and Autonomy', *Ethics*, 92 (1981).
ROSS, DAVID, *The Right and the Good* (Oxford: Clarendon Press, 1930).
ROTHBARD, MURRAY N., *The Ethics of Liberty* (Atlantic Highlands, NJ: Humanities Press, 1982).
RUSSELL, BRUCE, 'On the Relative Strictness of Negative and Positive Duties', in Bonnie Steinbock (ed.), *Killing and Letting Die* (Englewood Cliffs, NJ: Prentice-Hall, 1980).
SCHEFFLER, SAMUEL, *The Rejection of Consequentialism* (Oxford: Clarendon Press, 1982).
SEN, AMARTYA, 'Rights and Agency', *Philosophy and Public Affairs*, 11 (1982).
SLOTE, MICHAEL, *Common-Sense Morality and Consequentialism* (London: Routledge & Kegan Paul, 1985).
SMITH, ADAM, *An Inquiry into the Nature and Causes of the Wealth of Nations*, ed. R. H. Campbell and A. S. Skinner, ii (Oxford: Clarendon Press, 1976).
SPECTOR, HORACIO, 'Acerca del presunto carácter esencialmente controvertido del concepto de derecho', *Proceedings of the Second International Congress of the Philosophy of Law*, i, La Plata, 1987.
—— 'Dale on Supervenience', *Mind*, 96 (1987).
—— 'Is Slote's Argument against the Practical Character of Morality Sound?', *Rechtstheorie*, 19 (1988).
—— 'Liberalismo, Perfeccionismo y Comunitarismo', *Cuadernos de Investigación*, 12, Instituto de Investigaciones Jurídicas y Sociales 'Ambrosio L. Gioja' (University of Buenos Aires) (1989).
—— 'Una nota sobre universalizabilidad', *Análisis Filosófico*, 8 (1988).
STEINBOCK, BONNIE, Introduction, in Bonnie Steinbock (ed.), *Killing and Letting Die* (Englewood Cliffs, NJ: Prentice-Hall, 1980).
STEINER, HILLEL, 'How Free: Computing Personal Liberty', in A. Phillips Griffiths (ed.), *Of Liberty* (Cambridge: Cambridge University Press, 1983).
—— 'Individual Liberty', in *Proceedings of the Aristotelian Society*, NS, 75 (1974–5).
SWANTON, CHRISTINE, 'On the "Essential Contestedness" of Political Concepts', *Ethics*, 95 (1984–5).
TAYLOR, CHARLES, 'What's Wrong with Negative Liberty', in Alan Ryan (ed.), *The Idea of Freedom: Essays in Honour of Isaiah Berlin* (Oxford: Oxford University Press, 1979).

THOMAS, LAURENCE, 'Acts, Omissions, and Common Sense Morality', *Canadian Journal of Philosophy*, suppl. vol. 8 (1982).

THOMPSON, JUDITH JARVIS, 'Killing, Letting Die, and the Trolley Problem', in *Monist*, 59 (1976).

—— 'Rights and Deaths', *Philosophy and Public Affairs*, 2 (1973).

—— 'The Trolley Problem', in *Rights, Restitution, and Risk: Essays in Moral Theory*, ed. William Parent (Cambridge, Mass., and London: Harvard University Press, 1986).

TOOLEY, MICHAEL, *Abortion and Infanticide* (Oxford: Clarendon Press, 1985).

—— 'Abortion and Infanticide', *Philosophy and Public Affairs*, 2 (1972).

—— 'An Irrelevant Consideration: Killing versus Letting Die', in Bonnie Steinbock (ed.), *Killing and Letting Die* (Englewood Cliffs, NJ: Prentice-Hall, 1980).

TRAMMELL, RICHARD LOUIS, 'Saving Life and Taking Life', in Bonnie Steinbock (ed.), *Killing and Letting Die* (Englewood Cliffs, NJ: Prentice-Hall, 1980).

—— 'Tooley's Moral Symmetry Principle', *Philosophy and Public Affairs*, 5 (1976).

TULLY, JAMES, 'Locke on Liberty', in Zbigniew Pelczynski and John Gray (eds.), *Conceptions of Liberty in Political Philosophy* (London: Athlone Press, 1984).

VON WRIGHT, GEORG HENRIK, *Norm and Action* (London: Routledge & Kegan Paul, 1963).

WALDRON, JEREMY, 'A Right to Do Wrong', *Ethics*, 92 (1981).

—— 'Theoretical Foundations of Liberalism', *Philosophical Quarterly*, 37 (1987).

WASSERSTROM, RICHARD, 'Rights, Human Rights, and Racial Discrimination', *Journal of Philosophy*, 61 (1964).

WILLIAMS, BERNARD, 'A Critique of Utilitarianism', in J. J. C. Smart and Bernard Williams, *Utilitarianism: For and Against* (Cambridge: Cambridge University Press, 1973).

YOUNG, ROBERT, *Personal Autonomy: Beyond Negative and Positive Liberty* (London and Sydney: Croom Helm, 1986).

ZIMMERMAN, DAVID, 'Coercive Wage Offers', *Philosophy and Public Affairs*, 10 (1981).

Index